SpringerWienNewYork

Horst Sondermann

Light Shadow Space · Architectural Rendering with Cinema 4D®

SpringerWienNewYork

Professor Arch. Horst Sondermann
Faculty of Architecture and Design
University of Applied Science
Schellingstr. 24, 70174 Stuttgart

© 2008 Springer-Verlag/Wien
Printed in Austria

SpringerWienNewYork is a part of Springer Science+Business Media
springer.at

Layout and Cover Design: Horst Sondermann
Typesetting in Tasse Regular Wide and Bold Wide
Translation into English: Pedro M. Lopez, 1050 Vienna, Austria
Printing and binding: Holzhausen Druck & Medien GmbH, 1140 Vienna, Austria

Printed on acid-free and chlorine-free bleached paper
SPIN: 11920137

CIP data applied for

With 1060 coloured Figures

ISBN   978-3-211-48761-7 SpringerWienNewYork

Table of Contents

Introduction

The depiction of architecture is an old art, it plays an outstanding role in the culture of architecture – not least of all with projects that were never realized. The desire to shape the sphere of what is possible, or even the visionary aspects of a building structure on paper, canvas or on screen – the omnipresence of computers having led to an exponential increase in this desire – is the underlying motivation of this art. This makes it ever more difficult for those creating these depictions to define, develop and hone what was earlier known as a "style," to perfection. The tools change all too quickly, and it isn't easy to keep things in perspective, or differentiate between what is useful and useless.

It therefore seems daring to try to make a helpful contribution to orientation in the confusing field of digital architectural rendering with a slim volume such as this. But there are, in brief, two important reasons for which I nonetheless made an attempt.

Firstly, I would find it a shame to not be able to use the potential of 3D software for one's own artistic purposes – major architectural aspects can be visualized with it all too well: space, color, materiality, light and shadow. The two last aspects are of special importance in my view since they make the use of 3D software most justifiable, while the other aspects could as well be displayed with currently available CAAD software.

The second reason for my work is the desire to separate what is practical and manageable from what is technically possible – in my office and teaching experience, architectural rendering in everyday planning is often a matter of a few days or hours. The technology involved has to meet these requirements, or it is useless otherwise.

I chose to use Cinema 4D by Maxon to address my first reason – not least because of the free language layouts it comes with. Additionally, it offers a broad spectrum of interfaces for both easy access to CAAD-generated material as well as several export formats for post-production purposes.

The desire to filter what is useful in everyday life results in a deliberate limitation of the contents; it might be baffling that I do not discuss the use of Radiosity (or Global Illumination) in relation to the most important subjects, light and shadow. But in my opinion, the additive, "lacquering," i.e. layering of individual lights with ray tracing is the more "craftsman-like" technique, which allows for easier control (esp. of the rendering time). Hence the exclusion of Global Illumination seems justified to me, especially since the new light sources available in Cinema 4D´s 10 version already offers very far-reaching realistic light visualization possibilities. Animation was also excluded – except for a detail in Chapter 3. In my opinion, it is a specialized field that should be discussed in a separate book.

In fact, the book concentrates on creating lighting sets for digital architecture models, which I supply, including prominent examples such as the new National Gallery in Berlin built by Ludwig Miesv.d.Rohe, or the remodeled Tomba Mambretti by Guiseppe Terragni, the interior of which is featured on the cover.

The subject is discussed in general introductory chapters on Cinema 4D, as well as those on handling polygon bodies, importing from and those on light and shadow types in Cinema 4D. In closing, the book includes a chapter on modeling, texturing and multi-pass rendering. The creation of lighting models is described step by step to make every step verifiable – this made the repetition of certain things unavoidable. I nonetheless chose this approach to enable the reader to work through each chapter as an independent unit without having to leaf through the book searching for references.

In some places it was important to me to show the post-processing possibilities Photoshop, Adobe's image-editing classic, offers. This is the case in chapter 16, Multi-Pass Rendering and Compositing, which would be incomplete without a reference to post-production possibilities.

The files needed to work on the individual chapters are also available as downloads on the Internet, please read the details at the end of the book.

Other important details you should make a note of are: the command key is referred to as the ctrl key (on a Mac, which I also use, it is the cmd key), the select key is referred to as alt (or opt key on certain Macs). I also assume that you use a mouse with more than one key. Measurements are always written in abstract units (without metric designations), since Cinema handles things the same way.

Light Shadow Space was first published in German spring 2006. The English edition, naturally, demanded illustrations being exchanged, which proved to be a good opportunity to present Cinema 4D´s revised interface in release 10. Accordingly, I felt obliged to rewrite increments of text too – which I hope gives this book enough actuality until the next major update.

With these things in mind, I hope you enjoy your reading.

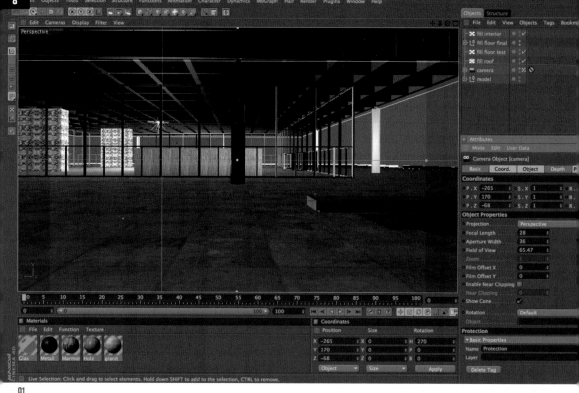

01

Cinema 4D · Overview and Navigation

In this chapter, I would like to make you familiar with Cinema 4D handling principles – a somewhat bold undertaking if one takes the scope of functions the program offers into account.

However, it seems sensible to me to choose certain fundamental aspects and present them to you to arouse your curiosity. Then you can explore the details in between with the help of the handbook, which I highly recommend for consultation purposes.

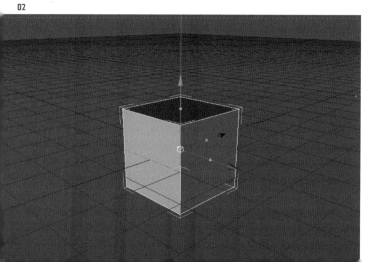

02

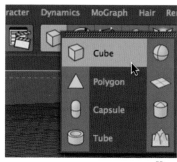

03

A Cinema 4D file looks like the image above on your screen (Illus. 01) – a large window in which you can see a model, surrounded by a number of smaller windows that seem to show details of the elements in the scene.

This type of file is referred to as a scene in 3D jargon, the large window is the viewport or Editor in which the scene is edited.

The other windows are known as managers, which display varying information on the scene and/or settings – they are equivalent to the panels you know from other programs.

When you start Cinema 4D the first thing you see is an empty scene. It is striking that each window has its own menu bar and that the windows are "stuck" to each other. You can change the size of two windows by sliding the line between them with your mouse cursor. This makes one larger and the other smaller.

Click on the button of the Primitive Objects menu (Illus. 03) and select the cube – it is placed in the center of your scene (Illus. 02). It is displayed in shaded perspective in the Editor. The visible axes show that the cube is selected for possible editing.

Click into the Editor viewport using the scroll wheel of your mouse (middle mouse key). Now you see four viewport windows which show the various views of the cube (Illus. 04) – the perspective image is shaded, the other images merely show lines. This is a default setting that can of course be changed (we will discuss that later).

If you click into one of the four windows with your scroll wheel again, only the clicked window will be shown (e.g. the window on the upper right that shows a top view).

A separate projection can be chosen for this and every other one of the four windows in the Editor Camera menu (Illus. 06). As can be seen in the four-window image, the default settings include a perspective, top, front and side view. (You can also select these four windows directly by pressing the F1-F4 keys, the four-window image can be set by pressing F5).

The way the views are organized can be set in the Editor View menu (Illus. 07). But use the default setting to begin with. The cube also appears in the Object Manager (Illus. 05).

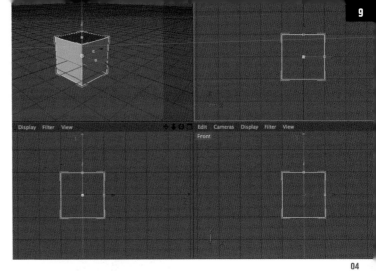

04

05

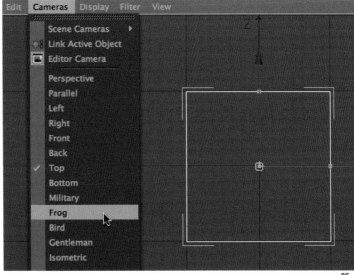

07   06

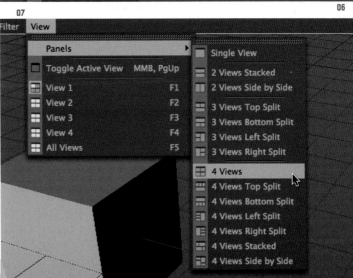

08

09

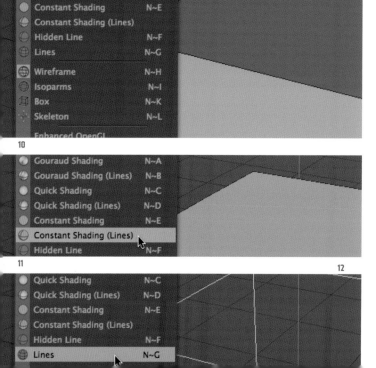

10

11

12

If more views are displayed, you notice that one of them has blue edges. That is the view which would be used for rendering (Render menu: Render View, Illus. 08). Any window can be selected for rendering by clicking into it.

If the program's interface has become confusing after sliding the windows or hiding various managers, click on the layout button at the upper end of the command bar on the left side and choose the Standard option from the pop-down menu.

Everything should then appear the way it did when you started the program – except for the things you see in the Editor (Illus. 09). You probably already guess that you can create various surfaces yourself and have them available at this point, but that isn't an issue yet.

We saw earlier that the perspective view was shaded, and that the other views were only shown in line mode.

The type of depiction can be set individually for each viewport window using the Display menu in the respective viewport. You can see the display alternatives in the second field from above – Gouraud Shading, Quick-Shading etc. – and in the field below you have the options for line display (Wireframe, Isoparms, etc.).

It is best to keep the line depiction set on Wireframe, but feel free to try the shading alternatives (Illus. 10-12).

Gouraud Shading takes the location of the object surfaces into account with regard to the lighting, either the Default Light in the more or less empty scene, or with regard to existing lighting sources.

Constant Shading doesn't react to light directions at all, instead, it shows all same-color surfaces with the same brightness. The lines show the polygon edges.

The viewport windows can show differing

Light Shadow Space · Architectural Rendering with Cinema 4D

views, but you can also use one viewport window to display selected and non-selected items in different ways.

Make sure your current view shows a perspective. It is best to hide the other viewport windows (F1). Select the Configure Command (as you can see, you can also choose default settings for all viewport windows, Illus. 13).

You can now see the available default windows in the Attributes Manager window on the lower right, sorted into a number of panels (Display, Filter, etc., Illus. 14).

You can choose settings for active and inactive objects in the Display panel. In the Inactive Object field, check the Separate Settings option and select the Lines option from the Shading menu (you may eventually have to click on the small triangle symbol near Inactive Object to access the settings.

Now, place a sphere selected from the Primitive Objects menu in the scene – it is shown as an active object, the cube – now inactive – is displayed in wireframe model (Illus. 15).

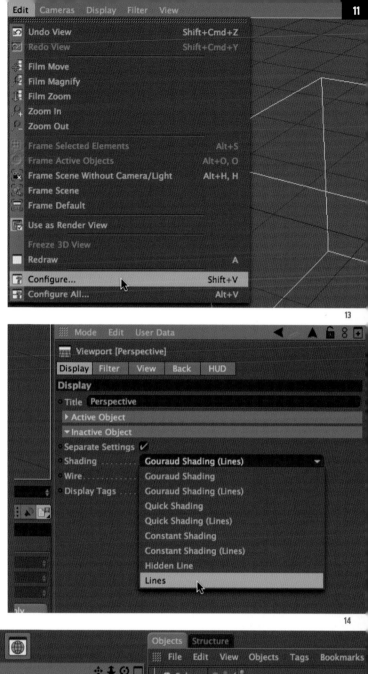

13

14

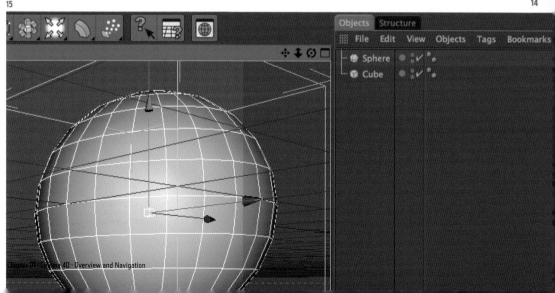

15

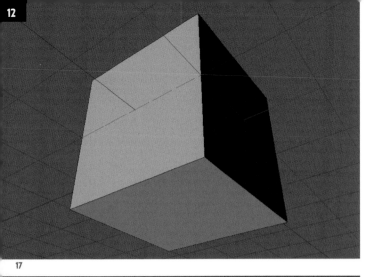

17

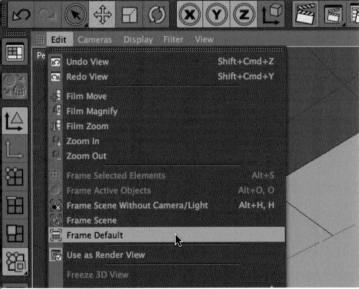

18

19

20

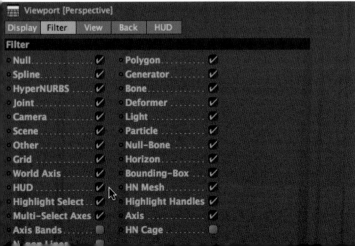

16

Now that you are familiar with the Editor display basics, it is time for you to learn how to move within your scene.

There are three buttons in the first place, which can be seen along the upper edge of the Editor window (Illus. 16; the fourth button on the far right can be used to switch between viewport windows).
One after another, please click on each of the three left buttons and keep your left mouse button pressed. Move the mouse – as you can see, the first button moves the view, the second helps you zoom in or out and the third allows you to rotate within the scene (for zooming, move your mouse left or right).

These actions do not change a thing in your scene itself, but the direction and distance of the view you take (Illus. 17). If you have lost your sense of orientation while navigating through the scene, simply select the Frame Default command from the Editor Editing menu – this resets the image to the default view (Illus. 18).

Of course a number of options you should know are concealed under the simple navigation tool surfaces – begin by imagining that you are viewing the scene through a camera (it is secondary whether these are "real" cameras you placed or the constantly present Editor camera – this subject is discussed later).

If you use the middle navigation button, you can change the size of the image – either by moving the camera or by changing the focal distance. To understand what

Cinema 4D does in this case, we should use a control tool, the so-called HUD (Head Up Display).

Choose the Configure settings from the Edit menu again (Illus. 19), and change to the Filter panel in the Attributes Manager. Here you can see which elements may be shown in the scene – the HUD is among them (Illus. 20). The Head Up Display can be used to show several scene and object parameters in the Editor.

Now change to the HUD panel. Here you can select the parameters to be shown – check the Camera Distance option to display the distance between the active object and the camera (Illus. 21).

Please keep the cube in your sample scene selected and reset the view with the Default Frame command (Viewport menu. The HUD shows a camera distance of 900 (Illus. 22).

Now zoom into the scene by clicking the middle navigation button and keeping the left mouse button pressed while moving the mouse to the right. The HUD shows how the camera moves towards the cube while the distance decreases (Illus. 23).

Select the Default Frame command again and zoom out of the scene, now using the right mouse button while clicking the navigation button – as you can see, the cube becomes smaller and smaller, but the camera distance remains constant (Illus. 24).

In this case you are not moving the camera away from the object but reducing the focal distance. Your viewing angle becomes wider, and the more you see of your scene in the Editor, the smaller the size of the individual objects will become.

These two possible ways of scaling the image are the same ones you may be familiar with in photography.

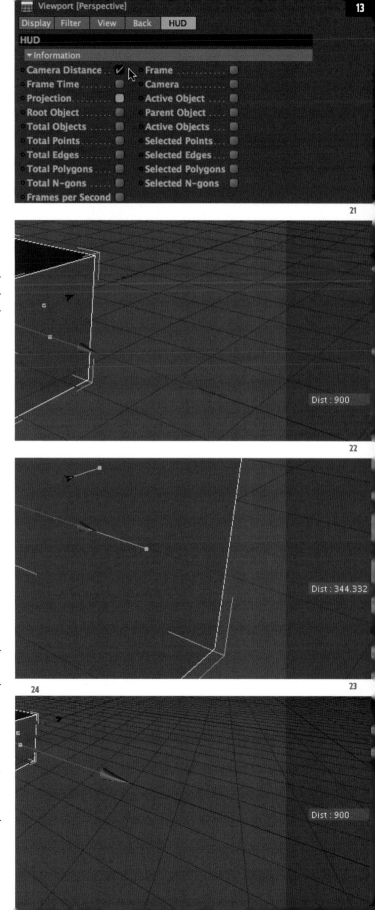

21

22

24

23

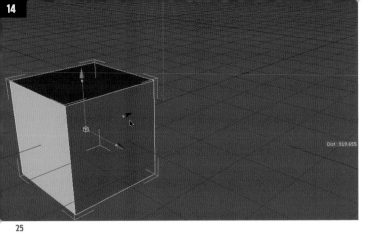

25

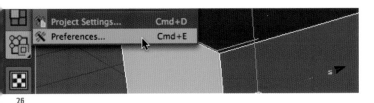

26

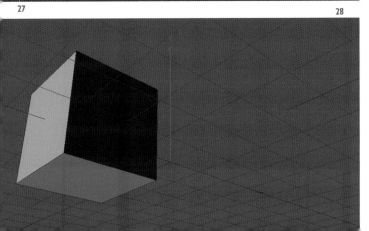

27

28

An alternative to the use of the navigation toggle on the upper edge of the Editor is the possibility of moving the scene with the help of the Alt key.

If you keep it pressed, you can rotate your camera with the left mouse button, shift the view with the middle mouse key (most common, it's the scrolling wheel) and zoom the camera in and out of the scene with the right key (as if you were using the middle Navigation button via the left mouse key).

Rotating the camera this way offers a number of options. To get acquainted, with them, move the cube out of the center of the scene; select it, click on the blue coordinate axis, and move the mouse to the left with the key pressed (Illus. 25).

If you turn your view now, you are rotating a virtual camera – as mentioned above. You can define which center the camera rotates around – the active object, the center of the viewport, the camera position or the point of origin of the entire scene.

The corresponding options can be selected in the program Preferences to be found in the Edit menu (under Document, Illus. 26). If, for Camera Rotation, the Object option is selected (Illus. 27), the camera will rotate around the zero point of a selected object – or around the common zero point of a number of selected objects.

If no object is active, the camera will rotate around the zero point of the scene (Illus. 28).

But that isn't all you can do – if you press the shift key as you turn, you will rotate around the center of the viewport, If you press the Ctrl instead, the camera will rotate around its own center.

As you can see, you are provided with several camera rotation options with only one option in the program preferences selected.

After zooming to and fro, you probably want to get an overall scene view again, so select Frame Scene Without Camera/Light from the Edit menu, or simply press the H key. Cinema 4D then fits your entire scene into your window (the Alt H short cut does the same for all your open viewport windows, Illus. 29).

Other helpful functions when working in a virtual space are the Undo View and Frame Default commands in the same menu (Illus. 30).

You have learned how to control your scene display using the Editor, and how to move inside your 3D world.

It is time to learn how to handle "real" cameras, which enable you to lock your view and thus get better control of your work's output.

If your model has been constructed in another CAAD Program, you might already have one of those cameras. You could then import them using Cinema 4D's 3ds format. However, let us for now assume you want to create a camera within your Cinema 4D scene.

To do this, use the Editor to navigate towards your favored camera position.

Then pick a camera from the Scene Objects menu (Illus. 31). You won't see a change in the Editor - Cinema 4D places the camera in the current Editor camera's position using the Editor camera display settings.

The new camera is listed in the Object Manager (Illus. 32), but it is still the Editor camera which is active. To refine the settings of your new camera, please select it by using the Scene Cameras command (Editor Cameras menu Illus. 33).

In the Object Manager, it is now marked in yellow (Illus. 34). The Attributes Manager reveals the camera parameters (Illus. 35).

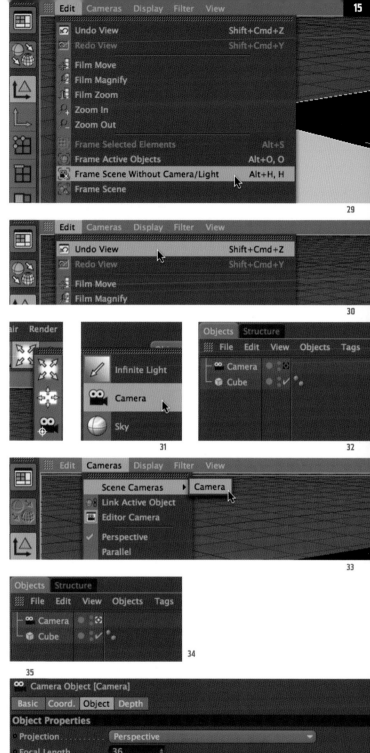

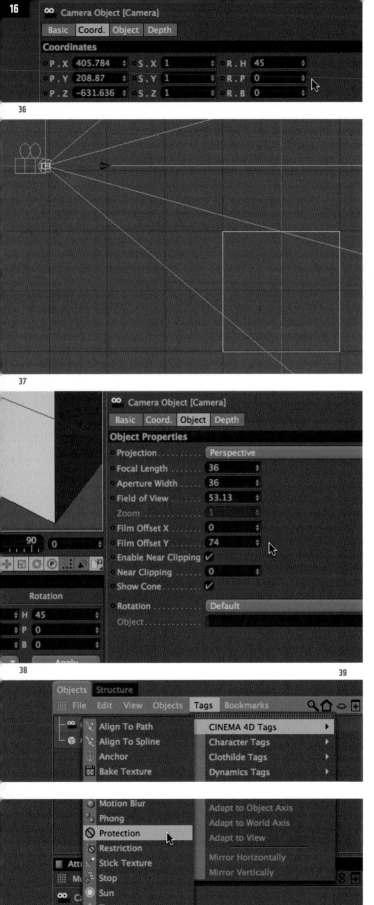

Here you can optimize the geometry of your perspective. In most cases, a good architectural image requires your model's verticals to stay perpendicular in view. To reach this, it is compulsory that your camera is precisely adjusted horizontally. (There are exceptions, of course – dramatically converging verticals can be fashionable in a scene dominated by sky scrapers, for example, or interiors.)

Have your camera selected and switch to the Coordinates panel in the Attributes Manager. Set the R.P and R.B. angles to 0° – the resulting perspective and the view windows show you that the vista axis is now horizontal (Illus. 36 and 37).

If part of the scene is no longer visible after leveling the camera, Cinema 4D offers you to shift the camera perspective vertically and horizontally. Keep your camera selected and switch to the Object panel in the Attributes Manager. Change the values for Film Offset X and Film Offset Y here. If you click on the double arrow next to the values and move your mouse while keeping its button pressed down, you can immediately see the effects in the Editor (Illus. 38). Using the offset only moves the image inside the viewport frame, the perspective's geometry remains the same.

When you're satisfied with your image's clipping, lock the camera by assigning a Protection tag (Object Manager Tags menu: Cinema 4D Tags, Protection, Illus. 39). You can identify the tag by the little icon beside the camera object in the Object Manager (Illus. 40). Now the camera is locked against changes in position and

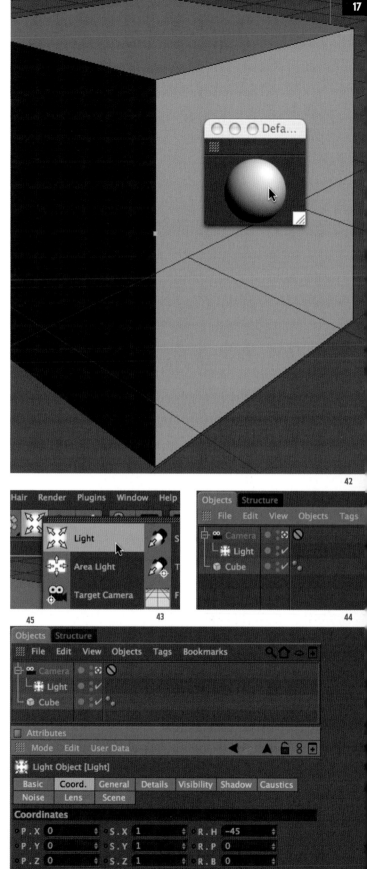

41

adjustment – Focal Length and Film Offset may still be changed.

Cinema 4D allows you to illuminate a scene with a variety of virtual light sources. This is of course a vast subject, of which some aspects are described in the following chapters. Having discussed display, navigation and the installation of cameras, I would like to at least give you a foretaste of this subject.

Up to now, there are no "real" light sources in your scene, but you can recognize the 3d objects, even when rendering it. Things are visible because Cinema 4D uses a so-called Default Light that provides sufficient lighting for each new scene – until we create our own lighting setup. Default Light is deactivated as soon as we install at least one light source.

Select the Default Light command from the Editor menu Display (Illus. 41) – you can change the Default Light position by clicking on the ball that appears, a right-click on the ball will reset the parameters, Illus. 42).

Now install a „real" light source in the scene (pick a Light from the Scene Objects menu in the upper command bar, Illus. 43). Drag the new light object onto the camera object in the Object Manager – this way the light becomes a sub-object to the camera (their hierarchical relation being shown in the Object Manager, Illus. 44). Have the light source selected and set the position coordinates P.X, P.Y and P.Z to 0 in the Coordinates panel of the Attributes Manager (Illus. 45).

42

45   43   44

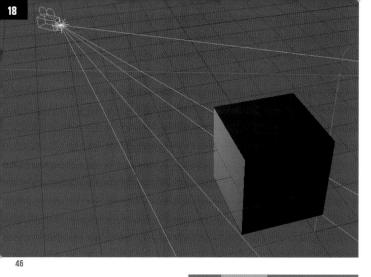

46

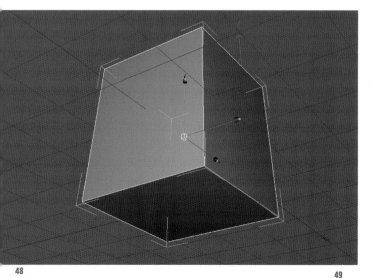

47

48

49

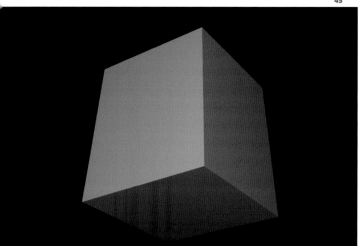

Switch to the Editor camera view again to see your new camera in its position, and the camera light attached to it (Illus. 46 and 47).

By dragging the light object onto the camera, its location is linked to the camera's – the Attributes Manager now shows its position coordinates related to the camera position, not to the scene's zero point. The X, Y and Z coordinates being zero mean that the position of camera and light is identical.

By default, the light source you installed is a so-called Omni that emits light in all directions and does not produce cast shadows.

Because of its position, everything is lit that can be seen through the camera. Such a setup is often necessary to give a scene additional lighting (or Fill, to put it more professionally).

Switch back to your camera, delete the Protection tag and rotate around the cube – as you can see, your new camera light follows every move, since it is linked to the camera (Illus. 48).

In line with the light subject, I'd like to briefly show you how to render an image in Cinema 4D, and how your objects may behave when doing so.

Everything you see in the viewport may also be rendered – just choose the Render View command from the Render menu (Illus. 50).

Cinema 4D now renders the complete image. For calculating the rendering, it takes into account every installed light, applied

50

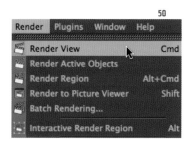

texture, together with shaders and other image effects – at this stage, of course, your image appears pretty simple (Illus. 48; you can find more on rendering in Chapter 16, Multi-pass Rendering and Compositing).

At present though, we are more interested in the very practical aspects of rendering, e.g. that you can hide objects from display in both Editor and rendering by clicking on the respective button in the Object Manager until it turns red. When the upper point appears red, the object is invisible in the Editor (Illus. 51), the lower point being red means the object will not be seen in the rendering (Illus. 52).
As you can see, an object such as Cube 2 may be visible in the Editor, but not be rendered – and vice versa, as is the case with Cube 1.

You may pool objects by grouping them – select both cubes in the Object Manager and select the Group Objects command from the Object menu (Illus. 53).
Now a so-called Null Object replaces the cube objects in the Object Manager. Click on the small cross beside its name in the list, and you can see the two objects again, having turned into sub-objects to the Null (Illus. 54). Their position is now related to the Null's position, as was the case with the light and camera before. You may hide the Null Object (which of course can be given a more meaningful name) from display too, the same way you dealt with its subordinate cubes before. When the Null itself is hidden, e.g. in the Editor view (Illus. 54), its subordinate objects may still be visible – the upper point next to the respective object (Cube 1 in your example), just has to be green.
The rules for the relationship between superior "red" and subordinate "green" objects applies to the rendering view accordingly.

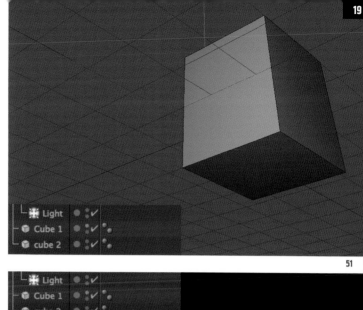

51

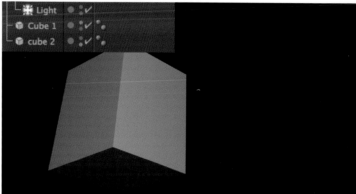

52

54

53

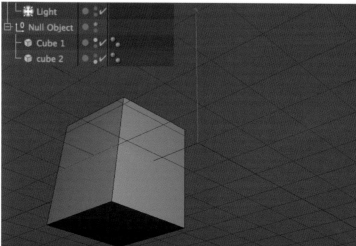

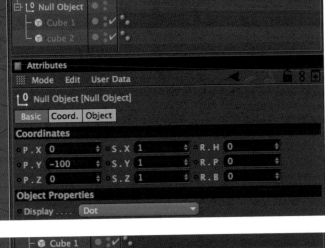

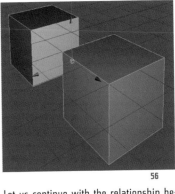

56

Let us continue with the relationship between superior and subordinate objects. Both the cubes and the superior Null Object have position coordinates (P.X, P.Y and P.Z in the Coordinates panel of the Attributes Manager).

55

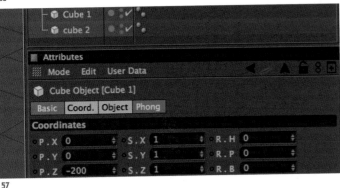

57

58

59   **60**   **61**

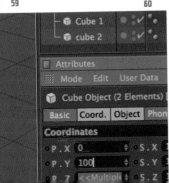

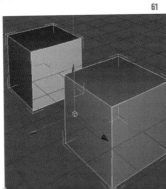

If you change the position of the Null, e.g. by dragging it down (P.Y = -100, Illus. 55), the cubes will also slide to the new position (Illus. 56). Since they are subordinate to the Null, their position now refers to the zero point of the superior object, instead of still being related to the global zero point of the global scene.

You can verify this by clicking on one of the cubes and read its coordinates – although the Null has been moved together with its cubes, the Attributes Manager still shows P.Y = 0 for the sub-objects, (Illus. 57) – this is correct, since the cube and the Null had the same Y value before and nothing has changed in their relation after changing their position.

If you want to find out the global location of the cube, you have to take a look at the Coordinates Manager, not the Attributes Manager.

The Y position is initially shown with value 0 as well (Illus. 58), but if you select the World Option from the pop-down menu below the position values, you can read the global elevation of your cube (Illus. 59).

You may also edit values for a number of

objects at the same time, e.g. their position coordinates – as an example, select Cube 1 and Cube 2 and change their P.Y to 100 (Illus. 60); both cubes will slide up together (Illus. 61).

The Attributes Manager is an allround panel used to display and set parameters for objects, tools, materials, etc. It always shows settings for the object, tool or material that is currently active: according to the item's potential, it does so in a number of panels and hierarchy levels.

Open a new empty scene and place a cylinder (from the Primitive Objects menu in the upper command bar, see beginning of the chapter). By default, a newly placed object is active, its parameters at display in the Attributes Manager (Illus. 62). The settings are sorted into a number of panels.

Now place an Atom Array object in the scene (pick it from the Modeling Object menu on the upper command bar, Illus. 63). Drag the cylinder onto the Atom Object in the Object Manager (Illus. 64).
In the viewport, you can see that your cylinder is turned into a skeleton, and its segment edges become tubes (Illus. 65).

What is crucial now is that you can edit the settings of both objects in the Attributes Manager, depending on which is currently active. E.g. you can set the Cylinder and Sphere Radius to the same value when the Array Object settings are shown in the Manager (=0.5, Illus. 64).

To change between parameter displays for objects recently treated upon, you can also use the arrow toggles on the upper right corner of the Attributes Manager instead of having to select the individual objects in the Object Manager or viewport.

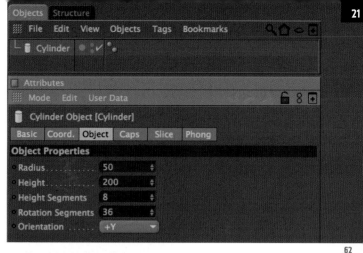

62

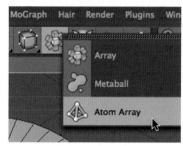

63

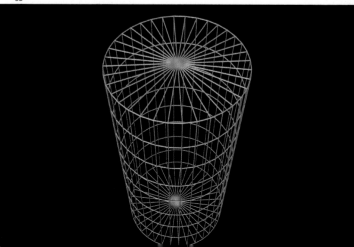

64

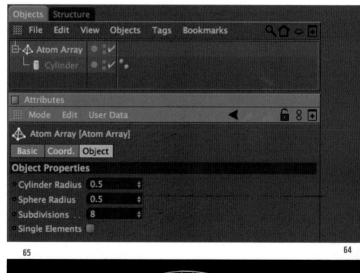

65

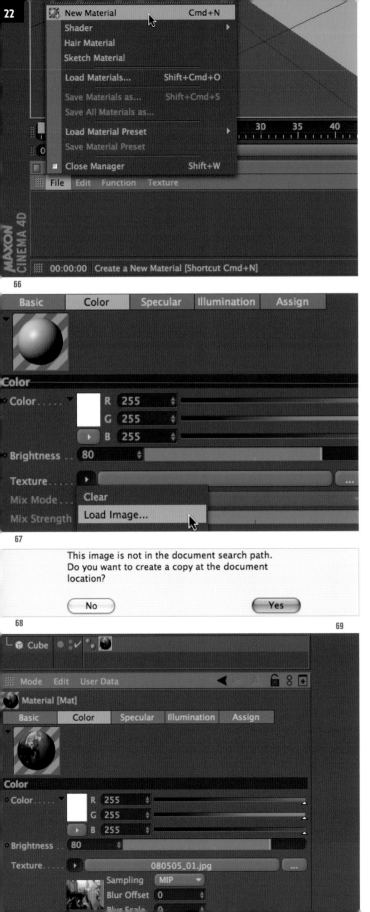

We have reached the end of our brief introduction, so it seems adequate to talk about file management in Cinema 4D.

You can save a scene (= file) you created using Cinema 4D at any time, the same way you save a file in any other program (menu File: Save). For files without bitmap textures, the only thing you have to keep in mind is version compatibility.

The situation becomes more complex the moment you use bitmaps (= pixel graphics) in your file – as a texture inside a material, for example. In Cinema 4D, textures are not embedded in files, but referenced. For processing a rendering the file has to "know" where the images are, so an index path is saved with the file.

Now if the path changes or gets lost, e.g. when a Cinema 4D scene is opened on another computer, the pictures cannot be found and an texture error message will appear while rendering.

In this respect, Cinema 4D works just like other programs that use referenced data: DTP programs such as Quark XPress or InDesign, as well as CAAD programs like ArchiCad, which use external object libraries.

Similar to these programs, Cinema 4D also lets you save your scene together with external texture files, but we will discuss that a bit later.

For a short test, you will assign a texture as a test to make things a bit more clear. Open a new scene in Cinema 4D and place a cube (from the Primitive Objects menu in the upper command bar, see beginning of the chapter).

Now create a material (Material Manager menu: File: New Material, Illus. 66) and assign it to the cube by dragging its Material Manager icon onto the cube in the

Editor or on the cube symbol in the Object Manager.

A small symbol appears next to the cube, a so-called Texture tag.

Double-click the Texture tag to see the material settings in the Attribute Manager – by default, the color panel is in the foreground (Illus. 67). Select the Load Image command from the Texture pulldown-menu and select an image file from the file dialogue box that opens up (make sure it isn't too big).

Cinema 4D "asks" you if it should copy the file into the index which also contains your C4D file (Illus. 67), – it makes sense to hit Yes if your scene file has been saved before (Illus. 68).

Cinema 4D will save the bitmap file in its root folder if that isn't the case. The texture can now be seen on the cube (Illus. 69 and 70; you will find more detailed information on this subject in Chapter 15, Texture and Object). It also appears in the rendering.

Here you have the situation I mentioned above – if you simply save the file using the standard command (File menu: Save, Illus. 71), neither the scene nor the bitmap file must be moved, otherwise the file path gets lost – an error message will appear while rendering, textured object surfaces appear in black color.

You can avoid this by saving the complete scene together with its textures (File menu: Save Project, Illus. 72). The program will then create a folder with your file and a sub-folder named tex, which contains the texture bitmaps used in the scene (Illus. 73).

This ends our short introduction. You probably feel there are many other variants, options and details aside from these basic techniques and settings, but with

the above mentioned things, you should be able to work with the Cinema 4D surface for now.

Don't forget that all the facets of the program are explained clearly and in detail in the very easy-to-read online manual coming along with the software (Illus. 73).

70

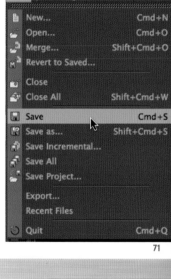

73   74   71

72

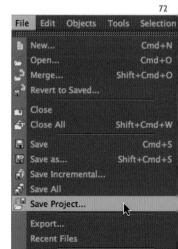

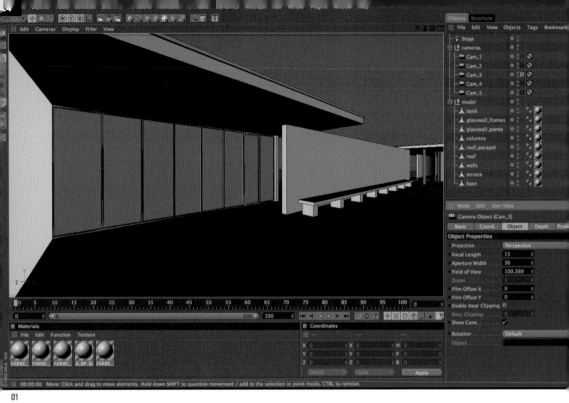

Handling Polygon Bodies

02

You are always working with arrays of polygons when using imported CAAD models. As you can see in the Illustration above, the Barcelona Pavilion model consists of a number of elements that are listed in the Object Manager marked with a small blue triangle. The blue triangle indicates that the objects are polygon bodies (Illus. 01).

At this point you cannot see how many individual surfaces each element consists

of. The criteria by which construction elements are compiled and named depends on the export format chosen in the CAAD-software (see Chapter 3, CAAD Import and Model Setup).

In practice, it is often necessary to repair, scale or move the imported model – sometimes polygons have to be removed, parts of it separated or merged.

We will practice handling polygon bodies in Cinema 4D now so you will be ready to deal with this type of objects further on.

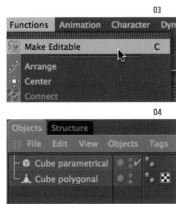

Light Shadow Space · Architectural Rendering with Cinema 4D

Open a new empty scene and place two cubes out of the Primitive Objects menu. Move them apart (Illus. 02).

Both of the cubes are so-called parametric objects, meaning they are units Cinema 4D describes mathematically using its own algorithm, modifiable with the help of object-specific parameters (Illus. 05).

As such, they are different to imported CAAD elements, which normally consist of "simple" polygon structures.

You can transform the cube into such a polygonal object, too (Functions menu: Make Editable, Illus. 03), and see how it loses its parametrical structure – the Attributes Manager doesn't offer any options for the object anymore (Illus. 06). Also the cube is now marked with a polygon symbol in the Object Manager (Illus. 04).

Only when an object is available in such a polygonal structure it is possible to edit it selectively.

Select the Use Polygon Tool command from the left command bar (Illus. 07) and the Live Selection tool from the upper command bar (Illus. 08).

Make sure the polygon body is selected (Illus. 06), and slide the mouse over the cube in the viewport – every polygon surface you "touch" this way is highlighted in a lighter gray (Illus. 09).

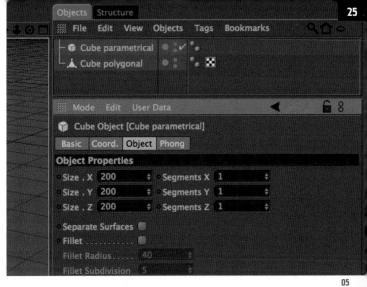

05

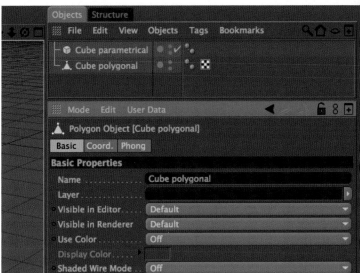

06

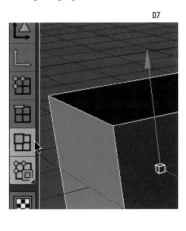

07

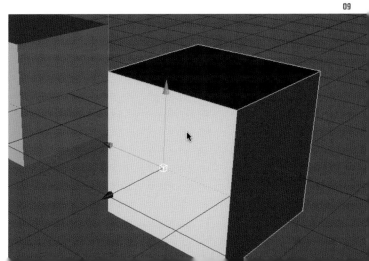

08

09

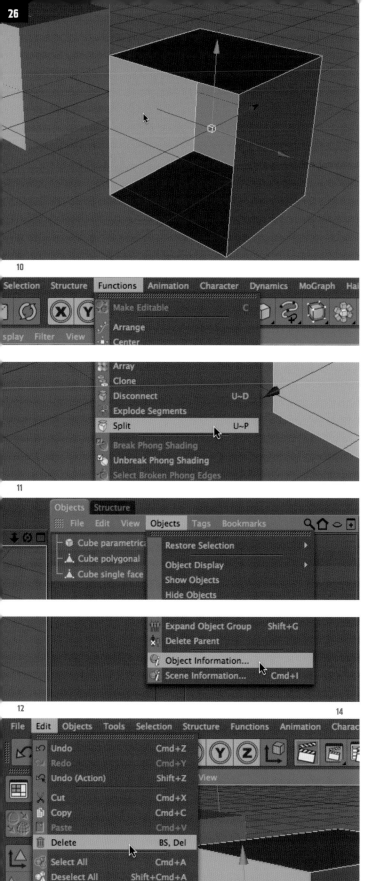

10

11

12

14

13

Now click to select a polygon surface – the respective surface is now displayed with yellow edges. You may now delete it, for example (Illus. 10).

Every now and then you might need to uncouple or separate a single polygon from the overall array in order to light it individually – it then stays in the same place, but turns into an independent object.

To practice this, please undo the delete action (CTRL Z) and make sure the formerly deleted surface that has turned back is selected.
Now choose the Split command (from the Functions menu; not to be confused with the Disconnect command, Illus. 11).
Cinema 4D will create a copy of the surface with the same name, the original still being active. (You should always rename the copy not to get confused, Illus. 12 and 13).

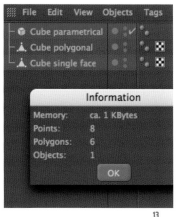

You can verify that it is a copy – and that the original still has six sides – by using the Object Information command (Object Manager: Object Menu, Illus. 13).

In order not to deal with two polygon planes at the same position, please delete the original surface now – make sure the original object is still active (Illus. 14).

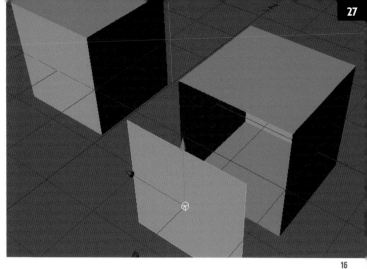

To see if you were successful check with the Object Information command (see above) – the original cube should only contain five polygons now (Illus. 15). Always keep in mind that you get un-

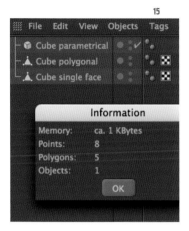

15

expected results during rendering if two polygons are in one and the same place. In our case, the most common reason to separate polygons is that it allows us to light them separately, but we are going to use this opportunity also to practice the exact positioning of polygons.

Move the single surface away from the cube by its Z-axis (Illus. 16).

For the two objects, assign colors before continuing your work – this is an easy way of breaking up the gray monotony of the scene.

Select one of the objects. You can activate the Use Color command in the Attributes Manager Basic panel – just choose the Always option from the pull-down menu (Illus. 17).

Double-click on the white spot beside Display Color to open the Colors panel in order to select a color (the panel's appearance depends on your operating system). Select the color you like – you may save it by drawing it into one of the white squares at the panels's bottom, so you can use it for other objects, too.

Do the same for the second object using a different color (Illus. 18).

16

17

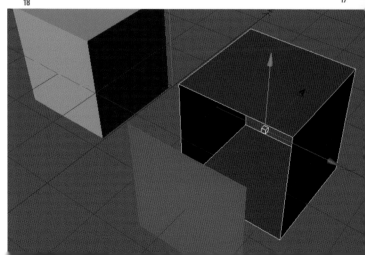

18

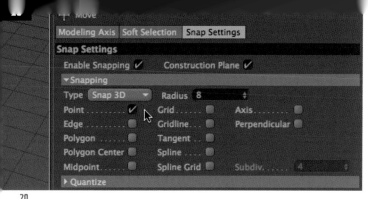

20

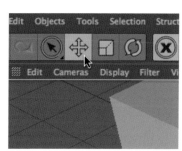

19

And now back to our task – we want to move the polygon precisely back into its former position and learn how to do this in Cinema 4D.

Now we need the Move tool – activate it in the upper command bar (Illus. 19).

To move an element in accurate increments, use the Snap function.

When the Move tool is selected, you will

21

22

find the corresponding settings in the Attributes Manager's Snap Settings panel (Illus. 20). Check the Enable Snapping option, select Snap 3D, check Point and remove the default checks for Grid and Grid line. This will make the Move tool snap to polygon points within a radius of 10 pixels.

To move the surface back so its four points will be placed exactly on the corresponding points of the cube, you first have to move the single surface's object axis to one of its corner points. (Each object in a Cinema 4D scene has its own set of coordinate axes, not necessarily positioned within the object; it can be moved independently from the object it belongs to.)

Change to the Use Object Axis Tool (left command bar, Illus. 21). When the single surface is selected (and the Move tool still at hand), you move its coordinate system until its zero point snaps to one of the objet's corners. (Just left-click somewhere into the Editor and move the mouse, you don't have to pick the very zero point; Illus. 22).

If this doesn't work properly, make sure your Snap settings are correct and match those described above – e.g. if you forgot to deactivate the Grid or Grid line options in the Snap settings, you will experience irritating skips while moving the axes.

Now you will move the single surface itself – all you have to do is change to the Move Object tool (Illus. 23). Now you

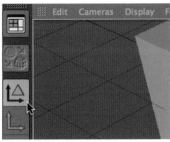

23

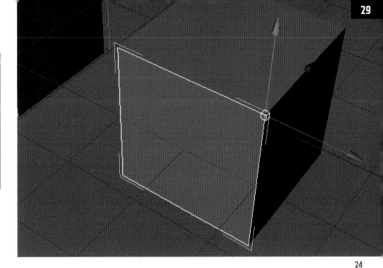

24

can move the surface to the right place the same way you moved the axes before (Illus. 24).

You have seen how polygon surfaces can be separated and how objects can be moved and placed precisely – an additional task which often needs to be solved is to scale an entire model to a greater or smaller size if something went wrong with the import scale.

Though the scale isn't really decisive for working in Cinema 4D, it is crucial your model isn't too small or to large to avoid problems in using lights and cameras, or navigating through your scene. (To my experience, you achieve the best results when Cinema's units match your model's centimeter units; see also Chapter 03, CAAD Importing and Model Setup).

When it comes to scaling, you normally have to do it for all your polygon objects together, so in our sample scene you'll have to scale the blue cube and the red surface.

In the first place, you will group both objects – select the objects in the Editor or the Object Manager (use the Shift key to select more than one item) and pick the Group Objects command from the Object menu (Illus. 25). This is a function you know from other programs (and chapter 01), but Cinema 4D can do a lot more here: it creates a container, a so-called Null Object in which the selected objects are kept as sub-objects (Illus. 25). The container can be renamed like a normal object (af-

ter double-clicking on its name in the Object Manager).

What is most important is that the Null Object also has a coordinate system, like other objects. All the edit commands – Move, Rotate, scale can be applied to the Null Object and the subordinate objects it contains.

26

25

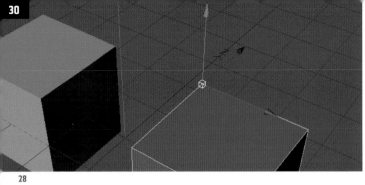

28

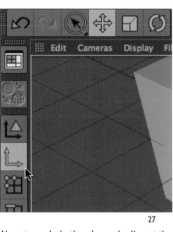

27

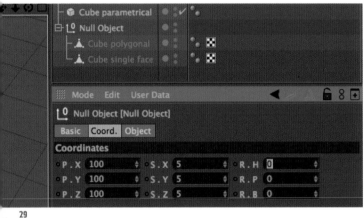

29

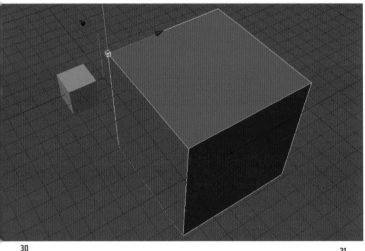

30

Now, to scale both polygon bodies at the same time and with the same factor, all you have to do is scale the Null object.

Before doing so, you should decide which point of the model should remain in its original position, and then move point zero of the Null's coordinate system to its position before scaling.
Make sure the Null Object is selected (Illus. 29) and that the Move tool and Object Axis tool are activated (Illus. 27).
Then drag the axis cross of the Null Object to the back upper corner of the cube (Illus. 28).

Have a look at the Coordinates panel in the Attributes Manager (the Null should still be selected) and use the same scale setting for all three axes (S.X, S.Y, S.Z = 5, Illus. 29). Each change will immediately be displayed in the Editor when you press the Tab key to reach the next entry. The result is correct (Illus. 30).

Another common problem coming along with polygon models is the geometry and number of polygons, since many CAAD program export filters break even object surfaces into triangles. This leads to an unnecessarily high number of polygons and makes restructuring objects more complicated; e.g. splitting single surfaces off objects (see above) is not very com-

31

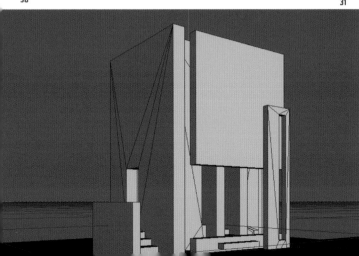

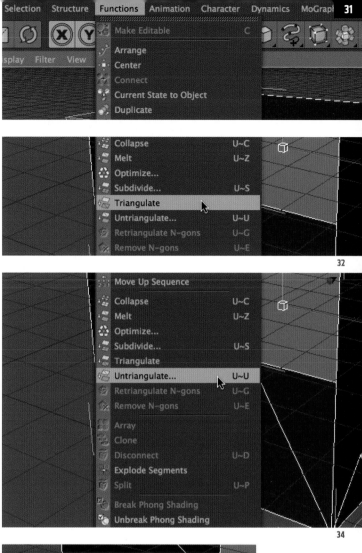

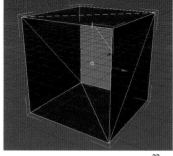

fortable when they consist of several triangles. (A typical example can be seen in
Illus. 31).

Turn the sides of your blue cube into triangles to practice handling this problem.
Make sure the cube is selected and
choose the Triangulate command from
the Functions menu (Illus. 32).
The sides of your cube are now divided
into triangles, so it looks like a typical
CAAD-generated object (Illus. 33).

The first way you can get rid of the triangles is using the Untriangulate command
in the same menu. This way, you can either correct the entire object, or single
surfaces – in that case, you have to select
them in the first place (Illus. 34).

When using the Untriangulate command,
Cinema 4D automatically assumes that
you only want to consolidate coplanar triangular surfaces with a maximum angle
difference of 0.1 ° (Illus. 35). You can also
consolidate triangles with a larger angle
deviation, though it doesn't make much
sense in our case.

What is more important is the possibility of avoiding the traditional limitation to
rectangles using the option Create N-Gons,
which makes it possible to get coherent
surfaces with more than four corners.

You can also try out the Melt command
(Functions menu, Illus. 36).

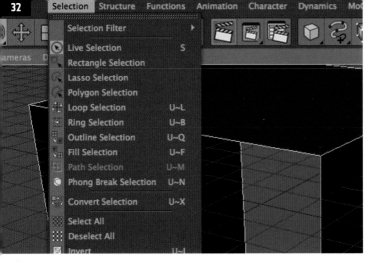

37

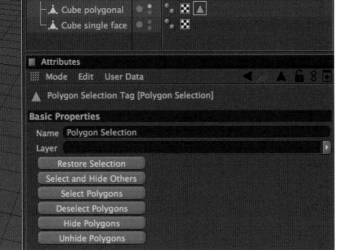

38

39

At the beginning of the chapter we saw how part of a polygon object can be stripped off and treated as an individual entity. This can be useful when creating a lighting setup in which single scene surfaces require individual lighting.

In principle, the same applies to texturing: sometimes you need to allocate a material to only a part of an object's surface – think of furniture such as the Rietveld chair, which has different color surfaces. Separating polygons the way you did it above is not necessary in such a case – it is more elegant to work with selections since Cinema 4D enables you to limit a material to a selected surface.

As an example, apply two materials to the cube – one material should only be visible on the right side, while the other should appear on the remaining surfaces. Click on the cube's right side to select it (remember: the cube object itself, the Live Selection tool and the Polygon tool have to be activated see Illus. 07,08) and choose Set Selection from the Selection menu (Illus. 37). This is how you save a selection in Cinema 4D.

The object that you have selected a side of is marked with a red triangle symbol in the Object Manager (Illus. 38).
This Selection tag allows you permanent access to the selection you made – you can redo the selection at any time now without choosing tools and click on the cube again, for example. You can also give the selection a name, but in our simple example we will keep using the default designation.

Now we want to apply materials to the cube, for the sake of simplicity we will use shaders. Choose the Shader command from the Material Manager's File menu. Select Danel as the first material and Nukei as the second (Illus. 39). Cinema 4D will list both of them in the Material Manager.

Now apply these two materials to the cube by dragging them out of the Material Manager and onto the object in the Editor or Object Manager – first the red, then the blue one.

In the Object Manager, additional, so-called Texture tags appear next to the Selection tag indicating that materials have

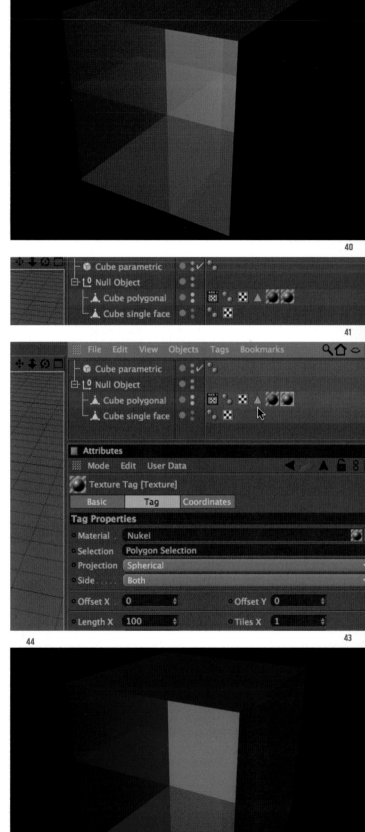

40

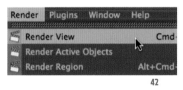

42

been assigned to the object, the last assigned material on the right. (Illus. 41).

After rendering the scene, you see that only the blue material is visible (Illus. 40) – i.e. the material furthest to the right in the Object Manager.

Precisely this material should now be visible only on the right surface, the one with the saved selection.

Click once on the blue Texture tag in the Object Manager (not on the symbol in the Material Manager). On the Attributes Manager's Tag Panel the Texture's characteristics are displayed – this is where you would normally define the geometry and scale of a texture projection.

However, we are only interested in limiting our material allocation to a single surface at the moment – just drag the Selection tag out of the Object Manager to the Selection entry in the Tag panel (Illus. 43).

Please render the scene – notice that now the blue material appears only on the right side, while the red shader is visible on all the other surfaces (Illus. 44).

41

44

43

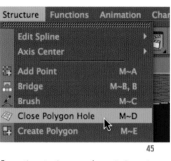

45

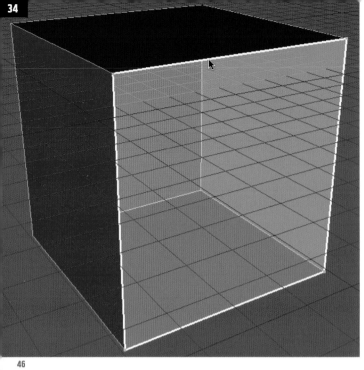

46

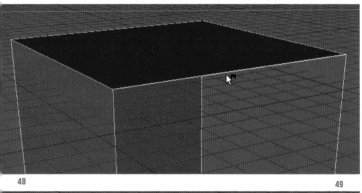

48   **49**

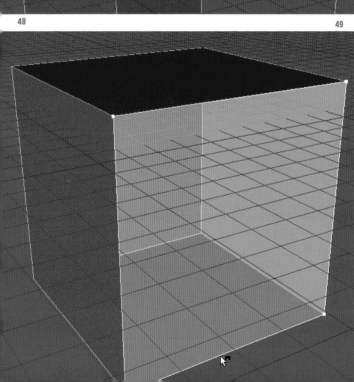

From time to time you have to invent new polygons when editing a CAAD model, e.g. to close openings that confuse your lighting setup.

The most obvious command is Close Polygon Hole from the Structure menu (Illus. 45). Once you have selected this command just move your mouse over one of the edges defining the opening – the new polygon closing the gap is shown in preview, a single mouse click will place it (Illus. 46). You don't have to use one of the Polygon, Edge, or Point tools to use this command.

The Bridge command is another tool in the Structure menu you can use to close openings, and it can be used to connect polygons as well (Illus. 47).
Pick the Edge tool (left command bar) after selecting Bridge, click on one edge of the opening (Illus. 48), then move your mouse to the opposite side.
The result will once again appear in preview. Click to close the opening (Illus. 49).

To conclude, we should discuss how you can unite a number of solitary polygon

47

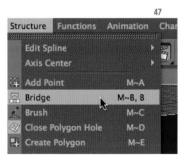

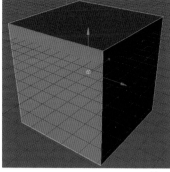

50

objects into one, since your imported CAAD model might contain more individual parts than you need.

For example, it's a good idea to combine all construction components that require the same texture; this makes work more easy, and you avoid making mistakes by texturing several items in different projection and scale.

In our example the single red surface and the blue cube (Illus. 50) should be reunited into one complete cube object.

Select both parts in the Object Manager and pick Connect from the Attributes Manager's Object menu (Illus. 51).

Cinema 4D will combine both objects, producing a copy (Illus. 52). As you can see, the new cube appearing on top of the Object Manager's list has inherited its name and color from the upper cube, the one with 5 sides and opening.

Now you can delete the original parts of course, but it may as well be sufficient to exclude the Null object from the Editor and render display by checking the small points right beside it (Illus. 52).

The new, complete cube is now the only visible object in the rendering viewport (Illus. 53)

These are the most important aspects of polygon management. More in-depth information is available in Chapter 14, Space and Object II.

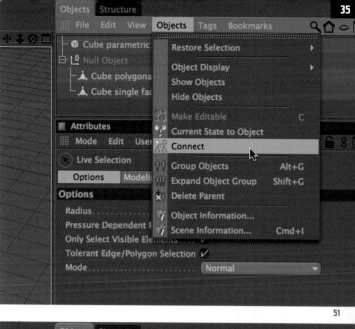

51

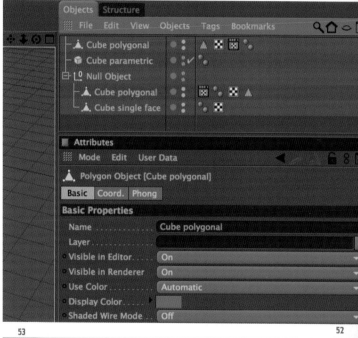

52

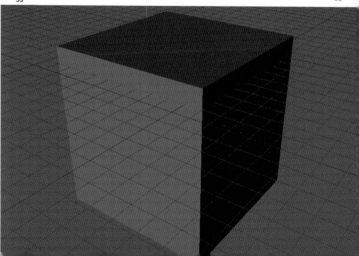

53

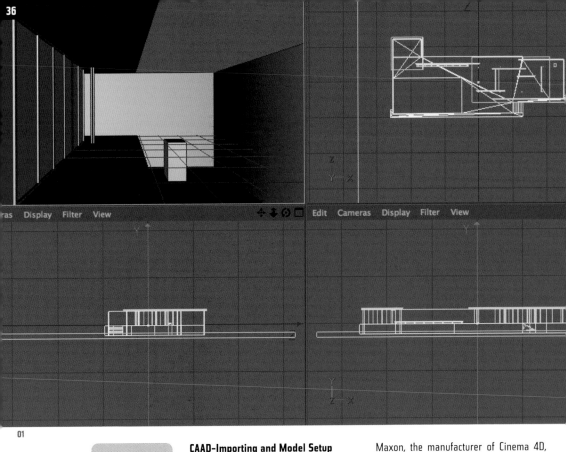

01

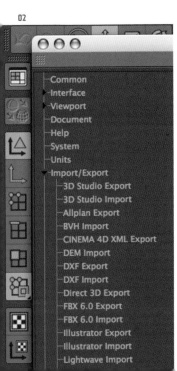

03

02

CAAD-Importing and Model Setup

For architectural visualization, 3d models are often created in a CAAD software, since such programs offer specific tools for architects, parametric objects, construction helpers and structuring systems, features we find not properly implemented in 3d software such as Cinema 4D.

On the other hand, refining an architectural model with texturing, lighting and rendering is easier in Cinema 4D, so exporting and importing 3D models is a rather important aspect of our work.

Commonly, CAAD programs offer standard export formats like dxf, 3ds, obj etc, which all handle export files in a different way.
E.g. ArchiCad models saved in obj format arrive in Cinema 4D together with correct layer names, but without cameras and lights.

Maxon, the manufacturer of Cinema 4D, offers plugins for ArchiCad® and Vectorworks® that allow exporting and, most importantly, re-importing models for additional construction.
But since these plugins cost extra money and this book is written not only for ArchiCad- and Vectorworks users we will try to achieve similarly satisfactory results with Cinema 4D's onboard capabilities.

A few introductory remarks: CAAD -generic "intelligent" building elements (e.g. walls with windows and doors) turn into "unintelligent" polygon structures when exported, though they still look like their predecessors in the CAAD program.

The model's global coordinate position is transmitted correctly (Illus. 01), but the model will rotate with some import formats (the horizontal Y axis in the CAAD program then turns into the vertical Y axis in the 3D program).

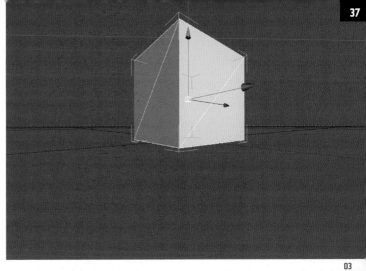

03

This has to be corrected using the respective export settings in the CAAD software. The size – or scale – the model appears in also depends on the export and import settings.

The scene is more difficult to manage and texture errors will appear in renderings if the size relation between the CAAD model and Cinema 4D's Scene Objects, the cameras and light sources, is incorrect (see also chapter 02, Handling Polygon Bodies, p.29).

In general, a CAAD file can be structured by layers, object type and texture allocation.

Most of the time, it is a good idea to rely on the layer structuring, since normally most architects use this to sort their construction elements in the CAAD program already.

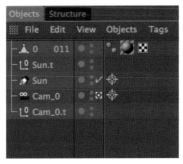

04

05

To address the question of model size, open the 03_cube.3ds file.

It contains a 10 x 10 x 10-meter cube that was built using ArchiCad and exported as a 3ds file.

The cube appears in the same perspective it was saved with in ArchiCad (Illus. 03). In the Object Manager, you see the cube is surrounded by rather some equipment – there is a camera, a light source and two Null objects, additional to the cube (which carries the name 0, Illus. 04).

The Coordinates Manager shows 10 for the cube size (Illus. 05).

Switch to the Editor Camera (Illus. 06) to view the entire scene from another point of view, including the imported camera – in relation to the camera the cube seems very small (Illus. 07) – this is an indication that the import factor has to be changed.

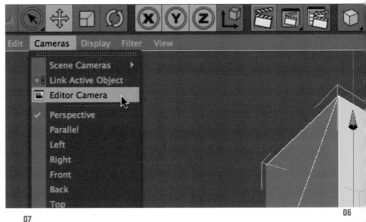

07

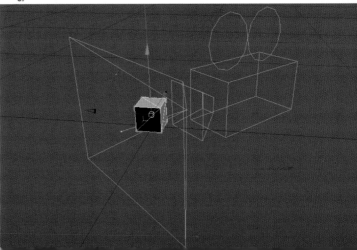

06

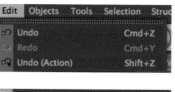

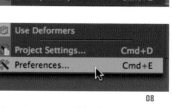

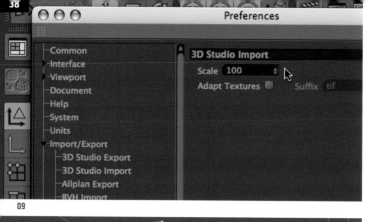

09

10

08

Managing a model always becomes a problem if it is too large or too small – Cinema 4D doesn't offer a 1:1 scale the way CAAD does, but there is a size range which is OK to work in. If you slip out of this range by making a mistake concerning the scale, some problems may arise, e.g. in handling and navigation, but also in texturing and rendering.

You will get a rather quick impression of whether the size of your model is correct by observing its relation to a Scene Objects like a camera which is always the same size in Cinema 4D. As we already mentioned in chapter 02, you get the best results when your CAAD centimeter units match Cinema 4D's units, which by the way have always the same size, no matter what unit index is written behind them (m, cm, mm, it's all the same.)

11

Now back to the cube you just opened: compared to the camera, the cube appeared too small, so you should do something about it.
Of course you may scale the cube, but you may also define the size before importing the file.

12

Close the scene without saving and select the program's Preferences settings from the Edit menu (Illus. 08). Click on Import/Export in the list and 3D Studio Import (3ds = 3D Studio) in the submenu. Change the factor from 1 to 100 in the Scale entry. (Illus. 09). Press the Return key to confirm

13

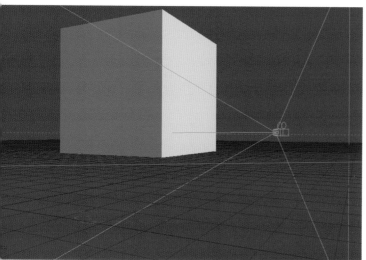

Light Shadow Space · Architectural Rendering with Cinema 4D

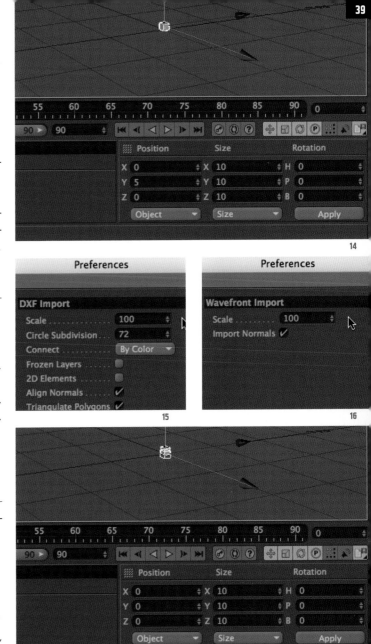

the change and close the window again. Now open the 03_cube.3ds again. The Coordinates Manager shows the cube is now 100 times larger than it was before (1000 units, Illus. 11),

The Editor camera view shows a correct relation between camera and object (Illus. 10).

By the way, you can change the measurement units from meters to centimeters in the Preferences settings (Illus. 13). As mentioned before, this doesn't change a thing in the scene, but the Coordinates Manager now shows a size of 1000 centimeters instead of the former 1000 meters (Illus. 12).

Now, please open the 03_cube.dxf file. Although it is the same cube, it appears in the standard Cinema 4D perspective, without camera and light sources. By now, you know that its size should be 1000 units to fit in the scene, but a look at the Coordinates Manager tells you it's only 10 units large (Illus. 14).

Close the file, open the program Preferences settings again and change the import factor to 100 with the Import/Export - DXF Import command. Now the scene opens in the right size.

Please repeat everything with the third file, 03_cube.obj. As with the 3ds and dxf cube, this will be too small too (10 units, Illus. 17). You have to set the Import Factor to 100 as well. (Notice that the format with the obj. suffix bears the Wavefront name, Illus. 16.)

Now let's talk about another model importing aspect: the question of how a model is structured. For the Wavefront file 03_cube.obj, you can see in the Object Manager that the polygon object is shown with a name containing the name of the layer on which the object was placed in ArchiCad, and the name of the material that was assigned.

Before exporting the file from ArchiCad, we had the choice to set the structure according to layers and materials. As you can see, the exported Wavefront model had to be turned (Illus. 18).

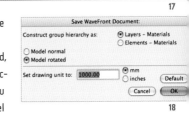

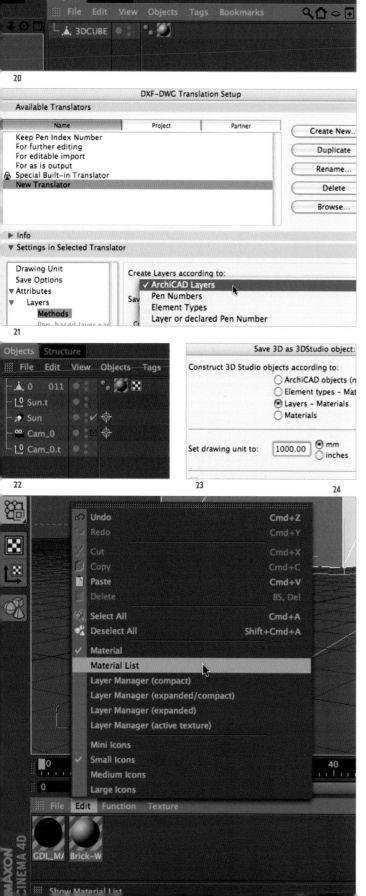

20

21

22

23

24

Coming in DXF-format, the cube is named 3DCUBE in Cinema 4D (Illus. 20).

With this file type you may export your model in a rather refined structure, sorted by layers, pen numbers and element types.

Typically for DXF files, the respective CAAD program settings are hidden in a hodgepodge along with other settings. (E.g. in ArchiCad, Illus. 21).

As you have already seen, the 3Dstudio format is the best-equipped one. It features a scene camera, scene lighting together with the respective target objects (and – what is completely useless – their materials, as you will see further along). The polygon object itself has an abstract name (0, Illus. 22).

To have 3ds export files structured, you may use basically the same criteria as in DXF (e.g. in ArchiCad, Illus. 23).

Make sure the measurement units are set correctly in all export format settings – if you worked with meters, for example, you should select metric units with the correct value (Illus. 11).

This guarantees the model will at least leave the CAAD software in the right size. As mentioned before, using the layer structure seems most reasonable, if you worked that way in your CAAD program in the first place.

Managing materials already assigned in CAAD software is another important item when importing an architecture model. Materials are displayed in Cinema 4D's Material Manager.

First, switch to list view to be able to decipher the names of the materials with greater ease (Edit menu: Material List, Illus. 24).

Now what kind of names are given to materials by the different export formats?

In ArchiCad, the cube was textured with a material called Brick, White – in Cinema 4D, this name only reappears with the 3DStudio- (3ds) and Wavefront format (obj, see Illus. 25 and 27), in 3ds combined with an additional, mysterious GDL_material2, which is probably related to the camera and light objects coming along.
In DXF, the material name incomprehensibly changes to ACI 255 (Illus. 26).

We should discuss one last problem before tackling a real architecture model. After reading Chapter 02, Handling Polygon Bodies, you know that rectangles can be unnecessarily displayed as two coplanar triangles, which naturally increases the number of polygons and makes work harder.

The cube imported in 3Dstudio format shows this phenomenon, as you can see in the Editor and verify using the Object Information command (Object menu in the Object Manager, Illus. 28).
This is not the case with the DXF and Wavefront cube (Illus. 29).

You should always try to dissolve the triangle structure when working with your own models, first for the entire object, using the Untriangulate command in the Functions menu (Illus. 30 and 31), and if still necessary, for crucial parts using the Melt tool (see Chapter 02).

By the way, you will see that Wavefront and DXF also triangulate in more complex models, but much less than 3ds.

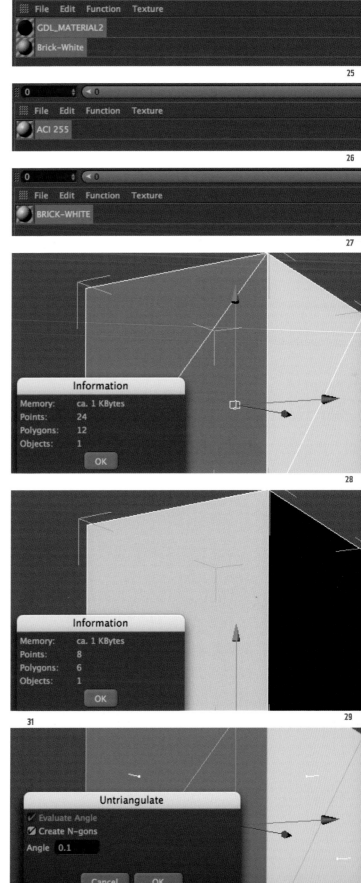

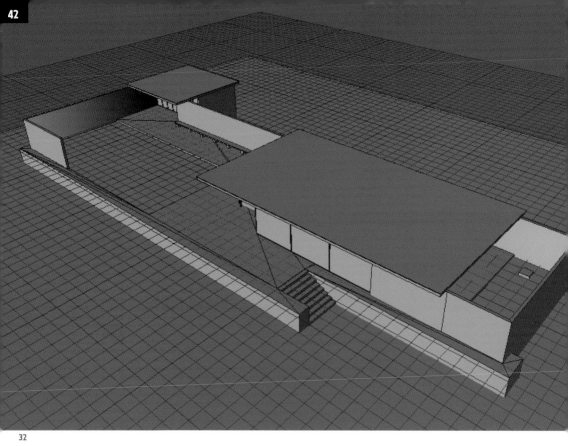

32

You are now ready to deal with a more complex architecture model in Cinema 4D.

Check your program's Preferences settings again and make sure the Wavefront import factor is set to 100.

Open the 03_bp.obj file. (As you can see, we prefer the Wavefront format since the correct element and material names make work just easier. If you are handling real huge models, you will see that the DXF files are much faster written than 3ds or Wavefront files; but our model still is not huge.)

A model of the Barcelona Pavilion by Ludwig Mies v.d.Rohe appears in the scene (Illus. 32).

It was made with ArchiCad, using an element-oriented layer structure. Materials were already assigned, yet they will only serve for color differentiation in this example.

Cinema 4D's Object Manager lists all the

33

34

polygon objects the model consists of, sorted according to the layers used, the sub-category being the materials assigned (Illus. 33).

A number of tags are displayed to the right. Among them, only the small gray spheres – the Texture tags – are of interest to us, since they represent assigned materials. The other tags are unnecessary, but don't do any harm.

The materials imported with the model are listed in the Material Manager on the bottom left (Material List being selected from the Manager's Edit menu, Illus. 34).

The first thing you should do is organize things a bit – select all the objects in the Object Manager and group them (Object menu: Group Objects, Illus. 35).

Name the Null Object, which now contains all your building components, Model (Illus. 36).

Open the Null in the Object Manager by clicking on the small cross icon in front of its name entry. Now you can view the individual objects and gather an overall impression.

Exclude the model group from the Editor view by clicking on the upper gray point to the right of the Null Object until it turns red – as you already know, this makes the model invisible in the Editor (Illus. 37).

Now you may display individual parts of the group (e.g. the Travertine Bank), by clicking on the upper gray point next to the respective object until it turns green (Illus. 37); only that object is visible in the Editor now.

Press the H key to have a larger view on the component (Illus. 38; H stands for the command Frame Scene without Camera/Light from the Editor's Edit menu).

Take your time and enjoy the look at all your model components individually, and from all directions.

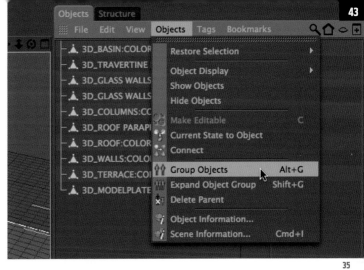

35

36

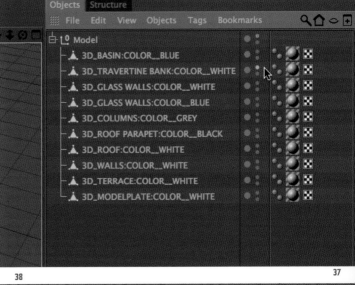

38

37

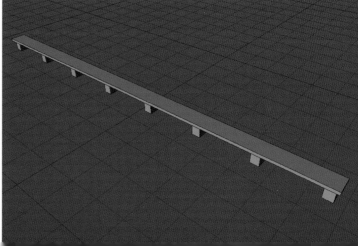

39

40

41

42

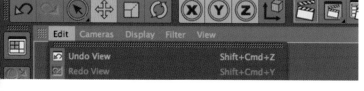

43

44

For a change, switch to another display mode: Constant Shading (Lines) from the Display menu (Illus. 39).

As a next step, you might want to install cameras in your Cinema 4D scene; this time we want to take the ones already used in the CAAD program.

As we discussed in the first part of this chapter, camera export is only possible in the 3Dstudio format. To have the five ArchiCad cameras in our Cinema 4D scene, empty scenes generated by those cameras were exported from ArchiCad, one scene for each of the five cameras.

You may now integrate those scene files into your existing Barcelona Pavilion set-up, using the Merge command instead of the Open command (File menu, Illus. 40).

Make sure the 3D studio import factor is set to 100 in the Preferences settings, the same as at the beginning of the chapter. Chose Merge and select the 03_bp_cam01.3ds file. As you can see in the Object Manager, the familiar list featuring a camera, a light and two target objects appears (Illus. 41).

Enforce a view from this new camera (Editor menu Cameras: Scene Cameras –

Cam_0, Illus. 42). The Editor should now display a perspective like the one shown in Illus. 45 – if this is not the case, the Wavefront (100!) or 3Dstudio format (100!) import factor has been set wrong.

Hide the World Grid display (Editor menu, Edit: Configure – Attributes Manager / Filter panel: uncheck Grid, Illus. 43 and 44).

Feel free to tune Default Light (Editor's View menu) to give the shading more balance.

Now load the rest of the cameras, one after the other (File menu: Merge, 03_bp_cam02.3ds to 03_bp_cam05.3ds).
As you see, the Object Manager has been stuffed with things, most of which you should immediately get rid of – select everything except the component group and the five cameras (these can be recognized by the small camera symbol, Illus. 46) and press delete.

You should group the cameras the same way you grouped the polygon objects (Objects menu: Group Objects, Illus. 47). Protect the cameras from accidental position change by selecting them in the Object Manager, and assigning Protection tags (File menu: Cinema 4D Tags, Protection, Illus. 48). But attention: fix the cameras only after grouping them, otherwise their position will change (Illus. 49). Now feel free taking a look through your various cameras (see p.44, Illus. 42).

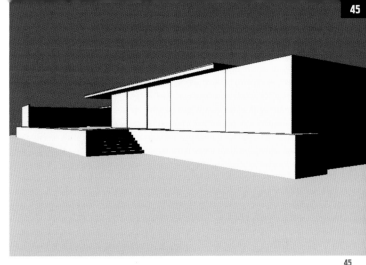

45

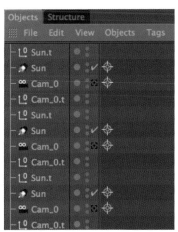

46

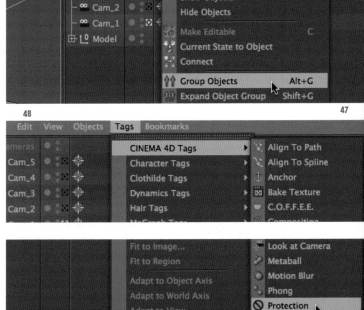

47

48

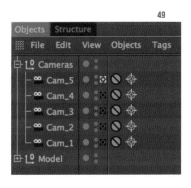

49

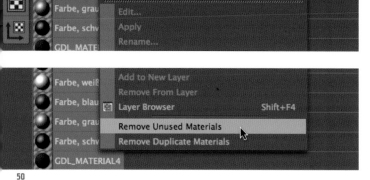

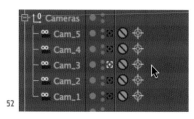

51

52

53

54

After importing the cameras a decent amount of materials have accumulated in our scene that are not assigned to any of the model's construction components. These materials can be removed swiftly with the Remove Unused Materials command (Material Manager Function menu, Illus. 50): as a result, the material list will only display the five materials used.

Coming to the end, I would like to touch the animation subject a little. To see what animation can do for you at the moment, you could for example set the five cameras on a time axis.

As you already know, Cinema 4D allows you to toggle between cameras using the Scene Cameras command in the Editor Cameras menu (Illus. 51). The camera in use is marked in the Object Manager (Illus. 52)

The animation we will now set up is meant to simplify the camera access.

If you want to animate the change between scene cameras, you need the so-called Stage object, which can be selected from the Scene Objects menu (Illus. 53). With the help of this object (its parameters being at display in the Attributes Manager), you can now choose the camera to be used for each of your animation's image. You have five cameras, so you have to set the camera to be used at five increments on the timeline using the Stage object.

To start with, let me talk about some basic animation concepts: the animations single images are called frames, the ones where decisive things happen are the keyframes.

Every Cinema 4D file is in fact a potential animation, i.e. a playable sequence of frames. 90 frames are available by default, each of which can show a different image. This is easiest to see by moving the small green slider in the timeline above the Material Manager, from frame

0 to frame 90 (Illus. 55). The number of frames and the frame rate that determines playback length can be set in the Project Preferences settings (Edit menu). Please enter 100 for Maximum here, so the timeline will show 100 at the end (Illus. 56).

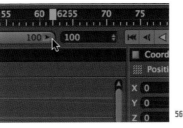

In an Animation, a different scene setting can be defined for each frame to create the impression of movement, growth, etc. To make things easier – and the animation smoother – you do this only for some decisive frames (called keyframes) and have your software interpolate between them.

Now you will start setting up an animation that will allow you to toggle cameras using the timeslider.

Note that the timeslider above the Material Manager is set to frame 0 (Illus. 57). Open the camera group in the Object Manager to view the complete list. Select the Stage object, make sure you see the Object panel in the Attributes Manager and move Cam_1 into the panel's Camera entry (Illus. 58). Now right-click on the word Camera (the one with the small circle beside it) and select Animation, then Add Keyframe from the Flyout menu (Illus. 59). The small circle should now have changed into a red dot (Illus. 60). It indicates an animation track has been set for

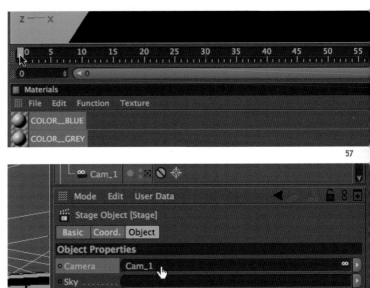

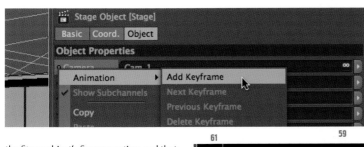

the Stage object's Camera option, and that this track has a keyframe at position 0.

You will have to repeat these steps four times using the remaining cameras. Move the slider to frame 21 in order to create the next keyframe (Illus. 61).

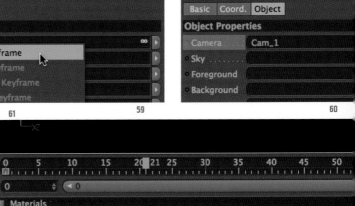

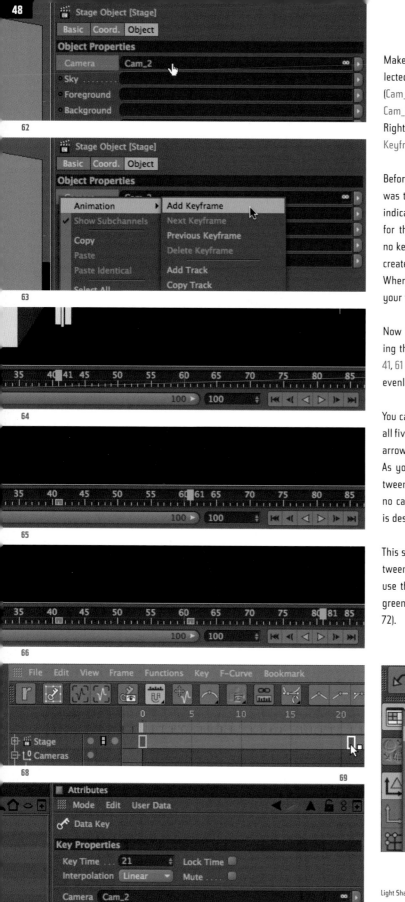

62

63

64

65

66

68

69

Make sure the Stage Object is still selected. Now drag the next camera object (Cam_2) into the Camera entry (Illus. 62). Cam_1 will be automatically replaced. Right-click on Camera and select Add Keyframe again from the flyout (Illus. 63).

Before doing this, a red circle, not a dot, was to be seen next to the word Camera, indicating there was an animation track for the camera in the Stage object, but no keyframe for image 21. Now you have created this keyframe.

When you move the slider, you can see your two cameras switching at frame 21.

Now repeat this process for the remaining three cameras using frame positions 41, 61 and 81 to distribute camera switches evenly over the time axis (Illus. 64-66).

You can play the animation after creating all five keyframes (click on the right green arrow to the right of the Time panel). As you can see, the camera position between the keys isn't interpolated, there is no camera movement - the Stage object is designed to create hard cuts.

This small animation helps you toggle between cameras easily; you don't have to use the Play button, just move the little green slider with your mouse (Illus. 70-72).

67

Light Shadow Space · Architectural Rendering with Cinema 4D

Just to have a look behind the simple, easy-to-use timeslider, switch to the Animation Layout (Illus. 67) to see the so-called Timeline panel that lists all animation tracks in the scene.

In our case we are looking for the camera entries in the Stage object. The keyframes are marked by small rectangles (Illus. 68), when you click on one of them, you can check the frame's entries in the Attributes Manager (Illus. 69). Don't forget to return to the Standard layout.

You have now imported your CAAD model, placed your scene cameras and cleaned up your Object Manager by grouping objects, sorted by the function the have in the scene.

Additionally, the little animation you installed will help you to keep visual control over your scene easily.

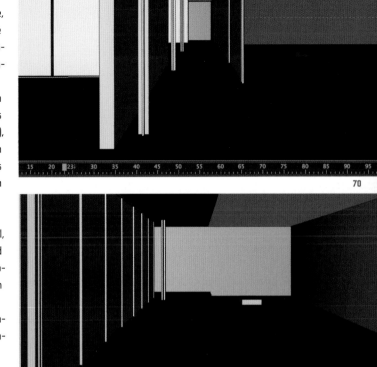

70

71

72

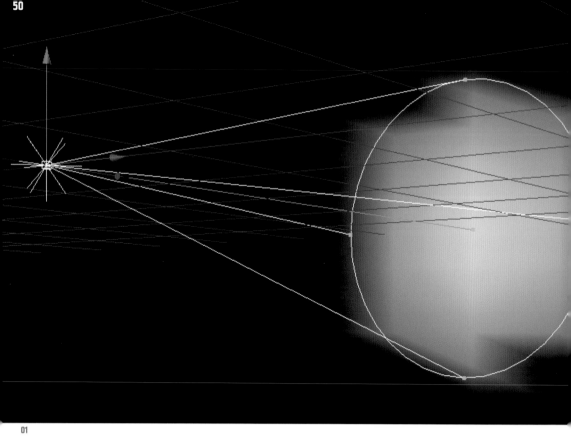

01

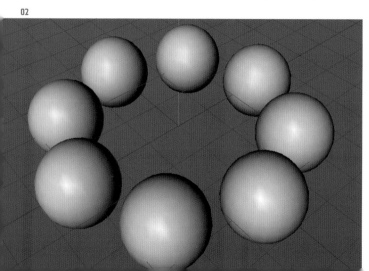

04

Light Sources in Cinema 4D

Since we are mainly discussing lighting for architectural models in this book, the light sources Cinema 4D offers are worth being introduced in a separate chapter. As always, we will only examine the most necessary aspects, further investigation of the details in the online reference being highly recommendable.

Open the 04_start.c4d file. You see a scene with a circular alignment of spheres (Illus.

02; this was created with the help of an Array object, Illus. 03).

Please notice that the elements in the scene are visible - also during rendering - although there is no light source in the scene yet.

The reason is that Cinema 4D offers a Default Light that replaces the missing "real" light sources.

The Default Light is an omni-directional light that is by default positioned slightly

02

03

left and above the Editor camera. If this camera rotates or moves during navigation, the Default Light follows it.

However, you are allowed to change the default setting: select Default Light from the Editor's Display menu (Illus. 04) and click around on the sphere image that is shown (Illus. 05). A right click on the sphere resets the default settings.

Default Light is deactivated the moment you place a light source in the scene, yet it becomes active again if the light object does not emit any light (Intensity=0). This feature, which is not desirable in certain cases while creating a lighting setup, can be turned off. The Auto Light feature is well-hidden in the Render settings's Option panel (Render menu), you may uncheck it there (Illus. 06).

Now we want to take a look at the light sources Cinema 4D offers.
Place a light source in the scene by picking the first object from the Scene Objects menu, or simply click on the menu icon in the upper command bar (Illus. 07).
The new light object is to be seen in the scene and listed in the Object Manager (Illus. 08 and 09).
As for the details, it is omnidirectional, emitting beams in all directions. The Attributes Manager's General panel shows that its type is Omni, its intensity (in this case: brightness) is by default 100, and that it does not create any shadows (Illus. 10).

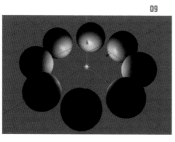

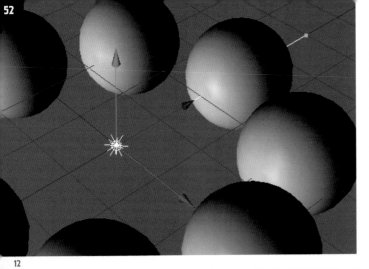

11

12

13

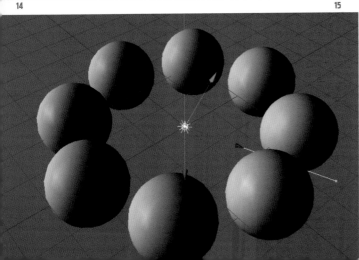

14

15

Due to its simple geometry, an omni is frequently used in architecture renderings, especially to lighten up dark areas.

However, another type of light source, the so-called Infinite, is indispensable to visualize sunlight. Just click on Type in the General panel of the Attributes Manager and choose Infinite from the pull-down menu (Illus. 11).

The position of the light source hasn't changed, but now it emits parallel rays. The direction of these rays is indicated by a white line that follows the global Z axis (Illus. 12).

When you render the scene you see that the position of the infinite light seems irrelevant, the only thing that matters is the light ray's angle (Illus. 13).

You can adjust the angle in the Coordinates panel of the Attributes Manager. Click on the double arrow next to the R.H value. Hold down the mouse key, move the mouse to change the value and notice the movement of the main ray in the Editor.

The R.H value lets you adjust the direction the light comes from (Illus. 14). Change R.P to adjust the rotation angle around the light's X axis (the ray's inclination). Notice that the value has to be negative if the light is meant to beam down.

You can watch the effect of your changes in the Editor (Illus. 15).

One additional feature in the Attributes Manager's light settings should be mentioned here: you can adjust the softness of the object's own shade borders.

Set the value, currently at 0, to 100 (Illus. 16), and render the scene. The transition from light to dark looks much sharper now (Illus. 17).

You can also set a negative value for the contrast, which would make the transition even softer than it does by default.

The Parallel light source works similar to the Infinite, the difference being that it lights only part of the scene – the area in the direction of its main beam - the other half in the back remains unlit.

Change the type of lighting to Parallel and render the scene: the difference is obvious in the rendering, although the scene remains unchanged in the Editor (Illus. 19).

The Parallel type is rarely used – at least in my work – a more defined variant on it, the Parallel Spot, is more common (see below).

To use spotlight sources now, hide the spheres from display (gray dots) and make the Plane visible (green dots, Illus. 20). Toggle Camera2 (Editor's Camera menu: Scene Cameras, Illus. 21).

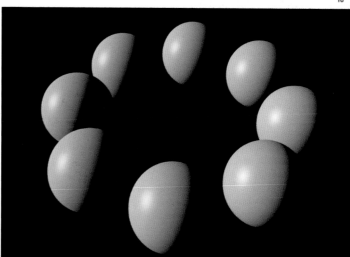

16

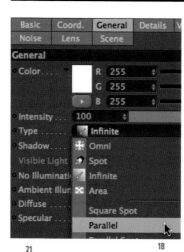

18

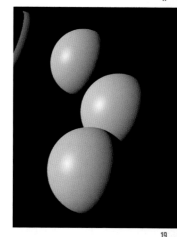

19

17

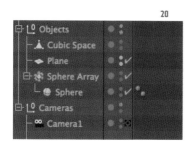

20

21

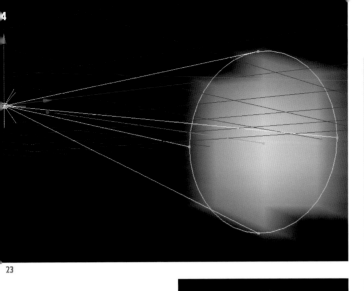

23

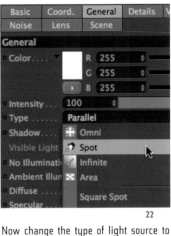

22

Now change the type of light source to Spot in the General panel (Illus. 22), and reset its direction (Coordinates panel: R.H and R.P=0).

As you can see, the Editor shows a circular cone (Illus. 23), the lit area is circular, or elliptic, as can also be seen in the rendering (Illus. 24). If the image displayed in your Editor differs from the one shown, you have probably selected a different shading type (e.g. Constant Shading), in your Display menu.

Cinema 4D allows you to define the spot's cone angle; in the Details panel of the Attributes Manager you can see that by default the Outer Angle is set to 30° (Illus. 25).

If the option Use Inner is checked, you can additionally set a value for the inner angle. Inner and outer angle will define the area where the circular lightbeam's brightness declines to 0.

The lightbeam's border will become sharper as the inner angle comes closer to the outer angle (Illus. 26).

The maximum inner angle value is equal to the outer angle value, the transition value between dark and light is 0 in this case.

The Square Spot is another light source that emits light from one point (Illus. 27).

24

25

26

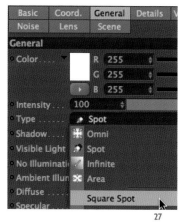

27

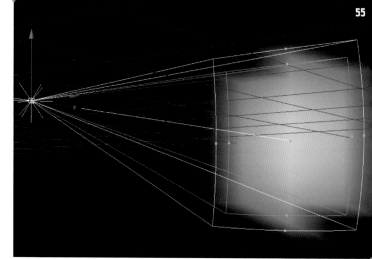

28

It emits a pyramid-shaped bundle of light and creates a spotlight with four corners (Illus. 28 and 29).

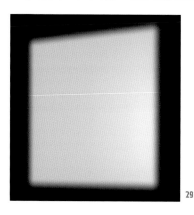

29

The Parallel Spot covers a segment of parallel light in the same way the Spot and Square Spot cover segments of omni-directional light (see above).

Change the type of lighting to Parallel Spot (Illus. 30). The Editor now shows a cylinder-shaped beam (Illus. 32).

The light patch is circular like a "normal" spot, but its size doesn't depend on the distance between the light source and surface. (Illus. 31 and 32)).

32

30

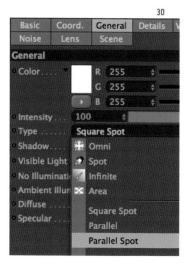

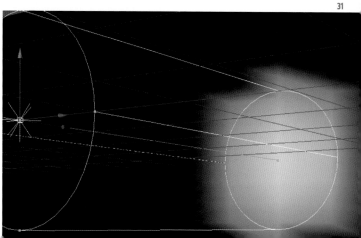

31

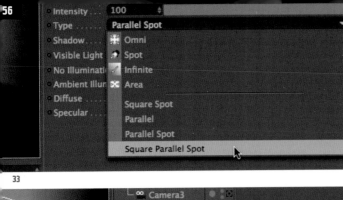

33

34

35

Since we often have to deal with orthogonal objects in architectural rendering, the Square Parallel Spot is an interesting tool, we use it to light pictures in Chapter 11, for example.

Change your lighting type to Square Parallel Spot (Illus. 33).
A prism-shaped body of light appears in the Editor, replacing the cylindrical body of the Parallel Spot.
The surface it lights is rectangular or trapezoid-shaped, depending on whether the light beams reach the surface at a right or oblique angle (Illus. 34).

The settings for square parallel spots are similar to the spot settings – you can define the size of the light bundle here too, but you have to do so with Radius settings.
As with the spots, you may define the maximum/minimum lightness transition by expanding or contracting the Inner Radius (Use Inner being checked, Illus. 35).

For the inner area of all spotlight types, you may decide to use a color other than white, and additionally define a color gradient for the transition to the outer edge.
All you have to do is activate the Colored Edge Falloff and Use Gradient options (Illus. 36 and 37).

36

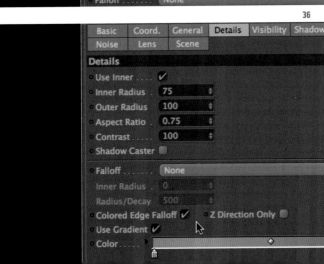

37

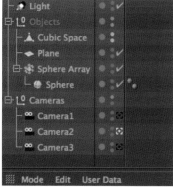

Now I would like to confront you with a phenomenon that can always been observed when lighting surfaces in Cinema 4D, an effect which gives rise to irritation at first.

Restructure the scene first by hiding the Plane object (gray dots) and show the Cubic Space (green dots, Illus. 38).
Toggle Camera3 (Cameras menu: Scene Cameras, Illus. 39).

Change your light source type back to Omni and make sure its intensity is set to 100 (Illus. 40).
Render the scene; all surfaces should be equally lit, the light should fade as is reaches the edges on each side (Illus. 41).

Now move the light source upwards by clicking and dragging the green arrow of the Y axis.
You can see how the ceiling surface becomes darker as you get closer with your light object. This effect can be observed in the rendering, too (Illus. 43).

This initially irritating phenomenon is to be explained: by default, the intensity of a light source in Cinema 4D does not decrease according to distance (as long as you haven't defined a Falloff), hence a surface doesn't become brighter the closer a light source gets to it.
The lighting gradient depends much more

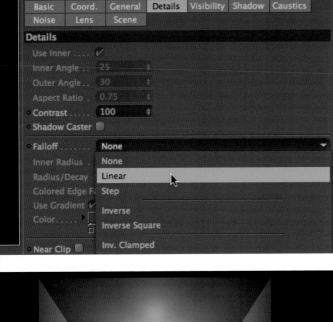

44

45

46

47

48

on the angle at which light beams meet the surface – light beams are strongest if they meet a surface at a right angle and weaker as the angle becomes more oblique. The light beam's angle falloff gets stronger as the light object approaches the surface, so on the other hand room surfaces appear brighter as light moves away from them.

But the distance between light and surface brightness does play an important role in real life since lighting energy decreases with distance.

So if you want to achieve a convincing visualization, you have to take this aspect into account.

Switch to the Details panel in the Attributes Manager and activate Linear Falloff (Illus. 44). Set Radius/Decay to 225 units and keep 0 for the Inner Radius setting (Illus. 45).

When you render the scene, the light effect in the room is completely different (Illus. 46). The Linear Falloff feature ensures a continuous reduction of lighting from the source until it equals 0 at the defined distance.

Now set a value for the inner distance (Details: Inner Radius=75, Illus. 47).

In the rendering you see that the brightness decrease is shown with much sharper contrast, since it does not begin directly at the light source and occurs over a shorter distance (Radius/Decay minus Inner Radius, Illus. 48).

You can check in the Editor that a falloff has been activated – take a look through the Editor camera and you can see how the falloff range is displayed with two spheres (Illus. 49).

Here you can conceive a more or less accurate impression of the light scene – i.e. normally you don't want the outer sphere to cut through the room body because that would lead to completely black areas in the corners of the inner space.

The introduction of Area light marks the end of this brief introduction.

Area light can be used in infinite geometrical variations since it can assume the shape of any object or spline.

First we will concentrate on a simple shape and light a room from the top with a square light surface.

Change the type of lighting to Area (Illus. 50), and make sure Falloff is deactivated (Details, Illus. 51).

The light should be rather bright (General panel: Intensity=200, Illus. 52) and should not create any shadows (Shadow: None).

Since by default an Area light is always a vertical rectangle, you should rotate it to a horizontal position (Coordinates: R.P=90, Illus. 52).

Drag it upwards so it is at one level with the ceiling (P.Y=100).

Cubes and area light are the same size in the X and Z direction, so we don't have to adjust anything here.

The rendered result doesn't look so bad (Illus. 53) – you will see that area light in this simple form is used for room lighting frequently.

Notice that the ceiling is completely black, which is understandable after the explanation above, since the lighting source is in the same place as the ceiling.

The floor is brightest, the walls show an even brightness gradient.

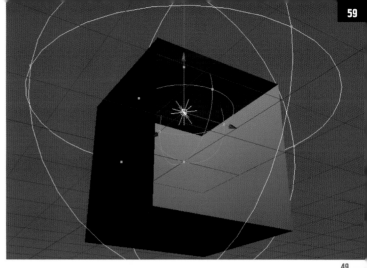

49

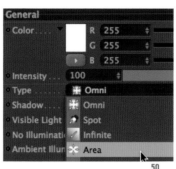

50

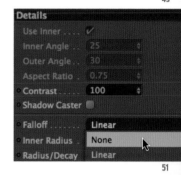

51

53

52

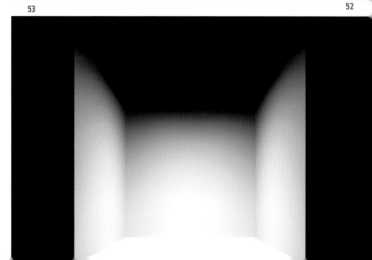

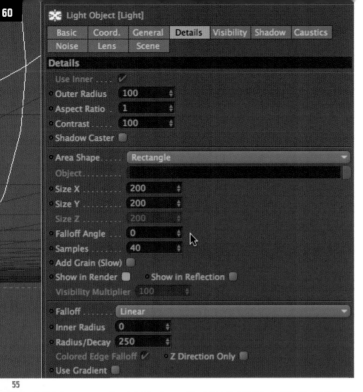

55

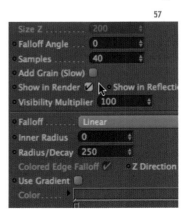

54

Now that you have installed a standard area lighting setup you might want to refine the result.

The first and most commonly applied option is to activate Linear Falloff to create a more dramatic brightness gradient on the dominating room surfaces, the walls.

Do this using the Detail panel in the Attributes Manager (Illus. 54).

Limit the falloff to 250 units (Radius/Decay=250, Illus. 55) - it should start directly at the light source, so keep using the 0 Inner Radius setting.

Make sure the Falloff Angle value is set to 0 (the default setting is 180!), otherwise the lighting on the walls will begin much further below and the entire scene will be too dark (you find the Falloff Angle entry in the Details panel, Illus. 55).

Render the scene; as you can see, the activated falloff makes a big difference (Illus. 56).

To simulate a light ceiling, you can make the light itself visible by activating the option Show in Render (Details, Illus. 57). The rendered result shows interferences that result from the fact that the area light

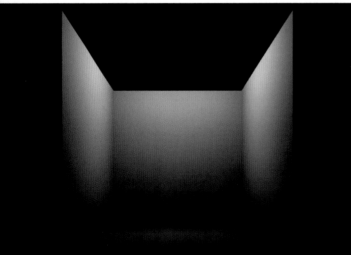

56

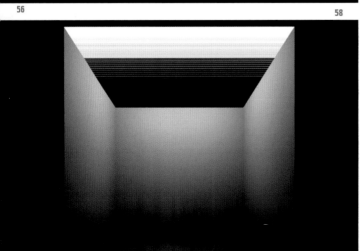

58

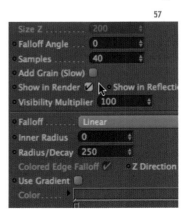

57

59

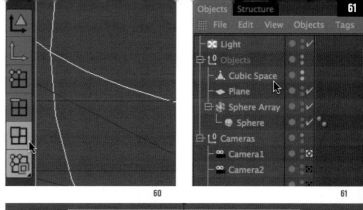

61

rectangle and the ceiling polygon are in the same place.

You could solve the problem by excluding the ceiling from lighting (using the Exclude Mode in the Scene panel), but for now it is OK to simply delete it since we don't need it anymore.

To remove the ceiling polygon without deleting the rest of the room, you have to cut it out from the room's polygon object first (listed as Cubic Space in the Object Manager).

Activate the Live Selection tool in the upper command bar (Illus. 59), and the Polygon tool in the left command bar (Illus. 60).

Make sure Cubic Space is selected by moving the mouse cursor over its surfaces, they should turn a lighter gray when "touched" (Illus. 61; if this is not the case you forgot to do one of the three things above.)

Click on the ceiling polygon (Illus. 62) and delete it (via the Delete command in the Edit menu, or using the backspace/delete key, Illus. 63).

Now render the scene; the light source will shine in pristine beauty and the area light setup is complete (Illus. 64).

As discussed, the area light is the most versatile light source in Cinema 4D, because it can assume any form and create every desired shadow. I think it's fine to end this introduction to light sources for now; you will get to know enough area light variants in the respective chapters, where they will be used for different lighting setups.

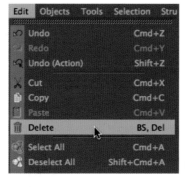

60

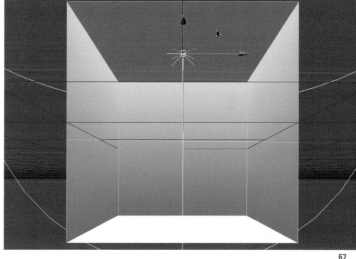

62

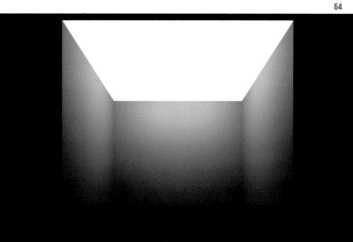

63

64

01

Shadows in Cinema 4D

05

In the previous chapter, we consciously omitted the subject of shadowing in the discussion of Cinema 4d light sources to keep matters simple. Now we will discuss the subject in a chapter of its own.

Again: you can only make creative use of the program's features when you take time to try things and learn by yourself. You will probably understand a lot of

things better if you use shadows in concrete lighting setups (see ch. 06-16).

Open the 05_start.c4d file and render the scene – you see a plane that casts a hard shadow (Illus. 02). The light source itself is invisible.

The Illustration above is of a different kind (Illus. 01) – the shadow has soft edges and the light source appears as a light spot with a slender aureole.

This kind of depiction requires a bit more

02

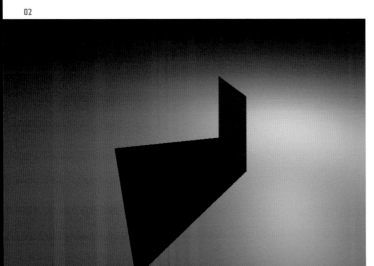

03

Light Shadow Space · Architectural Rendering with Cinema 4D

dedication during setup, but it is much more realistic, we will learn how to do this a bit further on.

Let's go back to our somewhat spartan first scene.

The first thing you notice is that the plane isn't completely black, although it is back-lit, thanks to a so-called camera light, an omni which was linked to the camera after placement.

Since its coordinates were set to 0 (Illus. 03), it is in the same place as the camera and lights the scene with reduced brightness (Intensity = 50).

The actual scene light that creates the shadow is an omni as well, the shadow type is set to Raytraced (Hard), in the General panel of the Attributes Manager (Illus. 04).

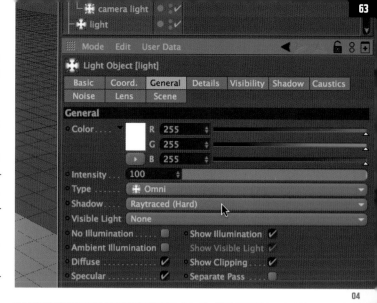

04

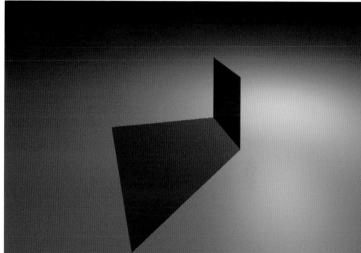

06

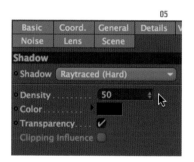

05

You can change a few settings in the Shadow panel, like the opacity level, for example (Density, Illus. 05 and 06).
Now set the shadow type to Shadow

Maps (Soft) and notice how the image changes (Illus. 07 and 08). It is apparent that the shadow does not begin directly at the object.

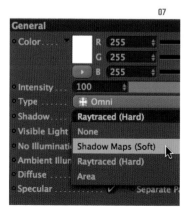

07

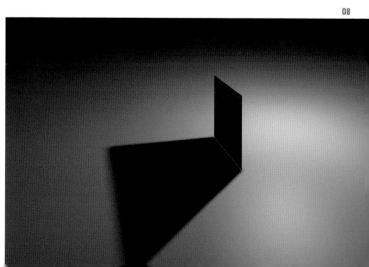

08

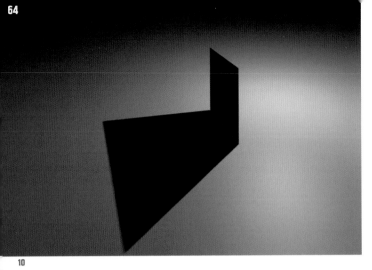

09

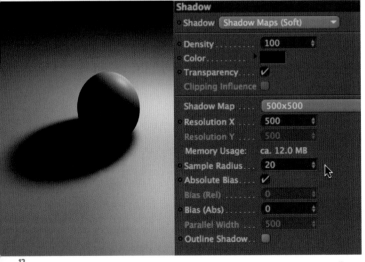

10

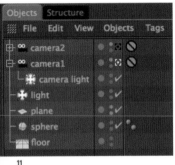

11

The fact that there is a gap between object and shadow at all results from the way it is calculated – as a grayscale bitmap that covers everything that cannot be "seen" by the light source.

However, the gap may be reduced a little in the Attributes Manager's Shadow panel, by setting the Absolute Bias value to 0 (Illus. 09 and 10).

The edge gradient can be controlled more effectively using the Sample Radius value – the lower the value, the sharper the shadow's edge (in our example: Sample Radius = 1, Illus. 10).

In general, soft shadow rendering times lie between raytrace and area shadow times.

Since they look more realistic than raytrace shadows you will want to use them at times.

The gap problem is no issue in certain object constellations, as can be seen on the left (Illus. 12; the plane object is hidden here and the sphere is shown, Illus. 11).

So both hard and soft shadows have certain imperfections, but they can both be rendered relatively quickly.

When you are in need for a visualization both realistic and geometrically correct, Area shadow is the first choice – the most important difference between Area shadow and the two beforementioned (hard and soft shadow) is that it reacts to the geometry of the light source that creates the shadow.

Change the light source's Shadow type from Shadow Maps to Area (Illus. 13) but keep the Omni for the time being.

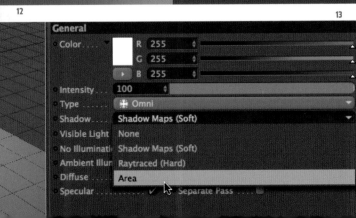

12

13

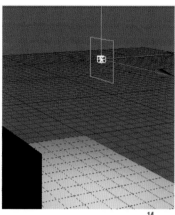

14

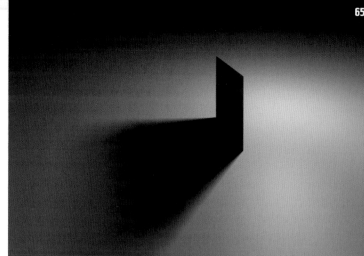

15

In the Editor, you can see that there is a square frame around the light source – area shadows obviously require a degree of light source stretching, even if you are using an omni (Illus. 14).

The rendering shows how the shadow image diffuses; there is a transition from the shadow's core to its edges, which becomes broader as the distance to the object increases (Illus. 15).

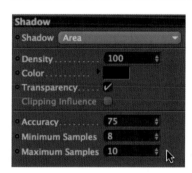

16

This realistic effect comes at the expense of a considerably longer rendering time. This problem can be minimized, at least during the setup phase, when frequent test-rendering is necessary.

You should for example lower the shadow's bitmap resolution considerably in the Shadow panel (Maximum Samples = 10, Illus. 16).

This will add grain to the shadow, but rendering is much faster and the image still gives you an adequate impression of your shadow's geometry (Illus. 17).

18

17

You have already seen that Cinema 4D assumes that even an omni stretches to a certain degree to create this characteristic spreading of a shadow.

Area light makes it easiest to control the ratio between light source geometry and shadow image (Illus. 18).

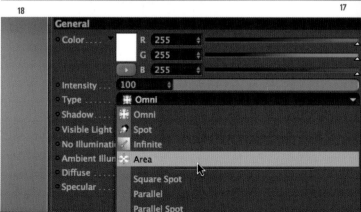

19

Render the scene – an irritating bold black strip appears on the floor directly under the area light (Illus. 19).

What happened? Although no falloff was defined, a starting angle applies to this non-active effect, influencing the brightness beamed onto the floor.

This problem can be solved by setting the Falloff Angle value to 0 in the Details panel of the Attributes Manager (Illus. 20).

This is certainly one of the more incomprehensible details Cinema 4D has to offer.

Whatever the case, the rendering is generated as desired after changing this parameter (Illus. 21).

21

20

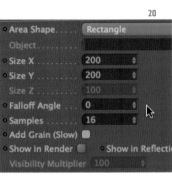

In the Details panel, change the Area Shape from Rectangle to Sphere, define an Outer Radius of 50, and check the Show in Render option (Illus. 22). The spherical light itself can be seen now in the rendering (Illus. 23).

22

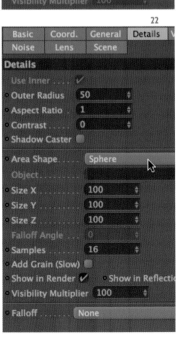

23

Now enlarge the sphere (Details: Outer Radius = 400) and render the scene again – as you can see, the core shadow becomes smaller and the gradient area grows considerably.

This is a good example of how the geometry of the light object determines the shadow image (Illus. 24).

Area light assumes the shape of any form of polygon object or spline – lets try a torus to begin with.

26

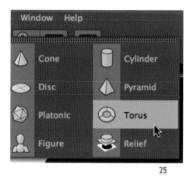

25

Place a torus in the scene (Primitive Objects menu, upper command bar: Torus, Illus. 25) and – in the Object Manager – move it onto the light object to make it a sub object to the light.

Set its position coordinates to 0, so it is in the same place as the light (Illus. 26).

Reduce its size in the Object panel (Ring Radius = 100, Pipe Radius = 15, Illus. 26).

In the Detail panel, please change the Area Shape to Object/Spline (Illus. 27). From the Object Manager, drag the torus into the Details panel's Object entry field, and the light source will assume its shape.

You see that you don't succeed doing so – you will have to change the torus into a polygon object before, since this trick only works with polygonal, not with parametrical objects.

Make sure it is selected and choose the Make Editable command in the Functions menu.

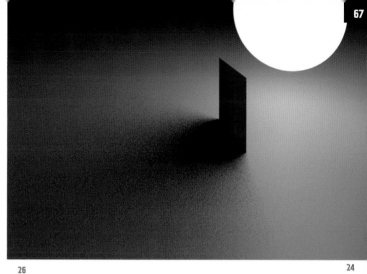

24

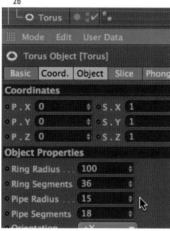

27

Select the light source again, drag the torus from the Object Manager and into the Object entry field in the Detail panel (Illus. 28).

To see the scene from a different perspective, switch to Camera2 (Cameras – Scene Cameras).

29

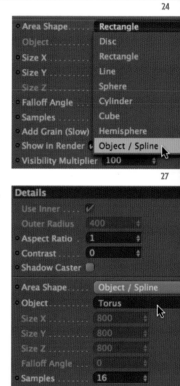

28

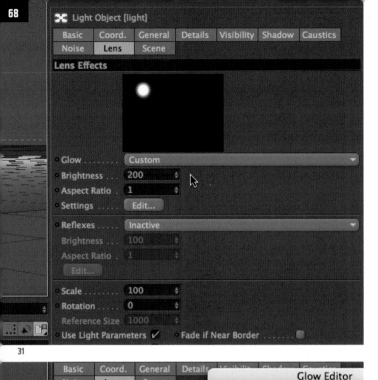

31

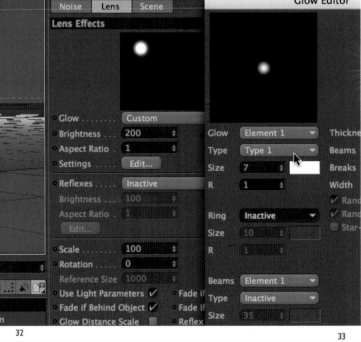

32

33

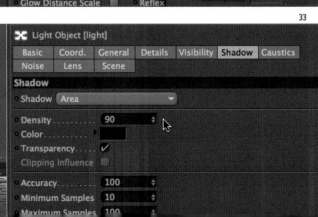

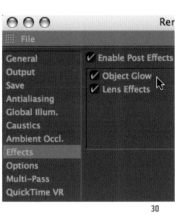

30

Make its camera light visible and hide the other.
Render the scene to see the shining ring (Illus. 29).

You have now seen how the three shadow types look like and how the light source's geometry influences the shadow image, which is interesting since area light can assume any shape.

In closing, I'd like to show you another function that almost always makes a light source look more realistic in a scene – a glow effect you can assign to the light source.

We have to differentiate between a general scene glow that can be limited to individual objects via their texture, and the glow that can be assigned to a light source out of a complex set of lens effects.

Since the general glow doesn't work well with light sources, we will look at the second variant.

For a light source to glow, Lens Effects have to be selected in the Render settings (Render menu, Render settings, Effects). The option Enable Post Effects has to be checked, in the list below you should find Lens Effects.
If not, pick it from the Post Effect pull-

down menu on the right (Illus. 30).
Make sure your light source is selected and switch to the Lens panel in the Attributes Manager.
Select Custom from the Glow menu and set Brightness to 200 (Illus. 31).

For Settings, click on the Edit button, choose Element 1 for Glow and Type 1 for Type. Set the size to 7.
Leave Ring and Beams inactive (Illus. 32). Confirm your settings by hitting OK.

Create a more elegant shadow effect before admiring the rendered result. After all, the test phase is over and the final rendering may take a bit longer now.

Set the shadow bitmap resolution to a higher value in the Shadow panel (Accuracy = 100, Maximum Samples = 100, Illus. 33).
Your rendering now shows a finer shadow resolution as well as a small aureole around the light sphere (Illus. 34).
These were some general remarks on the methods to create shadows in your scene. The following chapters on lighting setups contain further information.

If you remember how difficult it was to create shadow images by analogue means (a complex chapter in Projective Geometry!), then you will appreciate that a program like Cinema 4D makes this work so much easier. However, you will notice that working with light and shadow is full of surprises that will put both your patience and technical comprehension to the test when working in this digital environment.

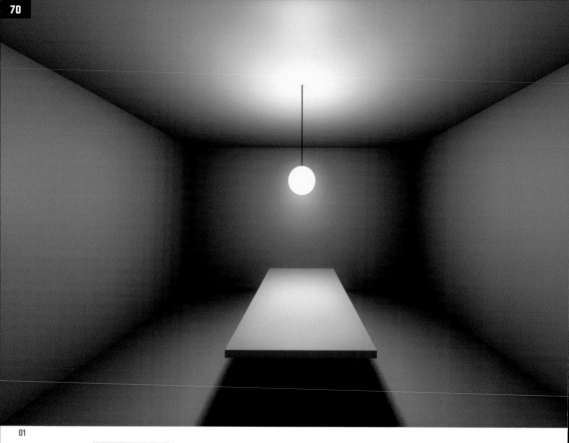

01

06

Space and Central Lighting

We will concentrate on a simple lighting model to get started: a spherical light source will brighten a room, a table will cast a shadow on the floor.

The aim is not to visualize a complex lighting dramaturgy, but become acquainted with parameters such as brightness, shadow graphics, brightness decrease, selective lighting and so forth, things we will be dealing with through-out the following exercises. You can see what the final result should look like in the example above (Illus. 01).

A sphere-shaped light will be our most important tool when reconstructing this lighting situation.

By using Area shadow, we will try to achieve a differentiated, soft shadow bitmap. Only two other fill lights will be necessary, one to light the ceiling and a camera light for the foreground.

Getting Started

Open the 06_start.c4d file (see p.236). It was created with C4D 10.

You see a room with a sphere object hanging from the ceiling that is meant to represent a light (Illus. 02).
There is a table directly below the lamp.
For Editor display Constant shading (Lines) was selected (Editor menu, Display), Grid

02

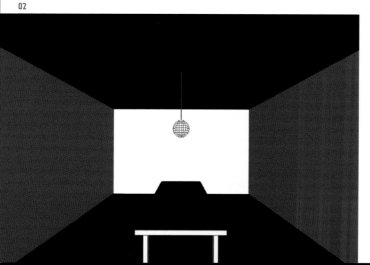

and world axis are hidden (Editor menu Edit: Configure – Filter).

For the view, a camera is in use, which is protected – it is listed in the Object Manager, and the Protection tag indicates its position and angle is locked (Illus. 06).

Switch to the Editor camera if you want to navigate within the scene (Editor menu Cameras).

Render the scene. Although there are no light sources in the scene, you can see the room, because Cinema 4D uses a Default Light that replaces missing light sources (Illus. 03).

After reading chapter 01, (Cinema 4D · Overview and Navigation) you know that the Default Light is emitting light omnidirectional from above and does not create shadows.

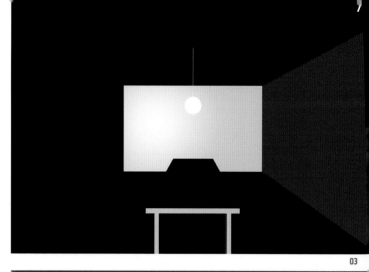

03

04

You can change the position of this lighting substitute by selecting the Default Light command from the Display menu (Illus. 04) and clicking on the sphere that appears (Illus. 05).

Right clicking on the sphere resets the light to its default settings.

The lighting sphere is white because it was given a material with a Luminance channel (Illus. 06).

You can examine the channel's settings by double-clicking the Texture tag next to the sphere object in the Object Manager (Illus. 07).

Notice that the material's luminance doesn't influence the scene, it just ensures the sphere is always white.

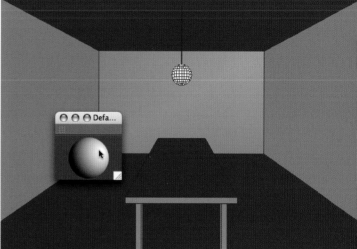

05

06

07

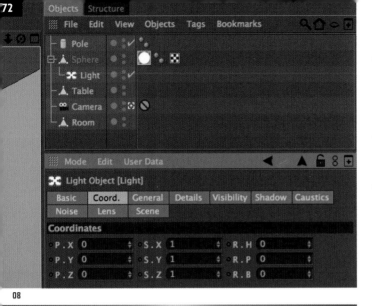

08

09

A Primary Light as Central Lighting

Place a light source in the scene by clicking on the Scene Objects icon in the upper command bar.

This light will be responsible for the overall lighting in the room, including the shadow cast under the table.

The new light source appears in the middle of the coordinates system, i.e. in the middle of the room, like any other new object will do.

Make the new light source a sub-object to the light sphere by dragging it onto the sphere object in the Object Manager (Illus. 08).

Make sure the light object is selected and set the position values to 0 in the Coordinates panel of the Attribute Manager (P.X, P.Y, P.Z = 0, Illus. 08).

Now the new light source is located exactly in the middle of the sphere.

(As you already should know, a sub-object's position refers to the position of the main object, the position offset values P.X etc are relative to the main object's. We already made use of this feature several times, e.g. for camera lights.)

Render the scene – the result already looks more like central lighting (Illus. 09), but it is still missing shadows.

Select the light source in the Object Manager and define hard shadows (Raytraced (hard)) in the General panel (Illus. 10).

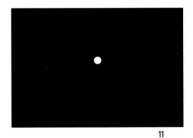

11

Now when rendering the scene again, everything is black except for the white sphere (Illus. 11).

10

The scene appears black because your light source cannot penetrate closed surfaces – like the sphere's shell – when you've defined shadows for it.

But Cinema 4D allows you to exclude objects from lighting, which keeps them from becoming obstacles for light rays.

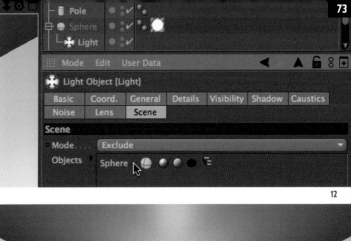

12

Make sure the light object is selected and take a look at the Attributes Manager's Scene panel, which allows you to limit lighting to individual objects.

For Mode, take Exclude – then move the sphere object from the Object Manager into the Objects field below. This will make this single object "invisible" to the light source.

Render the scene again – the light illuminates the room and creates a hard shadow under the table (Illus. 13).

However, the shadow is too jagged; it will get smoother edges when you use area shadow.

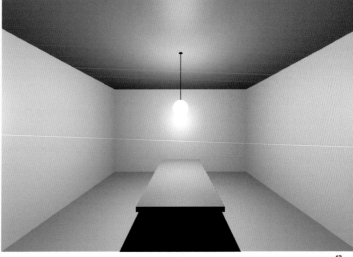

13

This type of shadow is working finest when it comes along with area lighting. From Cinema 4D 9.5 upwards, an area light can assume the shape of any object, e.g. your sphere object.

Make sure the light source is selected and change the light type from Omni to Area in the General panel of the Attributes Manager (Illus. 14).

In the Details panel, for Area Shape you choose Object/Spline (Illus. 15). Your sphere object is still parametrical, so you will have to convert it into a polygon object before using it for the light source's geometry.

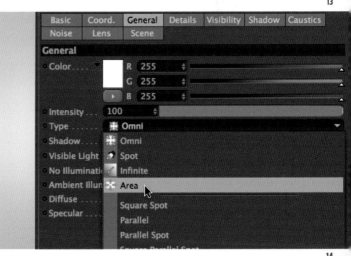

14

16

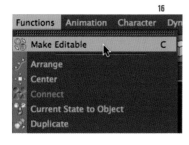

15

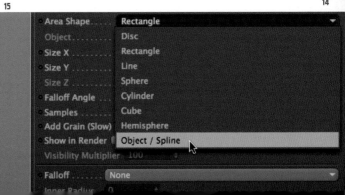

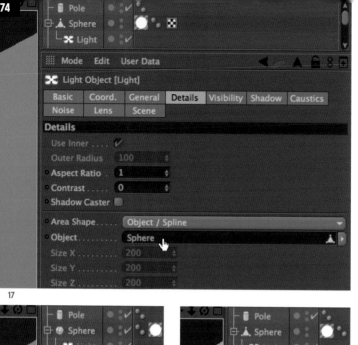

17

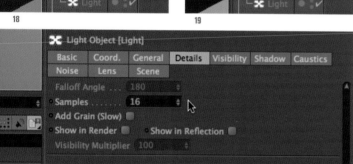

18   19

20

21   22

Make sure the sphere object is selected and choose the Make Editable command from the Functions menu (Illus. 16).

In the Object Manager, the sphere is displayed in a different way now (Illus. 18 and 19).

Now select the light source, bring the Details panel to the front, and drag the sphere object into the Object entry underneath the Area Shape selection menu (Illus. 17).

As desired, this will give the light source the same shape as the sphere.

Area light enriches a scene with a more realistic ambience, especially when it is used with area shadows.

The price you pay is longer rendering time, which can be annoying both in your setup phase and for your final rendering. This makes knowing the proper settings that bring quality and rendering time to a reasonable balance even more important.

In the first place, it's the accuracy of the light source itself that is important here. You can adjust it in the Samples entry in the Details panel. Set it to the minimum (16, Illus. 20).

Let's work on the shadow now. Select Area Shadow in the General panel (Illus. 21) and set a low bitmap resolution value in the Shadow panel of the Attributes Manager (Minimum Samples and Maximum Samples = 10, Accuracy = 75, Illus. 22). Reduce Density as well so the shadow isn't completely black (Density = 80).

Render the scene – the shadow now has a soft edge, but a very grainy one, too (Illus. 23) – this is due to the low sample values, and can be corrected later.

The transition gradient is too wide as well, but you can also solve this problem later on.

But let's look at a more important aspect of your lighting – it is still much to uniform for such a small light that is lighting the room all by itself.

A slight brightness decrease is visible along the wall edges that results from the fact that light beams weaken as the obliqueness increases.

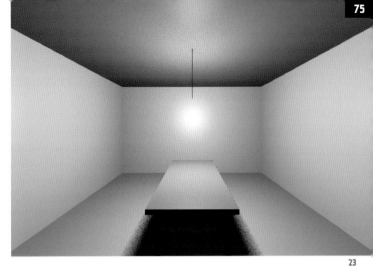

23

This decrease can be made more dramatic by using the Falloff function.

Select Linear Falloff in the Detail panel of the Attributes Manager, set the Inner Radius to 50 and Radius/Decay to 475 (Illus. 24).

This makes the light decrease continuously, starting with 100% 50 units off the center. You can check the result immediately in your rendering (Illus. 25).

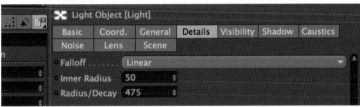

24

Now that the sphere has become our light's reference, it's not white anymore, the luminance channel of it's material doesn't work anymore.

To make it visible again, copy the sphere

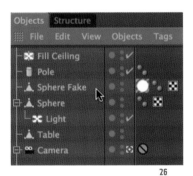

26

25

object (by pressing the Ctrl key and dragging it inside the Object Manager), delete the sub-object in the copy and rename it using Sphere Fake.

To see a white sphere again, you will also have to move the original sphere's Texture tag to the copied sphere (Illus. 26).

Render the scene again, and the shining sphere will reappear (Illus. 27).

27

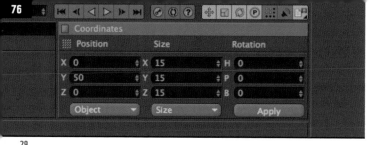

29

28

Now that you have separated the white sphere and the actual shadow-casting light source you can modify the edge of the shadow surface.

The transition from the shadow to the remaining floor surface is too wide, the

tabletop isn't that far from the area of the floor the shadow covers.

You have to edit the geometry of the sphere to create a narrower transition – the smaller the sphere, the sharper the contours of the shadow graphics.

Select the Sphere polygon object in the Object Manager (Illus. 28). In the Coordinates Manager, choose Size for the Size display (in the small pull-down menu below the Size entry fields, Illus. 29), enter 15 instead of 30 for all three axis values and click on Apply, or press Return.

The light emitting sphere is smaller now, the shadow edge gradient has become smaller too (Illus. 30 and 31 show a rendering before and after the change).

About the size change: the sphere which is in use as the reference for the light's shape, is a polygon object now that it has been converted, not a parametrical object any more.

Accordingly, its radius cannot be edited in the Attributes Manager Object settings any longer.

As a polygon body, it consists of surfaces which together only appear to be a perfect sphere because of its relatively high resolution and the Phong tag assigned to it.

It can be edited via its X, Y or Z measurements, either by changing a factor (you can do this in the Attributes and Coordinates Manager) or by changing the actual measurements (this is only possible in the Coordinates manager via Size mode, as shown above).

30

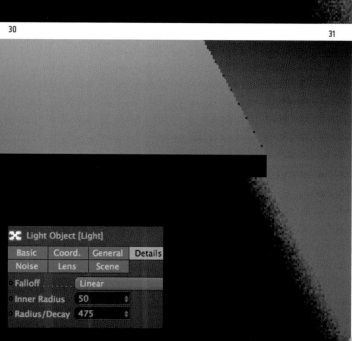

31

Your results should be satisfactory. Our primary lighting looks good, except for the somewhat grainy resolution of the shadow.

A look at the rendering shows that the scene still isn't perfect: the ceiling should be a bit brighter than the floor since it is closer to the light (Illus. 32).

Why is it darker at all? Because lights in Cinema 4D shine brighter on a surface the closer their beams are to being perpendicular to the surface.

Light sources with diverging (i.e. non-parallel) rays, create ever sharper angles the closer light and surface are to each other.

(This phenomenon becomes particularly apparent if no falloff is defined, but can be observed even then.)

32

33

Fill Light for the Ceiling

The ceiling should be made brighter, the rest of the room is well-lit.

You already know that you can make a light source shine exclusively on selected objects, but you have to make the ceiling a separate, individual object before.

It has been part of the polygon object that represents the whole room until now.

Select the Polygon tool from the command bar along the left edge of the screen and the Live Selection tool from the upper command bar (Illus. 33 and 34).

Select the Room object in the Object Manager (Illus. 35) and move your mouse cursor over the ceiling surface in the Editor.

Click on the surface when it turns a light gray, the red edge indicates the ceiling polygon is selected (Illus. 36).

Now select the Split command from the Functions menu (not to be confused with Disconnect, Illus. 37).

You can see a new polygon also called

34

35

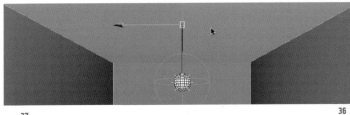

37

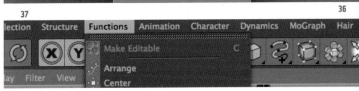

36

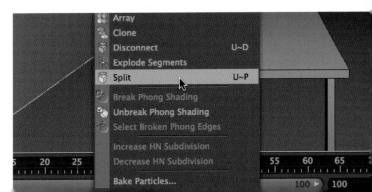

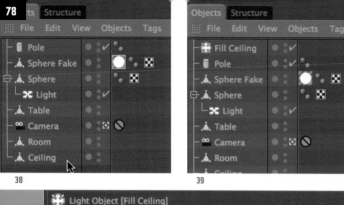

38

39

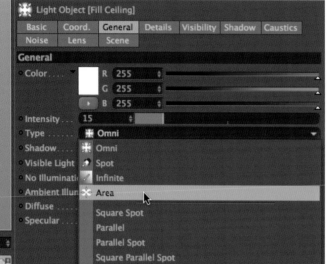

40

Room in the Object Manager – it is a duplicate of the selected ceiling polygon.

However, the original still exists and needs to be removed.

It is good that it is still selected (unless you have clicked on something else in the meantime), so all you need to do is press Delete.

If the whole room disappears by mistake, press Ctrl-Z, select the ceiling polygon again and try deleting it again. Call the new polygon Ceiling (Illus. 38).

Check with Object Information (Object Manager's Object menu) to make sure the original ceiling polygon is really gone since there can occur a number of problems if two identical polygons are in the same place.

Now that the ceiling is an individual object we can take care of brightening it with an additional light source.

Place another light source in the scene and name it Fill Ceiling (fill = fill light, Illus. 39).

For its type, select Area in the General panel of the Attributes Manager; shadow casting isn't necessary (Illus. 40 and 41).

A rectangle is preset as shape in the Details panel, which is exactly what we need in this case.

41

42

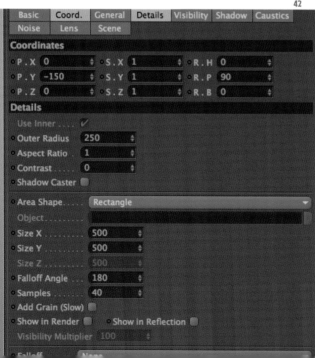

But rotate the rectangle into a horizontal position and drag it down (Coordinates panel: R.P = 90 and P.Y = -150, Illus. 42), to bring it to ground level (keep in mind, the further a light is from the surface, the brighter it's lit.)

Change the measurements of the rectangle here as well by setting the Outer Radius to 250, the Size X and Size Y val-

43

ues will follow automatically. Falloff isn't necessary (Illus. 42).

Switch to the Scene panel of the light source's settings.
Make sure the Include mode is set, then drag the ceiling object from the Object Manager into the Object entry field below (Illus. 43).
Since we want to brighten just the ceiling, we only need a low brightness setting (General panel: Intensity = 15, Illus. 44).

Render the scene. The ceiling's brightness appears correct now, matching the other room surfaces.
Aside from the shadow resolution, there is one flaw left: the front surfaces of the table are completely dark (Illus. 45).

Camera Light

We will use a low-key omni to solve this problem. This light will brighten the scene from the camera's point of view.

Place a new light source, call it Camera Light and make it subordinate to the camera by dragging it on to the camera in the Object Manager (Illus. 46).
This links the light to the camera's position – set the light source coordinates in the Coordinates panel (P.X, P.Y, P.Z) to 0, to make its placement identical to the camera's.

Set the brightness (Intensity) to 45 in the General panel and keep the Omni type. Shadow should stay deactivated (Illus. 46).

Choose Linear Falloff (Radius/Decay = 350) in the Details panel to create a more dramatic brightness decrease on the table surface (Illus. 47).

44

45

46

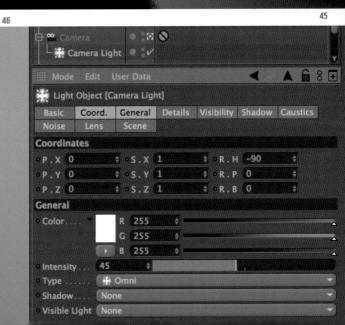

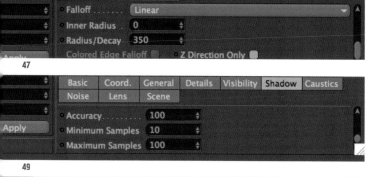

47

49

48

50

51

52

Set the Include mode in the Scene panel of the Attributes Manager and drag the Table object from the Object Manager into the Objects entry field so it is the only thing lit by the camera light (Illus. 48).

Now we finally want to refine the shadow graphics. Activate your first light source and set the Maximum Samples value to 100 in the Shadow panel of the Attributes Manager, and the Minimum Samples value to 10 (Illus. 49).

Render the critical image segment using the Render Region command (Render menu). The table is a bit too bright, but the shadow surface has a much finer grain (Illus. 50).

So now we should be satisfied with out lighting setup and can move on to the final rendering settings.

Final Settings

Since the light setup is done, we can focus on rendering the scene for a presentation.

A few settings have to be adjusted to improve the quality, rendering time isn't as important now as it was in the setup phase.

Open the Render settings panel (Render Menu).

In the Render Setting's General panel, select Best for Antialiasing to ensure optimum corner smoothing (Illus. 51).

In the Output panel, set the rendering measurements in pixels (Resolution) – the given measurements result in a picture with a resolution of 300 dpi over the entire page range in this book (Illus. 52).

Ambient Occlusion (Illus. 53) leads to a somewhat more realistic image, since this function darkens areas in which surfaces meet, e.g. room corners.

Keep the given settings, only click on the black square on the left end of the gradient and choose a mid-range gray from the color palette.

An aureole around the light sphere would be nice – you can create this effect using a Post Effect, an effect that is calculated after actual rendering (and therefore lengthens rendering time).

Activate the Post Effects option in the Effects panel and either check Glow in the list below, or pick it from the pull-down menu on the right.

This effect brightens the overall scene and creates an aureole around our light (Illus. 54).

The effect can be controlled with a number of settings, but we will leave the default settings for the sake of simplicity.

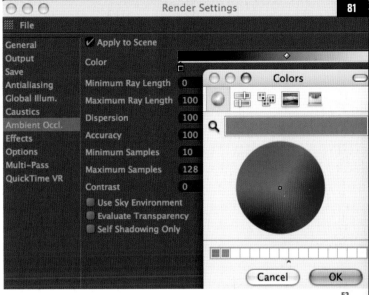

53

You have now adjusted your settings to improve the quality of your rendering, but keep in mind these changes also result in longer rendering times.

Before rendering in the Picture Viewer (Render menu, Illus. 55), be sure to render crucial image segments with the Render Region command (Render menu) before.

54

55

Single Space and Central Lighting

01

07

Sun and Diffuse Light I · Interiors Spaces

Sunlight casts a defined and contoured hard shadow in a room and on object surfaces when it reaches an interior space. The shadow's geometry is defined by the sunlight's entry angle.

Diffuse daylight gives the room additional light, even if the sky is overcast. This light also casts shadows, although these shadows seem soft and airbrushed.

In the image above they can be observed on the ceiling near the window frames (Illus. 01).

Sunlight is parallel light that creates parallel shadows, whereas diffuse light can be considered as an infinite amount of errant omnies – a portion of the light rays they emit enters the room via its windows and creates diverging shadows inside.

In principle we need two light sources to visualize this kind of situation, which have to simulate these differing light and shadow geometry characteristics.

Getting Started

Open the 07_start.c4d file (see p.236). It was created using Version 10.

You can see a room with windows – there are no "real" light sources yet (Illus. 02). Constant Shading (Lines) was chosen for the Editor display (Editor Menu: Display).

02

We look at the interior from a fixed camera.

Switch to the Editor camera if you want to navigate through the scene (Editor menu, Cameras).

Distance Light (Sun)

A sunlight source should be created first. From the Scene Objects menu in the upper command bar, place a light source in the scene.

An omni appears in the middle of the scene. Call it Sun (Illus. 04)

Make sure your new light source in the Object Manager is selected, and choose Infinite for Type (Attributes Manager – General panel, Illus. 03). You can see how the icon changes in the Object Manager (Illus. 05).

The position of this light source in the scene is completely irrelevant, the only decisive aspect is the direction of its light rays (see Chapter 04, Light Sources in Cinema 4D).

By default, the light shines in Z direction. Change the direction by setting the rotation around the Y axis (R.H) to 45° and around the X axis (R.P) to -25° in the Attributes Manager's Coordinates panel (Illus. 06).

Click on the double arrow next to the corresponding value with your mouse cursor, keep your mouse button pressed and move your mouse. You can see how the light direction changes in the Editor (of course you may also type in the value).

Choose hard shadow for the light source in the General panel (Raytraced (Hard), Illus. 06).

Render the scene to see how your first light source illuminates the room.

Notice that only the directly lit surface are visible (Illus. 07), and that the rest of the scene is completely dark.

03

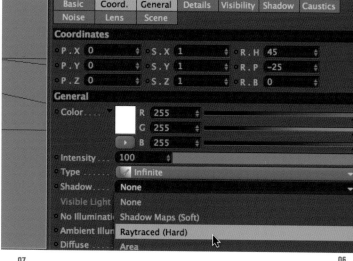

04

05

07

06

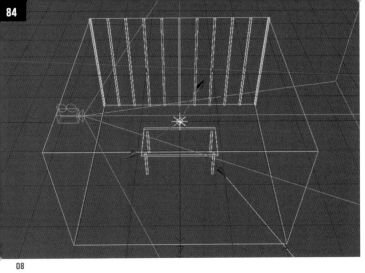

08

Keep in mind that you have to experiment with the light source a bit yourself in a comparable situation before you achieve a satisfactory shadow casting effect.

As we said, the only relevant aspect is the direction of the light source's own Z axis when using infinite lighting.

Look at the scene from the Editor camera perspective – the lighting direction is shown by the long white line with the orange-colored dot at the end (Illus. 08).

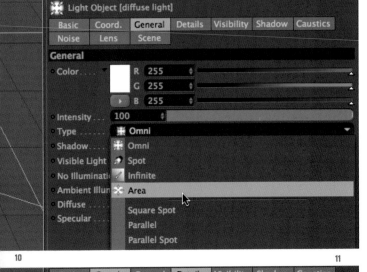

09

10

11

Area Light (Diffuse Daylight)

It is best to use area lighting, which creates a soft and relatively pale shadow, to visualize diffuse daylight in our example.

Place another light source in the scene and call it diffuse light (Illus. 09).
For Type, select Area in the General panel of the Attributes Manager (Illus. 10).

Move the new light source 250 units to the left, so it is one level with the window (P.Z = -250, Illus. 11). Make it as wide as the window facade (Details panel: Size X = 500, Size Y = 300).

It is decisive to enter a Falloff Angle of 0 (Details too), contrary to the default 180. The angle set to 0 guarantees that the room surfaces will get the most light closest to the window wall and become darker as the distance to the light source increases.

The rendering shows that the room is brightened by the new fill light (Illus. 12), although there is little differentiation – the right wall is much too bright and the brightness decrease on the roof and floor is not satisfying.

This is due to the Cinema 4D rule you already know: light rays make a surface

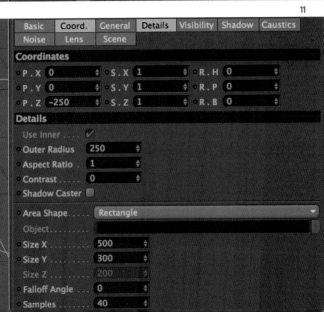

brighter as their perpendicularity increases – hence the high brightness values for the right wall.

You will now give the new light source some falloff to achieve a more dramatic image, i.e. make sure the brightness decreases over the room distance.

Make sure the diffuse light source is selected in the Object Manager and select Linear Falloff in the Attributes Manager's Detail panel (Illus. 13).

Keep the 0 Inner Radius setting and set Radius/Decay to 575 (Illus. 14). This will turn down the area light's brightness to 0% at a distance of 575 units – since our room is 500 units wide, almost the entire brightness decrease will take place within the room.

But do turn up the Intensity control in the General panel (Intensity = 250, Illus. 15).

For the view through the window, you could add an image, a sky background

12

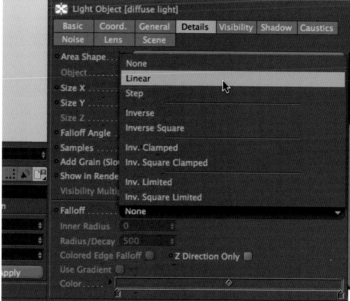

13

14

for example, in later compositing – e.g. in Photoshop.

You may as well do something about the windows in our scene file, the easiest being to brighten the window planes.

Just check the Show in Render option (Details panel, Illus. 16), and the rendering immediately looks better (Illus. 17).

17   15

16

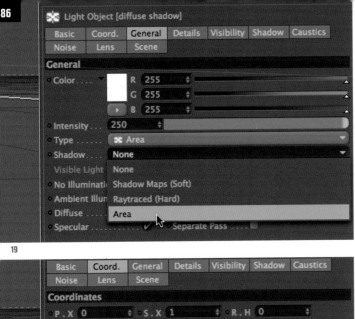

19

20

21

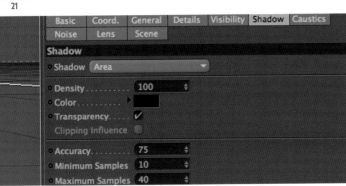

22

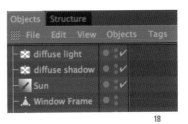

18

Diffuse Shadows

As you have certainly noticed, your area light doesn't create shadows yet.

A shadow the way you imagine it (see Illus. 01) requires a light source that is placed a bit further off the facade.

However, the light source you just placed just had the advantage that it was in the same place as the window wall, which made it easy to control the brightness decrease – not to mention the opportunity to use it for brightening up the window surfaces.

Taking this into account, it seems a good idea to divide light and shadow casting between two light sources.

The advantage this solution offers is the ability to set the brightness decrease along the room surface and the appearance of the shadow independently from one another.

Cinema 4D allows you to make light sources create shadows without contributing to the illumination.

In this case, the intensity and falloff settings define only the strength and brightness progression of the shadow image.

It isn't always necessary to take the extra step of controlling light and shadows separately – it wasn't necessary when you visualized sunlight at the beginning of this chapter, for example.

It makes things easier for you to use a copy of the area light already in use for the diffuse light.

Copy the light object by dragging it in the Object Manager while pressing the Ctrl

23

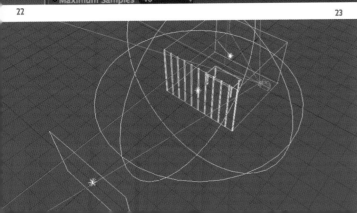

key – or use the common copy & paste function by pressing Ctrl C and Ctrl V. Name it diffuse shadow when done (Illus. 18).

Keep Intensity at 250 and select Area as shadow type (General panel, Illus. 19). Move the light source away from the facade by 750 units (P.Z = -1000, Illus. 20). Check the Shadow Caster option in the Details panel (Illus. 21). This simple, inconspicuous check ensures the third light source will create shadows without contributing to the lighting.

Area shadow requires a lot of render processing. To avoid losing too much time while test-rendering, set very low sampling values in the Shadow panel (Minimum Samples = 10, Maximum Samples = 40, Accuracy = 75, Illus. 22).

Your rendering shows - beside the graininess that is caused by the low bitmap sample rate - that the diffuse light's shadow darkens the right part of the room to much (Illus. 24).

You can correct this using two tricks: in the first place, define Linear Falloff for he shadow-casting light source (Details,

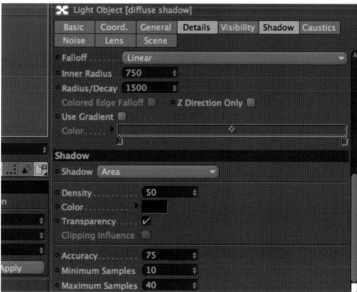

24

25

Illus. 25) - the falloff should start at 750 units (i.e. on the facade level) and end at 1500 units (see also Illus. 23). In this case, falloff will diminish the shadow's inten-

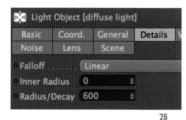

26

sity with increasing room depth.

Another trick is to set Density to 50 in the shadow panel - this makes the overall shadow lighter.

You may also raise the falloff distance for the light-generating area light to brighten the right part of the room (Radius/Decay = 650, Illus. 26).

Now the rendering is almost perfect (Illus. 27).

27

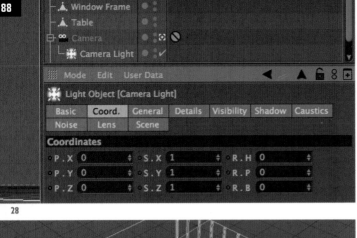

28

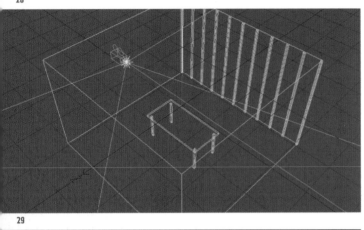

29

Examine both the shadow the table casts on the right wall and the shadows the window frame casts on ceiling and floor. They show you whether your light set is OK - they should be recognizable, but not too strong.

Camera Light

One flaw still needs to be corrected: the front surfaces of window frames and table are almost black, since both of the "active" light sources barely reach these objects (the infinite sun light not at all).

A camera light is helpful here, i.e. an omni in the same position as the camera.

Please, place a fourth light source in the scene (Camera Light).
Drag the light source on to the camera object in the Object Manager. This makes it subordinate to the camera (Illus. 28), which makes the light follow the camera when you change its position.
In the Coordinates panel, set all the light's position coordinates P to 0 (see also Il-lus. 29).
Lower the Intensity setting to 10, so this camera light doesn't outshine the scene (Illus. 30).

The lighting setup is complete now. Before rendering the scene for the last time, you should adjust a couple of settings to improve the quality of your final result.

First you should increase the resolution of the area shadow (created by your shadow caster light) by raising the sampling rates to 50 (Minimum Samples) and 200 (Maximum Samples).
You should also set Accuracy to 100 (Il-lus. 31).

Other ways to optimize the image are

30

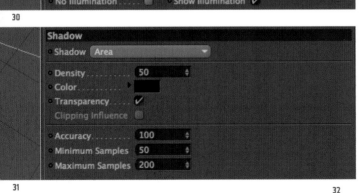

31

32

available within the Render settings (Render menu: Render settings).

Set the desired image size in pixels in the render setting's Output panel. (Our file uses a resolution of 1945 x 1323 pixel, so with 300 dpi the image will fit into my page layout; Illus. 32).

In the General Panel, choose Best Antialiasing to ensure perfect contour smoothing (Antialiasing should be tuned off during testing, Illus. 34).

Make sure you also check Ambient Occlusion to simulate a slight dirt effect in the corners (Illus. 33).

Check critical segments of your scene once again using the Render Region command (Render menu) before you start your final rendering (Illus. 35).

When you think everything is OK, render your scene in the Picture Viewer (Illus. 36) – from here you may save your image afterwards.

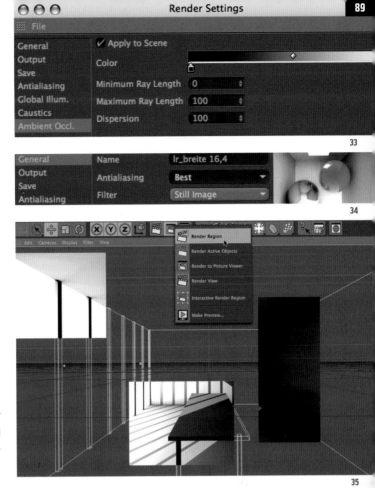

33

34

35

36

01

08

Rooms and Indirect Lighting

Bright light entering a room indirectly - e.g. through a gap between ceiling and wall, is a special lighting situation.

You see the main shadow starts sharp-edged and becomes softer the further the distance to the gap becomes.

The brightness decrease in the room itself is rather dramatic (Illus. 01).

We will reconstruct this lighting situation in the following chapter.

A cylinder-shaped area light is the most important tool here. It will be positioned in the gap's area and should create differentiated, soft shadow graphics using the area shadow.

Two fill lights, one to brighten the ceiling and a camera light for the foreground are the only other tools needed.

Getting Started

Open the 08_start.c4d file (see p. 236). It was created with version 10.

You can see a room whose ceiling leaves a gap to the wall at the right, which again is higher than the room, so its upper end is out of sight (Illus. 02).

Gouraud shading (Lines) was selected for display in the Editor (Editor's Display menu), You may hide Grid and World Axis if you feel like it (choose Configure from the Editor's Edit menu, then uncheck the two items in the Attributes' Manager's Fil-

02

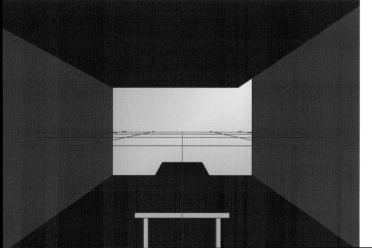

ter panel).

As for the view, a camera is in use – it is listed in the Object Manager, the Protection tag indicating it's position and angle is locked (Illus. 03).

Toggle the Editor camera if you want to navigate within the scene (Editor menu Cameras).

Cylinder as Primary Light (Key)

For light entering a room via a longitudinal gap, a light source placed in line with the ceiling opening is recommendable. For this purpose, Cinema 4D offers two types of area light, Line and Cylinder. However, since the line shape will cause only a very sharp-edged shadow, you're left with the cylinder.

03

Place a light source (from the Scene Objects menu in the upper command bar). Name it "Key" (it is the so-called key lighting source in the scene, Illus. 03).

Select in Area the General panel's Type pull-down, and choose Cylinder as shape in the Details panel's Area Shape menu. (Illus. 04 and 05).

Toggle the four-viewport view (F5, Illus. 07) and open the Coordinates panel in the Attributes Manager (Illus. 06). Move the light cylinder upwards (P.Y = 155) and to the right (P.Z = 225). Rotate it around the Y axis (R.H = 90). Click on the double arrow next to the value field and move your mouse to see the changes in real time.

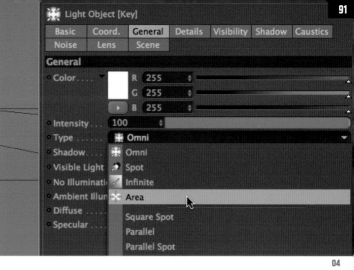

04

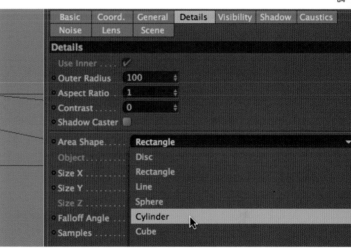

05

07   06

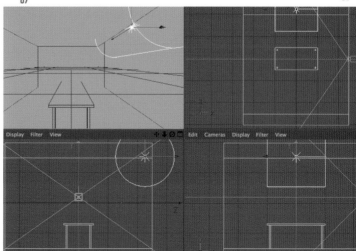

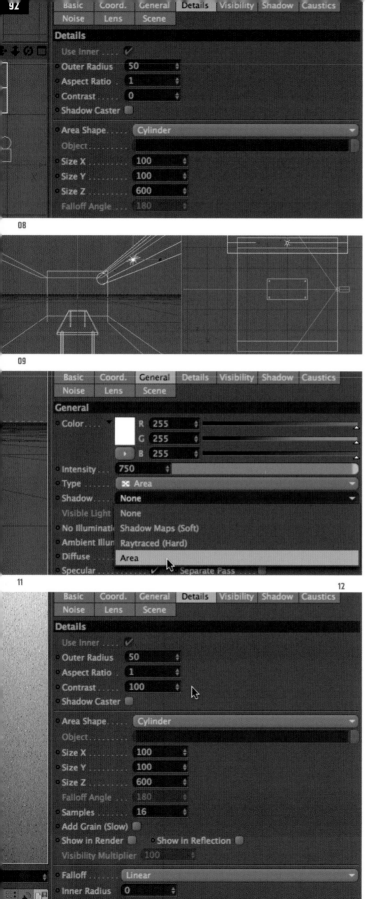

08

09

11

12

The shape isn't right yet. Make sure your light source is selected and toggle the Detail panel in the Attributes Manager (Illus. 08).

Adjust the thickness of the cylinder (Outer Radius = 50). This should make the X and Y sizes change to 100 automatically (Illus. 08).

Make the light cylinder a bit longer than the width of the room (Size Z = 600, Illus. 08, 09).

Position and dimension of the cylinder are of decisive importance for the lighting effect in the room, but they are also of pivotal importance for the appearance of the shadow graphics.

The settings I suggest here are the result of a long testing phase. You should bear

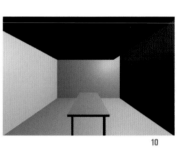

10

in mind that you will have to play around with these settings when you deal with a comparable situation before you achieve a satisfactory result.

Render the scene – the light source still doesn't create a shadow, so it isn't possible to assess its quality (Illus. 10).

Set Area shadow in the General panel – this is the only type of shadow we can use in our example (Illus. 11).

Increase the brightness (Intensity) of the light source to 750. Switch back to the Detail panel, adjust Contrast to 100, the light's sample rate to 16 and define a Linear Falloff of 0–650 units (Illus. 12).

Now render the scene again. The shadow spreads over the room surfaces in shades

of gray, you can also see how the brightness decreases from the gap as it pro-
gresses into the depth of the room (Illus.
13).

You may reduce the shadow's grain later
on, but the current settings make for tol-
erable rendering times.
But since the shadow can be a bit stronger,
increase its Density to 120 in the Shadow
panel of the Attributes Manager (Illus. 14).

You can see the difference in the rendering (Illus. 15) – the shadow along the front
wall is much more pronounced now.

The ceiling is still too dark, although – in
reality – it should be getting enough light
since light reflects from the wall.

13

15

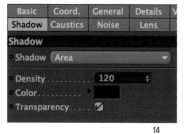

14

Using another Cylinder as Fill

You will now invent an additional light
source that will only light the ceiling
without lighting any other surfaces.
It seems a good idea to take advantage
of the work you've already done and use
a cylindrical light source again. This light
will feature the same dimensions as the
one we have already placed in the scene.
Copy the existing light object by dragging
it in the Object Manager while pressing
the Ctrl key, and call it Fill Ceiling. Move it
down (Coordinates panel: P.Y = 0, Illus. 16).
Your new light cylinder is exactly in the
middle of the room now (Illus. 17).

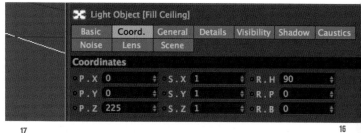

17

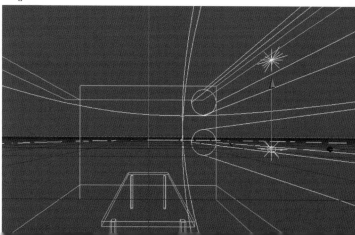

16

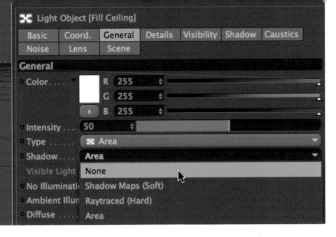

18

19

For this new light, you should deactivate the shadow and reduce it's brightness (Intensity) considerably since you only want to light the ceiling (General panel, Illus. 18).

You should also reduce the falloff distance, to create an even more dramatic brightness decrease for this light. (Details panel, Radius/Decay = 550 units, Illus. 19).

Up to now, the fill affects the entire room, which of course leads to a complete change in light distribution.

However, Cinema 4D enables you to make a light source affect selected objects – in your case it would be desirable if only the ceiling profits from the fill.

Separating Room and Ceiling

To make use of this feature you'll have to separate the ceiling from the polygon structure, since ceiling, walls and floor are a unit so far.

Pick the Polygon tool from the command bar on the left side of the screen, and also the Live Selection tool from the upper command bar (Illus. 20 and 22).
Select the polygon object called Room in the Object Manager (Illus. 21) and move your mouse over the ceiling surface.
Since Cinema 4D expects you to work on the active object's polygons, it marks every surface you "touch" in light gray, including the ceiling. Click on it, the orange-colored edges indicate the ceiling polygon is selected (Illus. 23).

Now choose the Split command from the Functions menu (not to be confused with Disconnect, Illus. 24).
You can see that a new polygon (also named Room) has been generated, and is listed in the Object Manager (please rename it Ceiling, Illus. 25,).

21

20

22

23

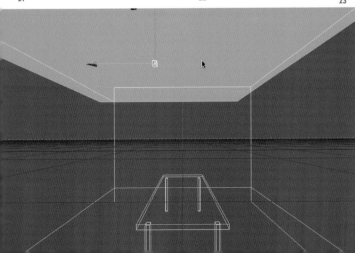

This object is a duplicate of the formerly selected ceiling polygon.

Keep in mind the original polygon is still there and needs to be removed. Reselect it the way you did above and press the

25

delete key.

Now that the ceiling is an independent object you can finish your fill's installation.

Be sure the ceiling is selected and toggle the Scene panel in the Attributes Manager.

Set Include mode and drag the ceiling polygon from the Object Manager into the Objects entry field (Illus. 26) to make sure it is the only object lit with your light source.

Exclude the primary key light from rendering (in the Object Manager, just set the lower dot on the object's right side to red) and render the scene using only the fill.

As you see, the ceiling is illuminated with a pronounced brightness progression (Illus. 27).

Turn the primary light on so it's part of the lighting scheme again and render the scene once more.

You can see how this additional ceiling light improves the scene's overall light arrangement – the ceiling's brightness now matches the other room surfaces (Illus. 28). Naturally, it is still darker than the floor.

One detail is still to be solved: the table's front surfaces are almost completely black, since they are barely reached by the existing lights.

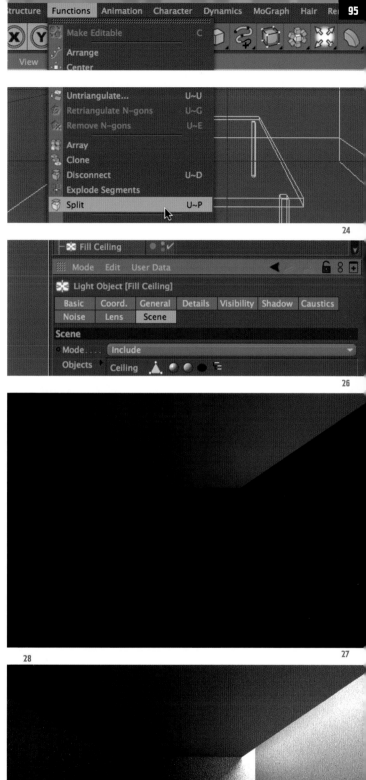

24

26

28

27

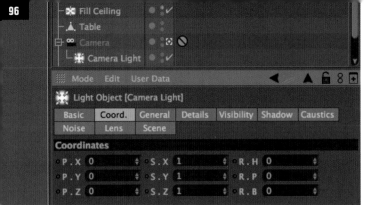

29

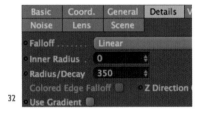

31

Camera Light

To lighten up the foreground, it's always a good idea to give the scene an additional camera light.

Place a new light source in the scene and make it subordinate to the camera by dragging it on to the camera in the Object Manager (Illus. 29.

As you know by now, this links the light source to the camera – set the light source position coordinates (P.X, P.Y, P.Z) to 0 so the new light is in the same place as the camera. You can check to make sure this worked by toggling your Editor Camera (Illus. 30).

Set the new light source's brightness (Intensity) to 75 – keep the Omni type and leave shadow deactivated (Illus. 31).

32

30

Define Linear Falloff with a 350-unit Radius/Decay in the Details panel so brightness decreases on the table surface (Illus. 32).

In the Scene panel of the Attributes Manager, choose Include mode and drag the table object from the Object Manager into the Objects entry field (Illus. 33), so it is the only item illuminated by the camera light.

33

34

Render the scene again to assess light distribution.

Now the front of the table is a bit too bright - as if the light was coming from a neighboring room (Illus. 34) - but you may leave this for now, and focus on your final rendering.

Final Rendering Settings

Since the light setup is complete, you can now launch a rendering for a presentation.

A few settings have to be adjusted to improve the quality of your rendering, though. Rendering time now isn't as critical as it was during the setup phase.

In the first place, you should increase the resolution of the shadow bitmap graphics. Activate the key primary light and set shadow Accuracy to 100 in the Shadow panel of the Attributes Manager. Minimum Samples should be set to 100, Maximum samples to 400 (Illus. 35).

Now, please open your default Render settings in the Render menu.

First choose Best Antialiasing in the General panel to make sure the edges are smoothened in the image - this will also improve the resolution of the area shadow (Illus. 36).

As for the Output size, set the Resolution in pixels - the values you see in illustration 37 will result in an image that covers the full width of a page in this book, with a setting of 300 dpi.

Use the Ambient Occlusion feature to darken room corners a bit (Illus. 38). You may keep the default settings.

Click on the black square on the left end of the scale and select a mid-level gray (Illus. 39), so the effect won't be overdone.

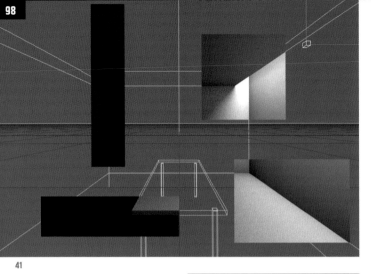

41

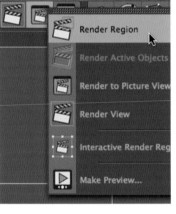

40

42

The settings you've made will lead to a significant boost in rendering time - especially the use of Ambient Occlusion, but also the high shadow graphics resolution you are using.

Before rendering the entire image, check smaller, critical areas in the Editor viewport by means of the Render Region command (Render menu, Illus. 40).
You can render small sections consecutively here (Illus. 41).

Keep always in mind that the settings I recommend here result from long testing, and that you will have to take into account enough trial-and-error-time for your own scenes.

Start your final rendering in the Picture Viewer (Render to Picture Viewer, Render menu) so you can export the image for further use (you will find more on rendering in Chapter 16, Multipass-Rendering and Compositing).

You probably feel an urge to process this image in Photoshop, for example.

In Photoshop, most of all adjust the brightness by using Levels (note: all corrections should basically done using Adjustment Layers),

Then, you might want to use a Gradient Map to give the grayscale image a decent color tone (Illus. 43 and 44) – this Adjustment layer may be turned to Multiply mode, it's opacity can be tuned down to weaken the effect.

You can experiment with Color Fills to create more coloring effects, also using Multiply mode.

You probably reproduce the things I described best if you look at the 08_final-render.psd file – also chapters 13 and 16 offer more detailed explanations of these steps.

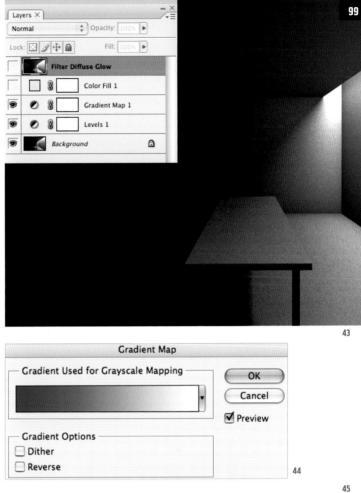

43

Gradient Map

Gradient Used for Grayscale Mapping

OK

Cancel

☑ Preview

Gradient Options

☐ Dither

☐ Reverse

44

45

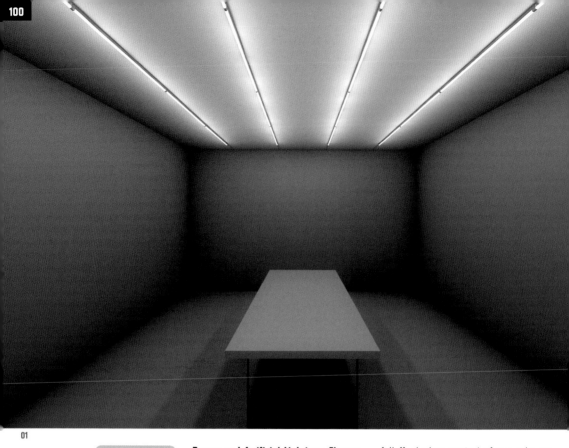

01

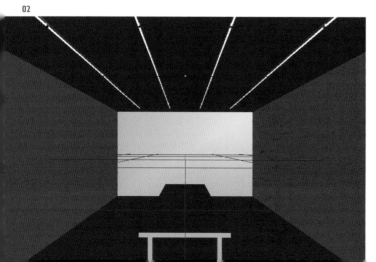

02

09

Rooms and Artificial Lighting · Fluorescent Tubes

We want to light our room with fluorescent light tubes in this chapter (Illus. 01). Multiple shadows on the floor and the peculiar light stains on the ceiling are typical for this lighting situation.

In principle, this lighting setup works with a number of copies of one original light source. The advantage of this setup is that changes to the parameters (brightness, falloff, shadow casting) of one tube are automatically applied to all duplicates.

There will also be two lighting sets, since room lighting and ceiling lighting require two separate setups.

We will also have to differentiate between modelled tube objects that only look like casting light, and the "real" lights which actually illuminate your scene.

A couple of fill lights will also be necessary to complete the image.

Getting Started

Open the file 09_start.c4d (see p. 236). It was created using version 10.

You see a room with objects on the ceiling – they represent fluorescent light tubes in their fittings –, still there are no "real" light sources yet (Illus. 02).

Gouraud Shading was chosen for Editor display, (Editor menu, Display). As for the view, a camera is in use – it is listed in the Object Manager, the Protection tag indi-

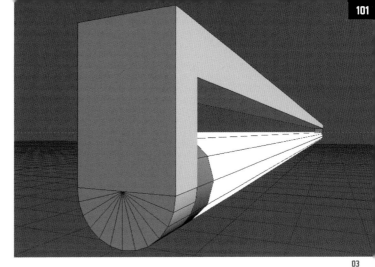

03

cating it's position and angle is locked. Toggle the Editor camera if you want to navigate within the scene (Editor menu Cameras).

The lights on the ceiling are polygon bodies. When you take a close look at one of these (Illus. 03), you can see that the cylinder surfaces have a relatively low resolution. The Cinema 4D default setting for cylinder resolution is 36 segments - in this scene we use a division

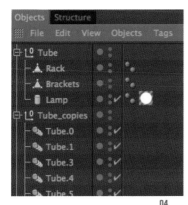

04

The neon lamp's model consists of three objects. One of them is the cylinder, which is meant to represent the actual lighting tube.

It was assigned a material with a Luminance channel (Illus. 04 and 05). This lighting material makes the tubes appear to be always white, although they will have no effect on the lighting of the scene. So far, the rendering only uses Cinema 4D's Default Light (Illus. 06).

There is a total of 16 lights in the scene. In the Object Manager, you can see there is one original object that was copied 15 times, the copies grouped into a Null Object called Tube_copies (Illus. 04).

The copies are so-called Instance Objects, meaning they are linked to the original - with the advantage that the original adjustment's are taken over by the copies automatically.

of 12, which is absolutely enough in this case. (You should always be careful not to create more polygons than necessary to avoid straining your graphics card while navigating through the image, and your patience while rendering.)

A Phong tag - to be recognized by the smalls balls icon in the Object Manager (Illus. 04) - gives the rendered picture its smooth appearance.

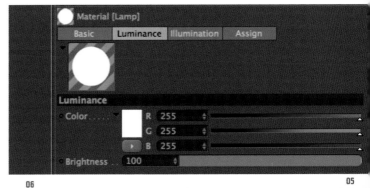

05

06

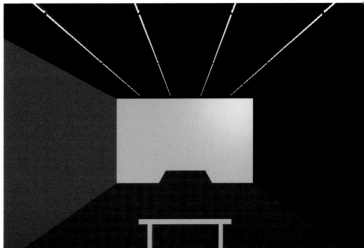

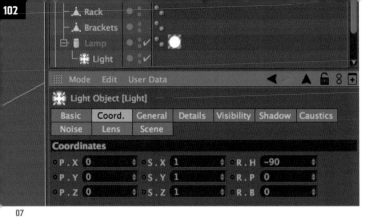

07

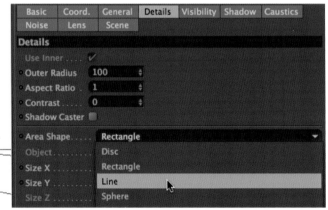

08

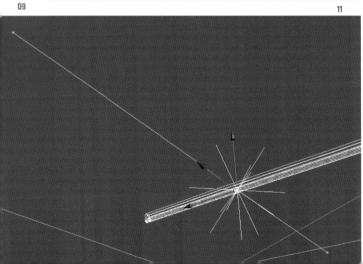

09

11

10

You will profit from this function, especially when creating the following lighting setup.

Line Light

As mentioned before, setting up a 16-light arrangement is most elegantly done by installing one original light and then creating 15 copies, so light adjustments for e.g. intensity, shadow characteristics etc. are passed on to all copies automatically.

In the first place, you should delete the copies of your initial lighting model – you will now exchange them with copies of a „real" light (which is yet to be installed, however).

Now please add a light object to the scene (from the Scene Objects menu in the upper command bar).
In the Object Manager, drag the new light source onto the Lamp object so their position is linked (Illus. 07).
In the Coordinates panel of the Attributes Manager, enter 0 for all position coordinate values (P.X, P.Y and P.Z) to make sure the new light is positioned exactly in the

center of the tube object Lamp.

Choose Area as your lighting type (Attributes Manager, General, Illus. 08) and Line as Area Shape (Details, Illus. 09).

Toggle the Editor camera view (Editor's Cameras menu, Illus. 10) and select Lines display (Display menu).
Navigate towards the original tube object. Notice that your light source still doesn't

point to the same direction and doesn't have the same length as the tube object (Illus. 11).

Rotate the light around its Y axis (R.H = 0) and shorten its length to 100 units (Details panel: Outer Radius = 50. Illus. 12).

Set shadow casting for your new light source in the General panel by selecting hard shadows (Raytraced (Hard), Illus. 13).

Switch back to your own camera. The room will completely turn black when you render the scene, because on one hand the light rays cannot pass through the tube model since it isn't transparent, and on the other hand Cinema 4D's Default Light is already deactivated since there is a light source in use.

You can solve this problem in the Scene panel of the light settings – dragging objects into the Objects field will either include them in or exclude them from lighting.

Make sure your light source is selected, toggle the Scene panel in the Attributes Manager, drag the objects contained in the Tube null object (Rack, Brackets, Lamp) from the Object Manager into the Objects entry field, then select Exclude mode (Illus. 14).

For what you've done up to now, the rendering should show a correct result – the area light illuminates the room and casts a hard shadow under the table.

Here, once again, you can see that the part of the room closest to the light – the ceiling in this case – is the darkest part of the image (Illus. 15).

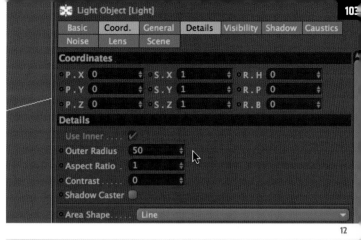

12

13

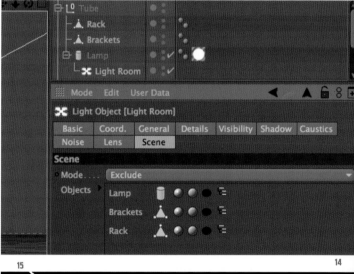

14

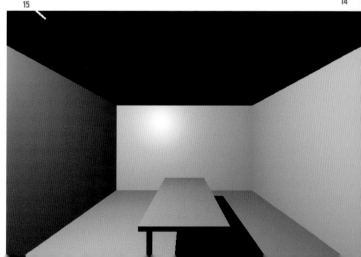

15

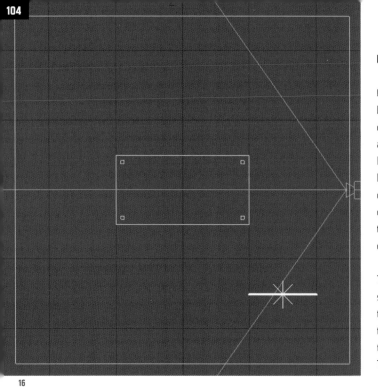

16

Duplicating Lights

Once tube object and light source have been linked successfully, they can now be distributed along the ceiling via copying as instances.

In the end, the scene should feature 16 lights aligned in groups of four. Copying is done first in Z-, then in X-direction - the Z distance (room width) should be 100 units, the X distance (room depth, between the objects' axis center) 100 units as well.

Toggle the top view (F2, Illus. 16). Make sure your Tube null object is selected in the Object Manager (Illus. 17), and select the Duplicate command from the Functions menu (Illus. 18).

The Attributes Manager shows the set-

tings you may choose for this command (Illus. 19). Be sure to see all of the panels by right-clicking on their tabs.

In the Duplicate Panel, set the number of copies to 3 and mark the Generate Instances option.

In the Options panel, choose Linear Mode to see additional parameters. Keep Per Step activated, allowing you to set an offset for the first copy.

17

18

For Position Move, set 0 for both X and Y direction offset, and 100 for the Z offset.
Scale and Rotation settings should remain deactivated, since they are of no use for you in this case.

In the Tool panel, click on Apply once you have completed your settings - the tube object will be copied in Z direction three times, together with the integrated light source (Illus. 20).

19

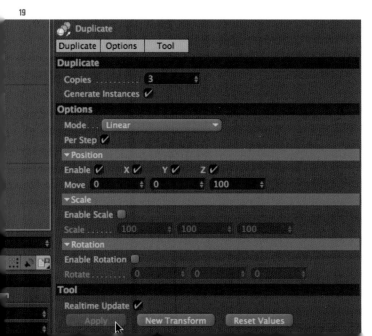

If what you did leads to different result, use Ctrl Z to return to your initial stage and check your settings – don't click on the Reset Values button, since that would only reset everything to the Duplicate command default settings.

You should dissolve the group of instances you just created before starting to copy the four lights (one original and three instances) once more in X direction.
In the Object Manager, select the null object called Tube copies and choose Expand Object Group (Object Manager's Objects menu, Illus. 21). The null object the instances were grouped in is empty now and should be deleted.

Now for the next step: mark the three in-

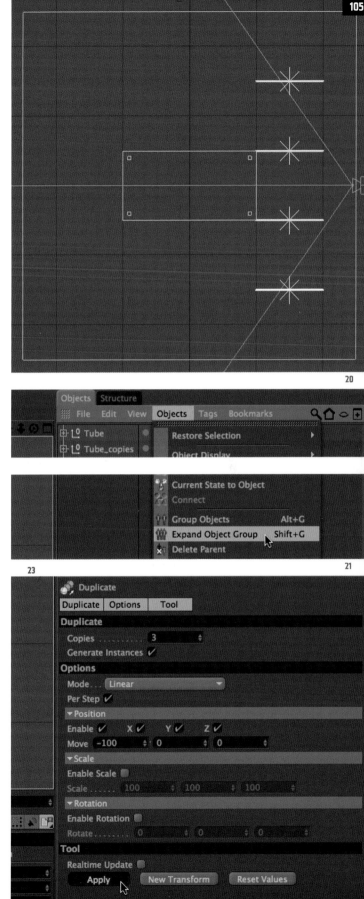

20

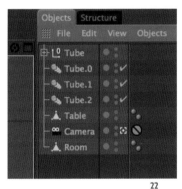

22

23

21

stances plus the original Tube for copying (Illus. 22).
Select Duplicate again (Functions menu). In the Attributes Manager you should still see the settings of your former copy action. Make absolutely sure the Realtime Update option (Tool panel) is deactivated (Illus. 23).

Now for Position Move (Options panel) set the X offset to –100 and Z offset to 0.
Now click on Apply (Tool panel) – Tube and it's three instances are now copied in negative X direction (to the left in the top view).
Now again, if your action has led to dif-

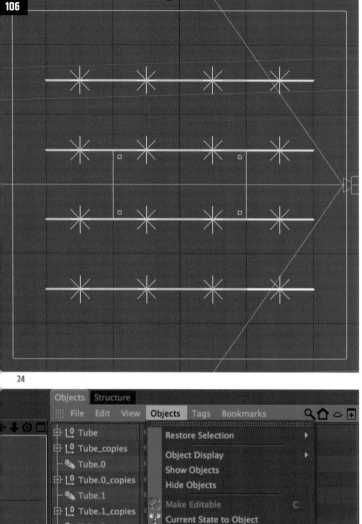

24

25

ferent result, use Ctrl Z to return to your initial stage and check your settings – generally the mistake is to be found in the Position Move settings.

You should clean up your Object Manager again – select the four new groups (Illus. 25), choose Expand Object Group (Object Manager Objects menu) and delete the empty null objects.

To finish the duplicating process, you should file away the copies since you only need the one original light source to make decisive adjustments for. (Remember, this was the reason why you are using a lighting setup with instances.)

Select all 15 light instances in the Object Manager and group them using the Group Objects command (Objects menu, Illus. 26). Change the null object's name to Tube copies (Illus. 27).

Now render the scene – notice that the ceiling is only dimly lit, while the rest of the room appears overexposed (Illus. 28). As you already know, light sources have much greater effect on room surfaces that are further away.

The other remarkable aspect is the expressive shadow on the ceiling. This will become less pronounced later, when we use area instead of hard shadow.
However, at present it's better to use hard shadow, since the shadow's geometry is easier to be controlled this way, and because it requires less rendering time.

26

27

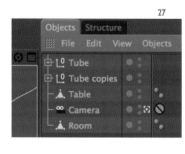

Separating Room and Ceiling

As you see, it'll make sense to differentiate between ceiling and room lighting.
You've already defined scene exclusion
for your tube object containing your first
light source.

You may as well exclude the ceiling, or
vice versa include room and table – and
later on install a second set of lights sole-
ly for the ceiling, with it's own intensity
settings etc.

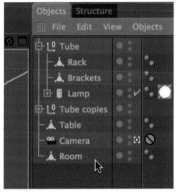

28

However, room and ceiling are still united
in one polygon object, so they have to be
separated first.

Select the Polygon tool from the command
bar on the left hand side of the screen,
and the Live Selection tool from the upper
command bar (Illus. 30 and 31).

Select the room object in the Object Manager (Illus. 29) and mouse over the ceiling
surface in the Editor.
Click on the surface as soon as it turns
light gray – the orange indicate the ceiling polygon is selected (Illus. 32).

Now choose Split from the Functions
menu (not to be confused with Disconnect, Illus. 33).
The Object Manager shows a new polygon also named Room (Illus. 34).
It is a copy of the selected ceiling polygon. The original polygon still exists and
needs to be removed.
Since it is still selected (unless you clicked
on something else in the meantime), you
just have to press Delete.

Should the complete room disappear
by mistake, Press Ctrl Z, select the ceiling polygon again and repeat the Delete.
Now rename the new polygon Ceiling (Illus. 35).

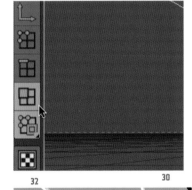

29

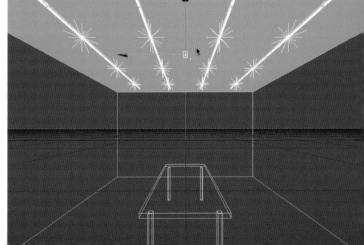

32   30   31

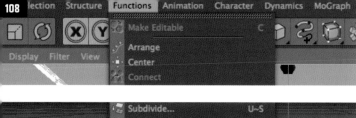

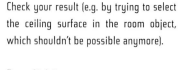

Check your result (e.g. by trying to select the ceiling surface in the room object, which shouldn't be possible anymore).

Room Lighting

Now we want to start optimizing light set-ups for both the ceiling and the rest of the room surfaces. First you will take care of the room, using the light set you have already created.

Select your original light in the Object Manager.
Set Include mode in the Attributes Man-

33

34

35

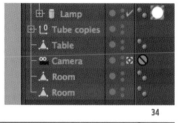

ager's Scene panel and drag both the room and the table object from the Object Manager into the Objects entry field (Illus. 36). This ensures only these two objects will be illuminated by your light source.

Remember that the room was overexposed in the last rendering, as opposed to the ceiling.
So in the General panel, reduce Intensity to a mere degree of 5. Keep in mind that hard shadow (Raytraced) is still selected (Illus. 37).

Before rendering the scene you should make sure it doesn't take too long.
Even though the light sources are line-shaped, they are still basically area lights.
Rendering this type of light doesn't only depend on the shadow type, but also on the light source's own resolution. You can adjust this using Samples in the Details panel of the Attributes Manager.

36

37

38

The default setting is 40, but you can reduce it to its lowest possible setting of 16 (Illus. 38). This will shorten rendering time to about a quarter - in this case.

The rendering looks better now (Illus. 39), showing a peculiar motive of multiple overlapping shadow rectangles on the floor.
However, light distribution is still far too regular, which leaves the image flat and sterile.
Falloff is one of the most elegant features to create a more natural and dramatic brightness progression in the room - allowing you to define a distance towards brightness intensity is coming close to 0%.

Make sure your light object is selected, and set Linear Falloff in the Details panel. Radius/Decay should be 650 units (Illus. 40).
This means brightness reduction will start directly at the light source and ends with 0% at a distance of 650 units.
The Front view (F4) shows circles which display this falloff distance for each light source (Illus. 41).

The result of choosing falloff is obvious in the rendering (Illus. 42).

You may dramatize the lightness decrease by reducing the falloff distance (Radius/Decay), but probably the corners will turn a little too dark then.
I suggest you stay with your settings, bearing in mind that you will still use area shadow later on.

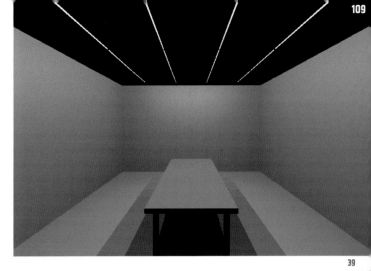

39

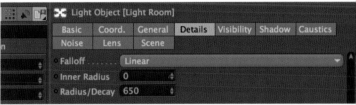

40

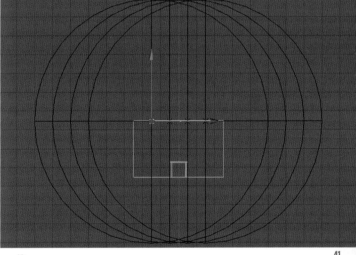

42

41

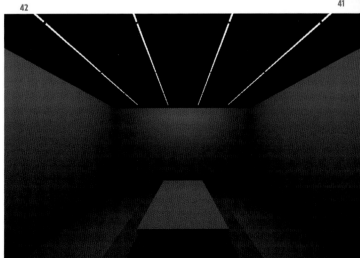

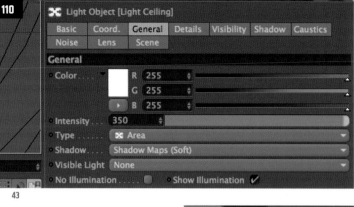

43

44

45

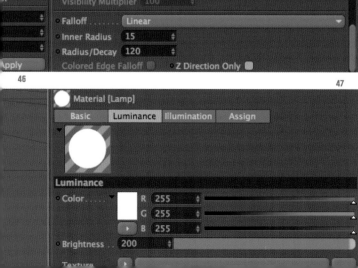

46

47

Lighting the Ceiling

Now you will take care of the proper ceiling lighting.

In our example, ceiling and room are handled separately, which requires two light sources – one for the room (the one you already installed), and a second light, line-shaped as well, for the ceiling.

This second light should also be a sub-object to the tube object, so that - via the already existing instances - it will be distributed all over the ceiling 16 times.

The easiest way to proceed is to make a copy of your first light - just drag it in the Object Manager while pressing the Ctrl key. (Make absolutely sure the copy stays on the same hierarchy level as the original, Illus. 44).

Name the new light source Light Ceiling and hide the other one (by clicking on both of the dots next to it until they turn red), which by now you should also have renamed Light Room.

Make sure the new light source is selected in the Object Manager and toggle the General panel in the Attributes Manager. Increase brightness (Intensity) to 350 and select soft shadows (Shadow Maps (Soft), Illus. 43).

Toggle the Scene panel. Set Exclude mode and drag room, table and lamp objects into the Objects entry field (Illus. 45). This ensures these elements will not be effected by the new light source.

Define Linear Falloff for Light Ceiling (Details panel, 15 to 120 units, Illus. 46) so the ceiling lighting won't appear too uniform. For the light stains on the ceiling, a somewhat finer resolution is desirable too – so raise the Samples value to 40 again (Details panel; a rate of 16 was initially sufficient for the room lights).

48

The fact that the tubes are displayed as white cylinders isn't due to the light sources. It has to do with the cylinder objects which were assigned a material with a Luminance channel.

To strengthen this white gleam, open the material settings by double-clicking the texture tag, toggle the Luminance panel in the Attributes Manager, and increase Brightness to 200 (Illus. 47).

The rendering of the ceiling looks pretty

49

good (Illus. 48), although the ceiling could be a bit brighter overall, though.

To assess this more precisely, we should look at the lighting of the entire room. Turn the other light visible again (in the Object Manager, click on both dots next to Light Room until they are gray again, Illus. 49) and render the scene.

Although both the distribution of light in the room and the expressive distribution of brightness on the ceiling are good for themselves, it is obvious that the ceiling appears too dark in relation to the room (Illus. 50).

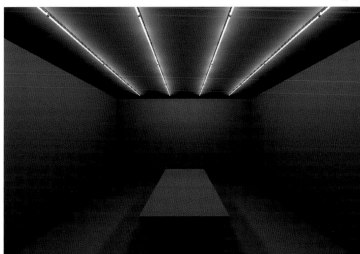

50

Brightening the Ceiling

The main lighting effects on the room surfaces are created by the lights you have placed so far – which is why they are called key lights.

To correct imbalances as to be seen in your rendering, you will have to place some fill lights.

Since they are only used to compensate and support key lighting, they are generally dimmer and do not create shadow.

Place a new light source and call it Fill

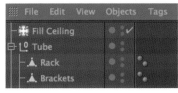

51

52

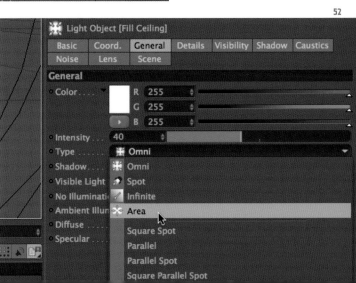

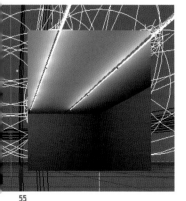

Ceiling (Illus. 51). For Type, select Area with an intensity of 40 (General panel, Illus. 52).

Bear in mind that a light source with non-parallel light emission (including area light) in Cinema 4D makes a surface

brighter with increasing distance, as long as no falloff has been defined.

Make sure Fill Ceiling is selected, then rotate it around its X axis by setting R.P to 90 (Coordinates panel, Illus. 53; click on the double arrow next to the corresponding value and move your mouse. You can see how the light surface rotates in the Editor. Of course you can also enter a numeric value).

Move the light downwards (P.Y = -145) and enlarge its surface by setting Outer Radius to 245 in the Details panel (which will make it almost as large as the floor surface, Illus. 53).

54

Make sure only the ceiling is lit by this fill; toggle the Scene panel, drag Ceiling from the Object Manager into the Objects entry field, and set Include mode (Illus. 54).

Render a segment of the ceiling – one of the critical areas along the wall – to check your results (Render menu: Render Region, Illus. 55). It seems the ceiling is properly lit now.

Camera Light

Additionally to the ceiling fill, it would do no harm to have the room appear a bit brighter from the camera perspective, at least the table would certainly profit from this.

Place another light (no.4 by now) and drag it onto the camera in the Object Manager (Illus. 56).

This links the light's position to the camera's. Set the light's position coordinates (P.X, P.Y, P.Z) to 0, so it is in the same place as the camera (Coordinates panel, Illus. 56).

Set Intensity to 40 and keep the Omni type (General panel). Shadow should remain deactivated.

Switch to the Scene panel of the Attributes Manager – drag the table object from the Object Manager into the Objects entry

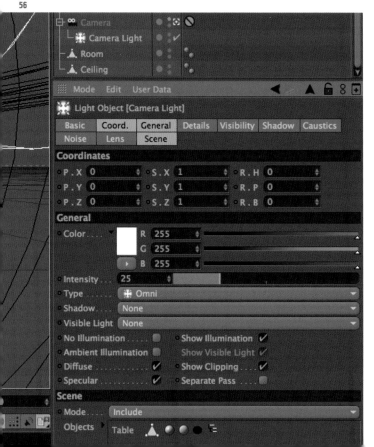

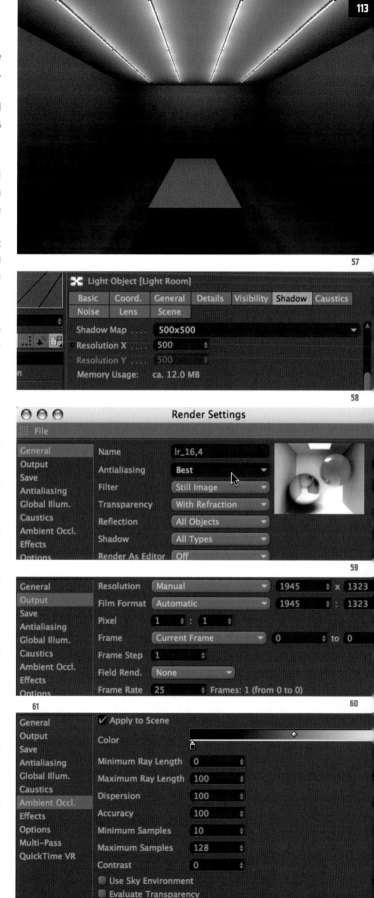

field, then set Include mode so only the table will be effected by the camera light.

Before you adjust settings for your final rendering you should define soft shadows for your room key lighting setup.

Select Light Room, toggle the General panel, define Shadow Maps (Soft), then switch to the Shadow panel and select a 500x500 Shadow Map (Illus. 58).
This value is responsible for the soft shadow's bitmap resolution – Cinema 4D uses a default setting of 250x250 – a little too grainy for our purpose.

Render the scene. The lighting setup is balanced now (Illus. 57). Additional fine-tuning can be done by choosing appropriate Render settings.

Rendering Default Settings

As in previous chapters, you will change some Render settings to improve your image, since rendering time isn't as decisive anymore.

Open your default rendering settings (Render menu: Render settings).

Select Best Antialiasing in the General panel (to ensure ideal contour smoothing, Illus. 59).
This option was meaningless during the setup phase, keeping it deactivated then saved you a lot of time.

Set the size in pixels in the Output panel (Resolution) – the values used will produce an image that covers the full width of a page in this book with a setting of 300 dpi (Illus. 60).

An effect that leads to a more realistic image is Ambient Occlusion (in the panel with the same name).

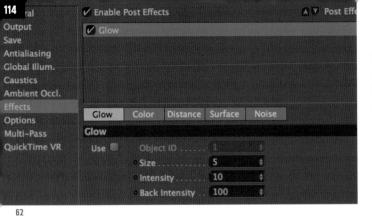

✓ Enable Post Effects

▲ ▼ Post Eff

☑ Glow

| Glow | Color | Distance | Surface | Noise |

Glow

Use ■   Object ID 1

○ Size 5

○ Intensity 10

○ Back Intensity . 100

62

It will darken areas where surfaces meet, e.g. room corners.

Use the default settings here (Illus. 61; this is one of the features that will cost you a lot of rendering time).

In our example, it would also be nice to have some mild glow surrounding the light tubes.

You can add this effect using the Glow Post Effect (Effects panel).

If it's not in the list already, click on one of the arrows in the upper right, and select the effect from the pull-down menu (Illus. 62 and 63).

You may stay with the default settings.

Render some of the critical segments before launching the final rendering (Render menu: Render Region, Illus. 64).

Keep in mind that the glow effect is calculated only after actual rendering (thus named Post Effect) and notice that it results not only in an aureole around the tubes, but also in overall scene brightening.

Multipass rendering would enable you to modify this kind of effect using an own image layer in postproduction (e.g. Photoshop, see chapter 16, Multipass-Rendering and Compositing).

The rendered image was processed and colored using Photoshop (Illus. 65 and 66).

Post Effect ▶

Remove Selected
Remove All

Load Preset
Save Preset

Highlights
Glow
Depth of Field

63

64

Structure   Functions   Animation   Character   Dynamics   MoGraph   Hair   Render

Render Region

Render Active Objects

Render to Picture Viewer

Render View

Interactive Render Region

Make Preview...

Chapter 09 · Rooms and Artificial Lighting · Fluorescent Tubes

01

Rooms and Visible Light

This chapter is about the use of bundled light to create a dramatic spatial effect.
The effect consists of stark contrasts between adjacent bright and dark areas.
The main factor creating the bright areas is the reflection of light on dust particles hovering in the room.
Illuminated fog in the lower part also contributes to this suggestive light dramaturgy (Illus. 01).

Parallel spotlights which emit visible light are needed to visualize this lighting situation.
As in the previous chapter, you will be using one original light and a set of instances again.
Without these „intelligent" copies which simultaneously adapt to the original light's adjustments you would have to deal with a rather large number of single lights; adjusting them all the same way would be as exhausting as it would be prone to errors.

Besides the light cylinders, there's fog created with a shader, and additional room lighting with rectangle-shaped area light.

Getting Started

Open the 10_start.c4d file (see p. 236). It was created with Version 10.
You see a high room with circular open-

02

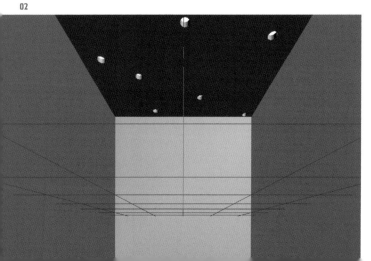

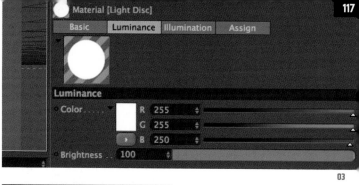

03

ings spread irregularly on the ceiling (Illus. 02). Gouraud Shading was selected for the Editor image (Editor's Display menu), As for the view, a camera is in use – it is listed in the Object Manager, the Protection tag indicating it's position and angle is locked.

Toggle the Editor camera if you want to navigate within the scene (Editor menu Cameras).

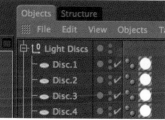

Render the scene. You can see white surfaces in the ceiling openings. These are disc objects with material assigned using a Luminance channel. They are just placeholders for the "real" lights that will be used later.

You may have a look at the Luminance channel's settings (Illus. 03) by double-clicking the discs' texture tag (Illus. 04).

04

Parallel Spots

To start with the light setup, place a light source and name it Key.

For Type, choose Parallel Spot in the General panel of the Attributes Manager (Illus. 05).

Rotate it into a vertical position by setting the R.P. value to -90 (in the Coordinates panel, Illus. 06).

This parallel spot should now be moved to the position of one of the lighting discs first.

In the Object Manager, drag the light onto Disc.1 (open the Light Discs group if necessary) so it becomes a sub-object of it (Illus. 07).

Make sure the spot is selected and set its relative position to 0 (P.X, P.Y, P.Z) – this ensures the position of light and disc will be identical (Illus. 06).

Now you have to create copies of the spotlight, one for each opening in the ceiling, and another three to be placed in the scene's foreground outside the room.

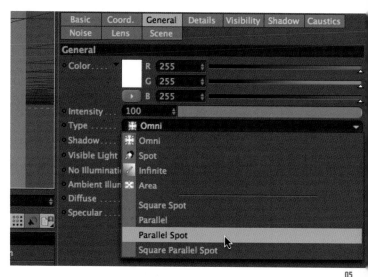

05

07   06

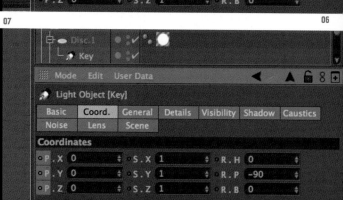

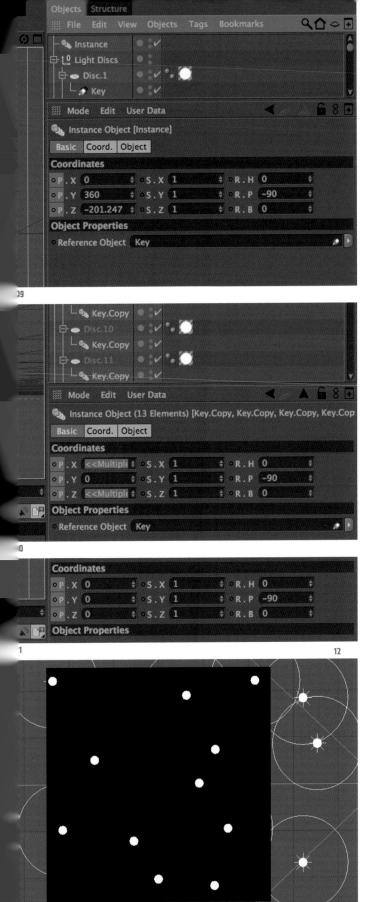

Their positions are also marked with disc objects.

As mentioned above, you have to make use of instances, i.e. "linked" copies that automatically react to changes to the

08

original's parameters, when you need a group of identical light sources,

Make sure your spotlight Key is selected and place an Instance Object (Modeling Object menu in the upper command bar, Illus. 08). Name it Key.Copy.

The instance object should be selected now. In the Attributes Manager you can see that your Key spotlight is entered as Reference Object (in the Object panel, Illus. 09).

Now you want to place one of your copies in each location marked by a disc.
You can't do this using the Duplicate command or any other trick. You have to do it individually for each copy.
But we will try to solve this as elegantly as possible.

Hold down the Ctrl key, and drag the Key. Copy instance onto the next disc object in the Object Manager (Disc.2).
Continue to create more copies by Ctrl-dragging Key.Copy onto the other disc objects as well, until each of them has a subordinate light instance object (Illus. 10).

Select all of the instances you thus created in the Object Manager (but not the discs! Make sure no other objects are selected by mistake) and enter 0 for P.X, P.Y and P.Z in the Coordinates panel of the Attributes Manager (Illus. 11).

This places all instances in the same position as their lead objects simultaneously, as you can see in top view (Illus. 12).

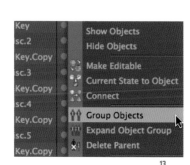

13

14

File away all the discs with subordinate light instances in a group (Objects Manager Objects menu: Group Objects, Illus. 13), and call this group Disc.Copies (Illus. 14).

Render the scene. You recognize that the spots work - they cast light spots on the floor (Illus. 15) But you are still far from the result you want to achieve.

The first thing you'll want to see are the light columns. Select the key light, and choose Visible Light in the General panel of the Attributes Manager (Illus. 16).

This makes the light's ray bundle visible when you render the scene - without this feature, you see just its effect on real object surfaces.

Of course this effect has to be tuned with a number of settings.

First you have to take care of the dimensions of the light cylinders. Set the spotlight radius to 14 (Details panel, Outer Radius, Illus. 17).

This should make it a bit thicker than the opening in the ceiling (its radius being only 10). But you can see that this is useful due to the decrease along the edges.

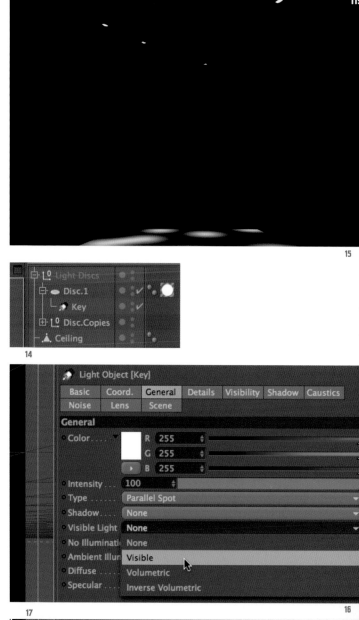

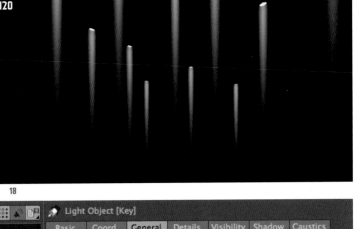

18

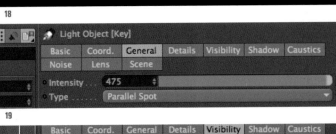

19

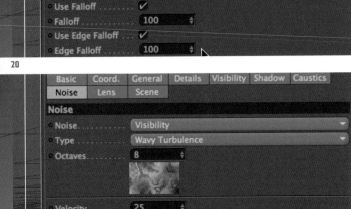

20

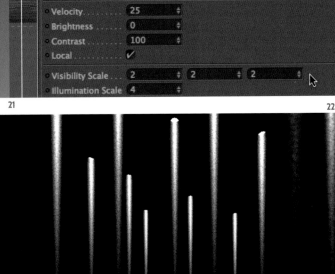

21

22

Render the scene. The desired effect can already be discerned, but the light isn't strong enough, and the cylinders are too homogeneous (Illus. 18).

First raise your brightness setting (General panel – Intensity = 475, Illus. 19).
Then emphasize the decrease in brightness from the cylinder's middle axis to its periphery – toggle the Visibility panel, and activate and set Edge Falloff to 100 (Illus. 20).

Noise is an effective tool when it comes to changing the appearance of your light cylinder (Illus. 21).
In the Noise panel, you assign Visibility for Noise, i.e. you make this effect work for you inside your light cylinders.
The following settings are, as usual, the result of a longer test phase – when you set up a scene of your own, keep in mind you'll go through a similar trial-and error phase.
Now to the noise settings: the small preview image gives you a first impression of the result. Set Wavy Turbulence for your noise type. Change the Octaves value to 8, and the Visibility Scale to 2 for all axis directions.

Render the scene again. Now the light cylinders look pretty good.
Notice that they do not contribute to the actual lighting, except for the light spots on the floor (Illus. 22).

This allows for two conclusions –
a) You need a few more fill lights to make the room visible,
b) You need another tool to create the impression of fog in the bottom half of the room: the fog shader.
But first we should focus on the now familiar task of giving the other room surfaces enough presence in the scene by using additional lighting.

Fill Light for the Ceiling

You'll handle the brightening of ceiling, walls and floor surfaces separately.

A horizontally aligned, rectangular area light source is the appropriate tool for all three cases.

We will start with the ceiling, because it is already separated from the room and it therefore doesn't require too much preparation to be lit separately.

Place a new light and name it Fill Ceiling (as opposed to the scene-defining spotlight, which is our key light).

For Type, choose Area (General panel), keep shadow switched off and reduce Intensity to 10 (Illus. 23).

Rotate the light rectangle (this shape being its default) into a horizontal position and move it downwards until it is at floor level (Coordinates panel: R.P = 90, P.Y = -150, Illus. 24). (You can set the values numerically or click on the double arrow next to the corresponding value field, press your mouse button and move your mouse.)

Change Outer Radius to 250 and keep the default rectangular shape (Details panel, Illus. 25).

To make sure the ceiling is the only surface lit by this light, set Include mode in the Scene panel and drag the ceiling from the Object manager into the Objects entry field (Illus. 26).

The rendering displays the ceiling dimly lit (Illus. 27). Whether the lighting is sufficient has to be checked within the overall context of the final result.

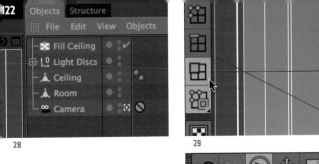

28

29

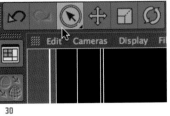

30

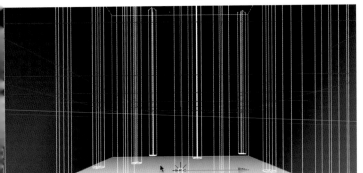

31

Fill Light for the Walls

The walls are the most critical of the three surfaces that need to be brightened, since they require a well-contrasted brightness progression from the bottom to the top.

The group of four walls has to be a polygon object of its own so you can light it separately. However, the walls are still linked to the floor.

Make sure Room is selected (Illus. 28), then choose the Live Selection tool (upper command bar, Illus. 30) and the Polygon tool (left command bar, Illus. 29).

If you mouse over the image in the Editor, you see how the surfaces of the room turn light gray as the cursor moves over them. Click on the floor surface to select it. It then appears with orange edges (Illus. 31).

Now choose Split from the Functions menu (not to be confused with Disconnect, Illus. 32).
You can see that a new polygon named Room is displayed in the Object Manager – a copy of the marked polygon.
Now you have to delete the original floor polygon. You can simply press the Delete key if you haven't clicked on anything else in the meantime.

If nothing happens or the entire room disappears, undo the deletion (Ctrl Z) and activate the original room object again in the Object Manager.
Mouse over the room surface again until it turns light gray, and press delete again.

Call the new polygon Floor, and the remaining surfaces Walls (Illus. 33 and 34).

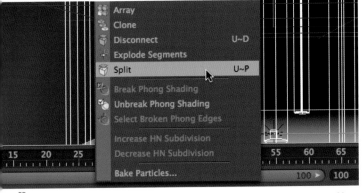

32

33

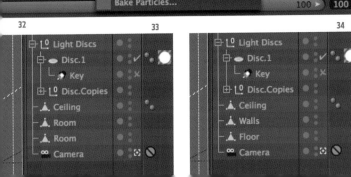

34

Now let's focus on the wall surfaces, the actual subject of this chapter.

Since you should use an area light for the walls as well, it is a good idea to copy the ceiling fill. You can do this via Copy & Paste, or by Ctrl-dragging Fill Ceiling inside the Object Manager.

Call the duplicate Fill Walls (Illus. 36).

Drag the new area light down to floor level (Coordinates panel: P.Y = -150, Illus. 35), the 90 R.P rotating angle is OK

Switch to the Scene panel (Illus. 37). Include mode is OK, but replace the ceiling with the walls object: drag Walls from the Object Manager into the Objects entry field, and delete Ceiling from the list.

Increase brightness substantially in the General panel (Intensity = 175, Illus. 38).

However, falloff is the most important design tool for this light, because it will create a richly contrasted brightness progression along the walls.

All of the relevant settings are to be found in the Details panel (Illus. 39).

Set the Falloff Angle to 0 first. This rather inconspicuous setting causes brightness to be strongest along the lower edge of the walls – the default 180 would create a completely different effect.

Make sure the light resolution is at its lowest possible setting (Samples = 16). This helps you avoid unnecessarily long rendering times.

Then select Linear Falloff ending a bit above the room's ceiling (Inner Radius = 0, Radius/Decay = 550).

Your rendering should show the desired result (Illus. 40).

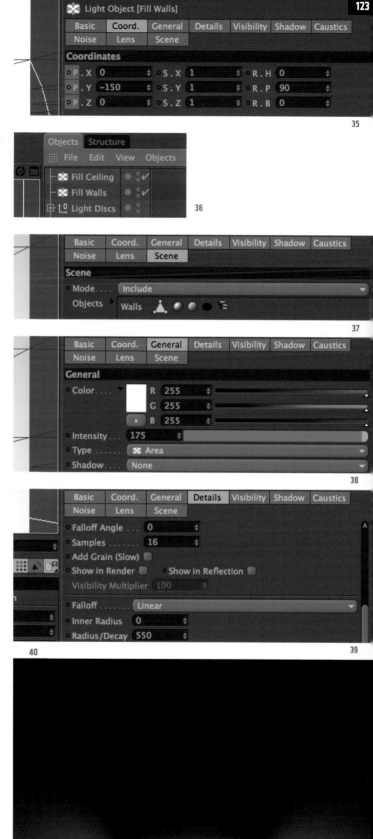

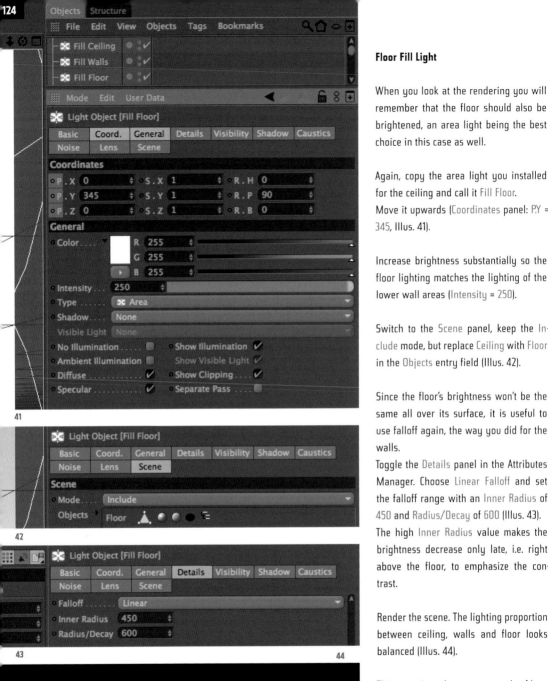

41

42

43

44

Floor Fill Light

When you look at the rendering you will remember that the floor should also be brightened, an area light being the best choice in this case as well.

Again, copy the area light you installed for the ceiling and call it Fill Floor.
Move it upwards (Coordinates panel: P.Y = 345, Illus. 41).

Increase brightness substantially so the floor lighting matches the lighting of the lower wall areas (Intensity = 250).

Switch to the Scene panel, keep the Include mode, but replace Ceiling with Floor in the Objects entry field (Illus. 42).

Since the floor's brightness won't be the same all over its surface, it is useful to use falloff again, the way you did for the walls.
Toggle the Details panel in the Attributes Manager. Choose Linear Falloff and set the falloff range with an Inner Radius of 450 and Radius/Decay of 600 (Illus. 43).
The high Inner Radius value makes the brightness decrease only late, i.e. right above the floor, to emphasize the contrast.

Render the scene. The lighting proportion between ceiling, walls and floor looks balanced (Illus. 44).

This scene is a showcase example of how to layer light sources to create a suggestive lighting situation. Every light assumes a clearly defined role, and each light can be optimized in its respective role.

Fog Shader Atmospherics

A scene like this requires the visualization of a room's atmosphere. A fog should give the room a subdued appearance, and leave the rear room area slightly blurred (see Illus. 01 at the beginning of the chapter).
These effects suit the slightly mystical light dramaturgy of this setup.

The Fog Shader is the ideal tool for this purpose.
Open a new scene and create a new material using the Material Manager.
But select Fog out of the Shader flyout menu instead of choosing New Material (Material Manager's File menu, Illus. 45).

Place a cube in the scene, and drag your fog thing onto it (similar to assigning a "normal" material, Illus. 46).

The rendering shows a cube with a three-dimensional white area pointing in positive Y direction (Illus. 47).

You can adjust the shader settings by double-clicking on the texture tag in the Object Manager.
If you set Exponential for Type (Illus. 48), the brightness progression will be somewhat more pronounced, and the inner edges will become recognizable (Illus. 49).

You can control the brightness and distance of the progression with the Thickness and Decrease settings (Illus. 50 - 53).

Keep this scene opened to be able to test more settings you may require.

Back to the room scene. You won't use the fog shader directly in the room. Instead you will apply it in a duplicate; this allows you to test its effect - even in a dif-

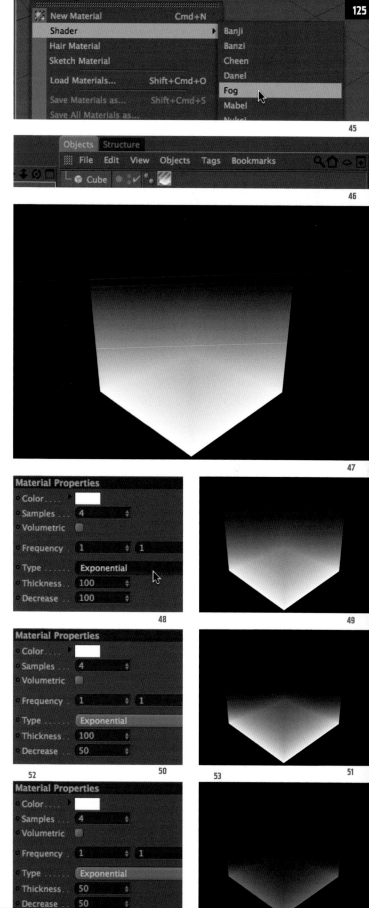

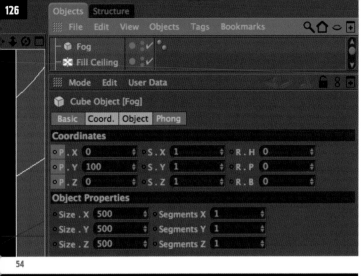

54

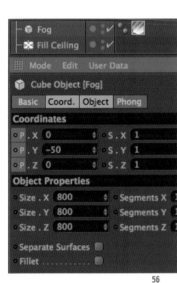

55

58

57

ferently sized space if necessary - without affecting the original room.

Place a cube, which is initially assigned the same measurements and position as the Walls cube (Coordinates panel: P.Y = 100; Object panel: Size X, Y, Z = 500, Illus. 54). Call the new cube Fog.

Now in the Material Manager, pick a fog shader the way you just learned.
Assign it to the cube and render the scene. The effect is basically correct, but a bit too strong (Illus. 55).

Changing Thickness and Decrease values won't help here, since it would make both fog and its progression darker, which would affect the entire room.

56

Scaling the fog cube so only part of the fog progression is visible within the room is the more elegant strategy.
Just enlarge its measurements (Object panel: Size X,Y,Z = 800, Illus. 56) and drag the cube down so it shares the same middle as the Walls object (Coordinates: P.Y = -50).

Toggle the Editor Camera - the rendering reveals how the large fog cube encompasses the smaller room object (Illus. 57 and 58).

Now finetune some of the shader settings. Double-click the texture tag in the Object Manager to display the shader settings in the Attributes Manager (Illus. 59).
First reduce the resolution (Material panel: Samples = 4), to avoid unnecessarily long rendering time.
Set – if not already done – Exponential for Type and reduce Thickness to 75.

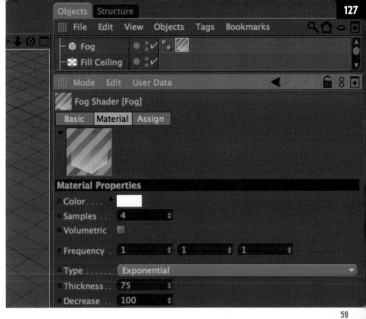

59

Render the scene – the image shows you a well-balanced brightness distribution in the room, the fog shader lightens the lower area as desired and makes the background slightly blurry (Illus. 60).

Now turn on the spotlights again. The rendering makes obvious that these lights play only a minor role in lighting the room surfaces.
Their effect is only visible on the floor, in the shape of little circular spots, which you wouldn't expect when the room dissolves into light and fog (Illus. 61).
Cinema 4D allows you to make lights not generate illumination, even though its rays remain visible.

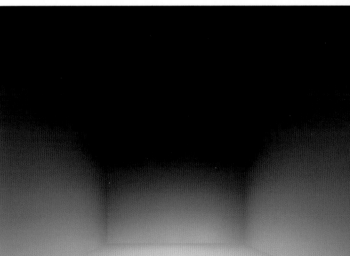

60

62

Select the original spot, and check the No Illumination option in the General panel of the Attributes Manager (Illus. 62).

The rendering demonstrates the change (Illus. 63).
The lighting setup is complete now, and you can focus on your final rendering.

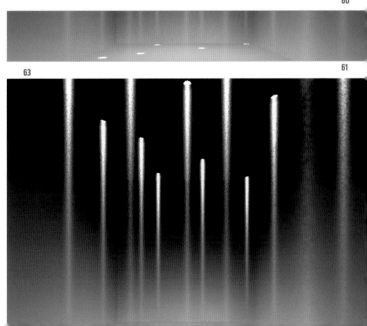

63

61

64

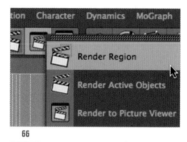

65

Final Rendering Settings

Now you have to make a few settings that will improve the final image – the rendering time isn't the most important criterion any more.

Set Antialiasing to Best (Render menu: Render settings, General panel) to achieve ideal edge smoothing (Illus. 64).
Antialiasing was completely deactivated while setting up and testing the scene since its absence only had a minor effect on the rendering's geometry and coloring.

Set the image size in pixels (Output panel, Resolution) – the given measurements lead to a 300dpi-bitmap as wide as a page of this book (Illus. 65).

We don't need Ambient Occlusion or any other post effect in this case.
Atmospheric refining can be more adequately achieved in postproduction, using Adobe Photoshop for example.

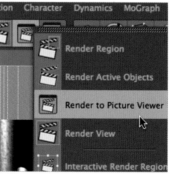

66

Before rendering the scene completely, take time to render critical segments using the Render Region command (Render menu, Illus. 66).
This allows you to check your lighting setup for wrong settings or other flaws (Illus. 67).

67

68

Then start your rendering in the Picture Viewer (Illus. 68), this will take a while (Illus. 69).

The rendered image was processed and colored in Photoshop (Illus. 69 and 70).

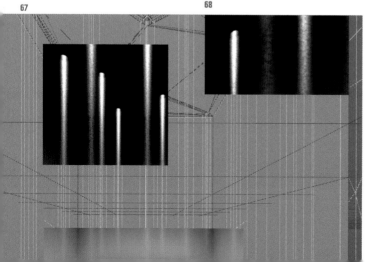

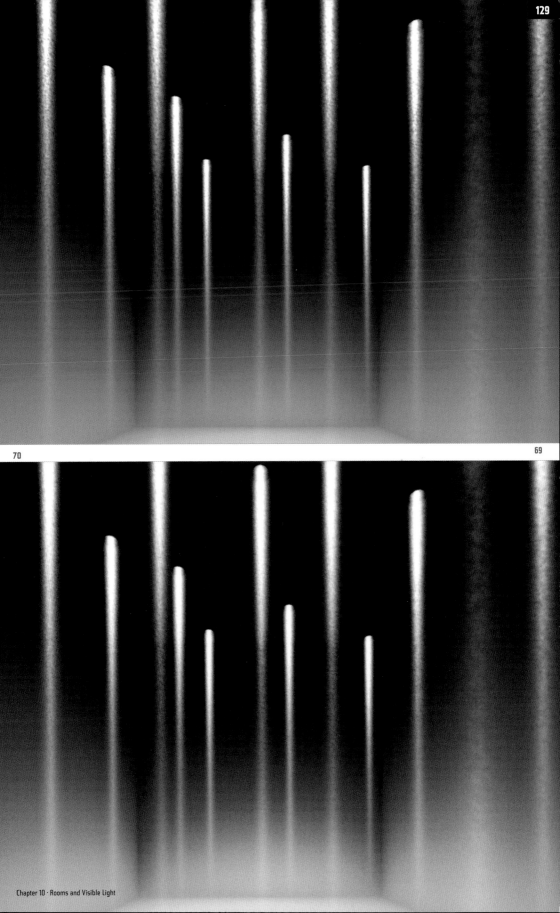

01

Rooms and Objects I · Gallery

In this chapter, the aim is to light a room with bright diffuse light entering the room through a suspended ceiling, and to light objects – pictures in this case – appropriately. The Illustration above shows you what the final result can look like (Illus. 01).

We will use a combination of area lights for the room, the exhibition items are given additional lighting with parallel spots. Hard shadows aren't necessary in this case since we will create the darker areas along the frames and room corners using Ambient Occlusion.

The photographs are mine, they show the highrise building built by Hans Kollhoff on Potsdamer Platz in Berlin.

Getting Started

Open the 11_start.c4d file (see p. 236). It was created with Version 10.

You see a room with a ceiling - consisting of frame and light panes - and pictures hanging on the walls. Quick Shading (Lines) is used for Editor display (Editor Display menu).

If you feel disturbed by the grid being displayed, you may hide it (Editor's Edit menu, Configure, Filter panel: uncheck Grid and World Axis).

For the view, a camera is in use, it's Protection tag in the Object Manager indicat-

02

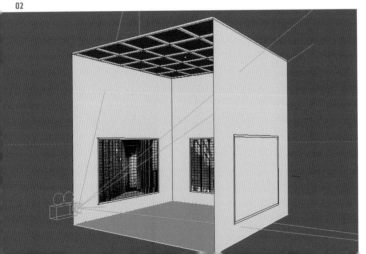

ing it's locked against position and angle change

Switch to the Editor camera if you want to navigate through the scene (Editor menu Cameras). This can be helpful from time to time to get an overview of your work (Illus. 02).

Render the scene. Although there are no light sources in the scene, you still can see the room. The Cinema 4D Default Light is active and serves as a replacement for the missing lights. (Illus. 03).

03

You also notice that the ceiling is completely white – it was assigned a material with a Luminance channel. You can check the Luminance channel in the Attributes Manager by double-clicking on the texture tag next to the sphere object (Illus. 04).

Keep in mind that the luminance doesn't contribute to the lighting of the scene, it just makes the ceiling appear white.

05

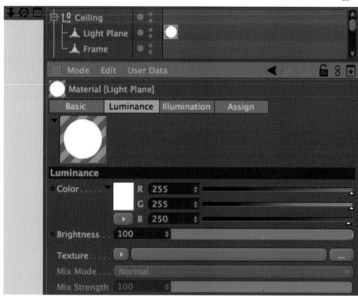

04

Area light as Ceiling Light

To begin working on the lighting setup, place a light object in the scene. By default, Cinema 4D will place an Omni light in the middle of the scene once you click on the Scene Objects icon in the upper command bar (Illus. 06).

Name the light Key Ceiling (Illus. 05). Decide for Area Type (without shadow) in the General panel of the Attributes Manager, and keep Intensity set to 100 (Illus. 07).

Area light allows you to choose any polygon or spline object shape for the light source. In our case it will be the shape of the ceiling.

06

07

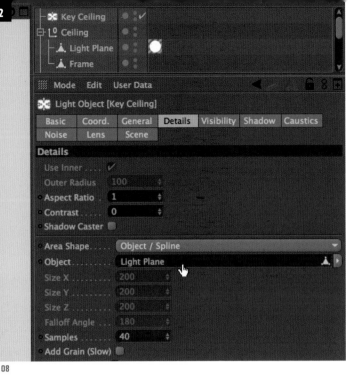

08

09

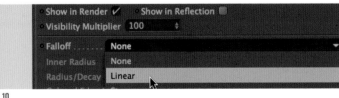

10

11

12

To select the shape, switch to the Details panel of the Attributes Manager (the light object should still be selected). Here you can define a shape for your area light (Illus. 08). Select the Object/Spline option in the Area Shape pull-down menu.

Note that Cinema 4D at this place only accepts polygonal, not parametric objects. However, the group of the ceiling's light planes already is a polygon object, as the icon in the Object Manager indicates (Illus. 08, top).

While the Attributes Manager's Details panel is still in front, please drag the light planes object from the Object Manager into the Object entry field (Illus. 08). This turns the ceiling light planes into a light source, no matter where the light you placed was initially located.

(As you see, you don't have to worry about the position, rotation and size of an area light with an Object/Spline shape; nonetheless it may be helpful to move it into the correct position, e.g. if you want to assess falloff range in the Editor.)

Still in the Details panel, check the Show in Render option, since you want to continue seeing the glass surfaces' white color. (This is necessary because Cinema 4D will ignore the light planes material's initially assigned luminance when using the object as shape reference for an area light.)

In the rendering you can see how the new ceiling light brightens the room, and the glass surfaces appear in shining white (Illus. 09).

Alas, there is still no brightness decrease from top to bottom. To achieve a higher brightness contrast, use Linear Falloff (Illus. 10) and set a range of 700 units (Radius/Decay = 700, Illus. 11).

Since this will result in a loss of brightness in the first place, you should increase Intensity significantly, to 250 (General panel, Illus. 12).

13

The rendering now looks much more differentiated (Illus. 13) – the direct lighting from above appears much more convincing now.

What is still missing is additional brightness coming from room surface reflections. E.g. the floor will reflect rather a lot of light initially coming from the ceiling, so that the lower parts of the walls will be much brighter. The light the floor "generates" this way won't be neutral, it will be slightly yellow, the floor's color.

Floor Area light

Use an additional area light to visualize the floor light reflection. Since there already exists an area light, you only need to duplicate it.

In the Object Manager, Ctrl-drag Key Ceiling, and call the duplicate Fill Floor.

As mentioned before. this light will assume the color of the floor since it is reflected by its surface, especially when it hits a white surface like the wall's.

Set a matching brown hue in the General panel (Color: R 255, G 255, B 200, Illus. 14). Enhance Intensity to 250, since you will define a strong falloff. But keep Area type, and shadow should remain deactivated.

Since the light is meant to simulate floor reflection, drag it to the same height (Coordinates panel: P.Y = -150, Illus. 15 and 17). Turn it into a horizontal position (R.P = 90; this was not necessary for the ceiling light since it was linked to the light planes polygon object).

Adjust the geometry of the floor fill in the first place (Illus. 16): for Area Shape, you choose Rectangle, its size should correspond with the room size (Size X, Y = 500). Make sure to set Falloff Angle to 0 (Illus. 16).

14

15

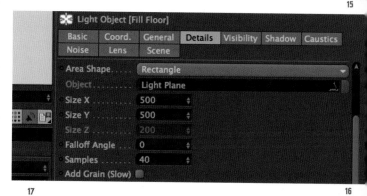

16

17

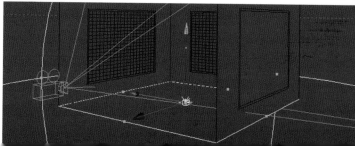

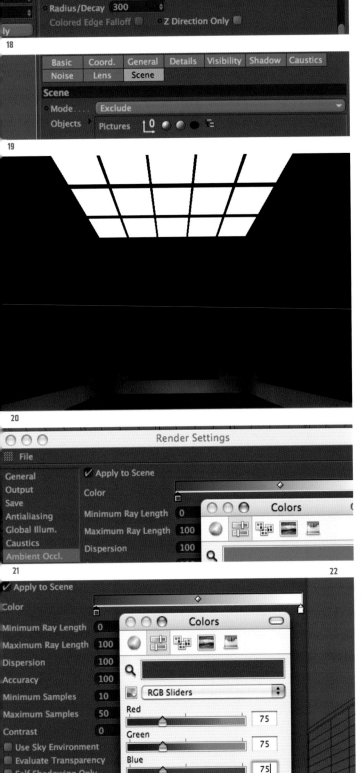

Having made your color, intensity, shape, measurement and location settings, you can deal with additional aspects of this light.

As the floor fill is supposed only to brighten the lower part of the walls, use falloff again, which you can set in the Details panel, too (Linear Falloff, Illus. 18). Limit this effect to approximately half of the room height (Radius/Decay = 300).

It is advisable to exclude the pictures from our floor reflection lighting, since you will work on their setup later. Switch to the Scene panel in the Attributes Manager, set Exclude mode and drag the Pictures null object from the Object Manager into the Objects entry field (Illus. 19).

Switch off the ceiling light and render the scene; the result should suit your needs (Illus. 20).

Darkening the Room Edges

An image of a room often seems sterile, even with a good lighting setup, because there are no imperfections as in real life. For this reason, Cinema 4D features Ambient Occlusion, which helps soften the somewhat aseptic character of a computer simulation.

Ambient Occlusion can be used to darken individual parts of a scene independently from the overall lighting. It is particularly useful for areas with bordering surfaces, e.g. room corners.

You can create this effect in several ways. In this case you might want to activate it globally for the entire scene. You can make the appropriate adjustments in the Render settings (Render menu).

Click on Ambient Occlusion in the left list and activate it by checking the Apply to Scene option (Illus. 21).

The darkening effect is adjusted with a gradient, its left-end color being the one applied to the darkest areas. Turn it a bit lighter by clicking on the small colored square and replacing default Black by Gray (e.g. R, G, B = 75, Illus. 22).

Close the Render settings, switch on the ceiling light again and render the scene once more.

If rendering takes too long, open the Render settings again and reduce Ambient Occlusion's Maximum Samples drastically – although this will make the darkened areas appear grainier.

The result (Illus. 24) shows an obvious improvement to the variant without Ambient Occlusion (Illus. 23).

Picture Lighting

The rendering reveals the pictures still aren't properly staged in the scene – the white background of the photographs is pale gray.

Hence we need additional light sources that only illuminate the pictures. Since the pictures are rectangular, it is recommendable to use rectangular parallel spots.

Place a new light and call it Fill Picture (Illus. 25); for its Type, assign Square Parallel Spot in the General panel (Illus. 26).

You can see how the spot works by looking through the Editor Camera – the light rays are parallel and create a square-shaped beam (Illus. 27).

Its origin lies in the middle of the scene (point zero of the coordinates system), and the default direction is identical with the global Z axis.

23

24

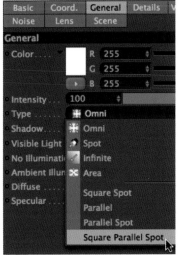

27

26

25

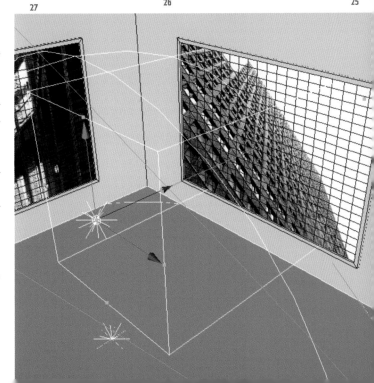

28

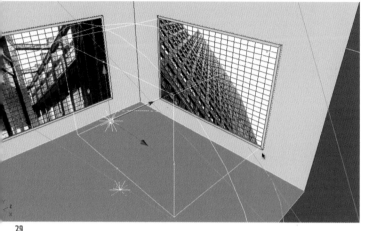

29

First we will work on the light dimension, since the picture is not square, but rectangular.

You can change the size in the Details panel – since the picture size is 200 x 300, you should set the light's Outer Radius to 150 and Aspect Ratio to 0.66 (Illus. 28).

Looked through the Editor camera, you can see that these adjustments result in dimensions matching the picture size (Illus. 29).

Turn off the other lights and render the scene with this one spotlight – disappointingly, you'll see only a circular stain of light in the image (Illus. 30).
Correct this flaw by changing your settings in the Details panel. Set Inner Ra-

dius to 150 as well (Illus. 31). Both radius values define beginning and end of the brightness transition, similar to the falloff settings.
If Inner and Outer Radius are the same, the patch of light will have the desired sharp edges (see Chapter 04, Light Sourc-

30

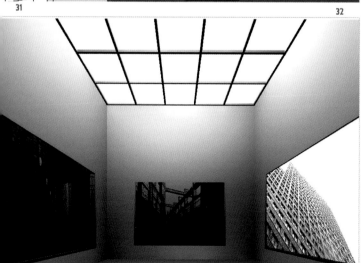

31

32

es in Cinema 4D) and appear in its correct measurements.
In the rendering you may notice the difference between the lit picture to the right and the other, non-lit pictures, even when the ceiling and floor lighting is turned on again. (Illus. 32).

To light the remaining two pictures the same way, you will use instances of the first spot instead of creating two addi-

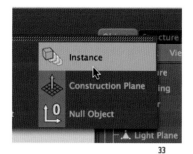

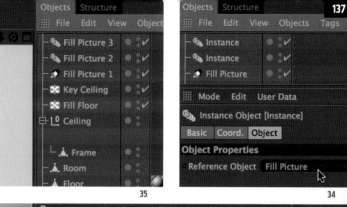

33

35

34

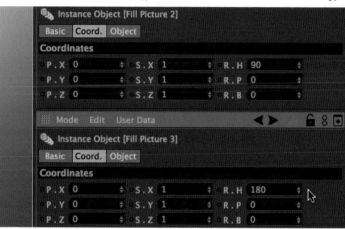

36

tional lights. Using the instance feature will guarantee that the copies adapt to the original spot's settings simultaneously (e.g. Intensity). This way of setting up lights eases your work and helps you avoid mistakes.

Make sure your Fill Picture is selected and place two Instance objects (from the Modeling Objects menu in the upper command bar, Illus. 33).

You can see that your original light is entered as Reference Object for the instances (Instance selected, check the Object panel in the Attributes Manager, Illus. 34). Rename the original light Fill Picture 1, and name the instances Fill Picture 2 and Fill Picture 3 (Illus. 35).

Original and copies are now in the same place and pointing in the same direction. Since the point of origin for all three lights is in the middle of the room, you only have to turn the instances in the right direction.

Turn Fill Picture 3 instance so it is pointing towards the left picture (Coordinates panel: R.H = 180, Illus. 36), and turn the second instance object so it is pointing towards the middle picture (R.H = 90, Illus. 36).

Reduce the original spot's brightness (General panel: Intensity = 50, Illus. 37). Now render the scene, with all your lights and light instances – the three pictures are illuminated with equal brightness (Illus. 38). Actually, they are almost a bit too bright now, as if backlit. But the result is satisfactory for the moment.

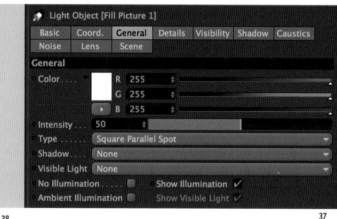

37

38

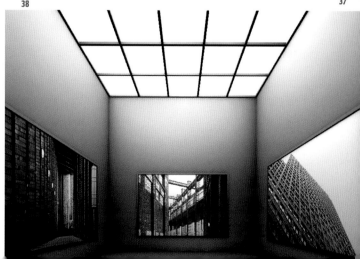

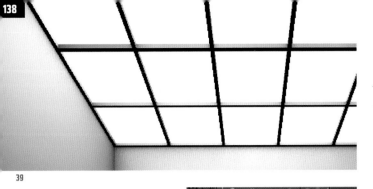

39

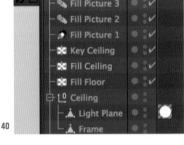

40

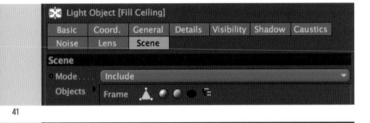

41

42

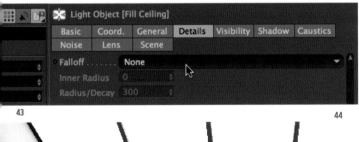

43

44

Fill Light for the Ceiling

The rendering reveals that the undersurface of the ceiling construction is completely black, which isn't surprising since it can't be reached by any of the existing light sources (Illus. 39).
Even though this appears to be a minor detail and the frame structure is actually backlit, we still want to brighten it a bit so the image doesn't have unnecessarily harsh contrasts.

The most appropriate tool for this purpose is, once again, an area light. In this case it is best to use a light that is positioned as low as possible with reference to the ceiling, like the floor fill.
(Remember: the further a non-parallel light source is from a surface, the brighter it shines on that surface, since the light rays' angle becomes more perpendicular as distance increases. The more oblique the angle, the darker it gets.)

Now copy Fill Floor, and name the duplicate Fill Ceiling (Illus. 40).
Select Include mode in the Scene panel and drag Frame from the Object Manager into the Objects entry field (Illus. 41).
Reduce brightness (General panel: Intensity = 35, Illus. 42) and deactivate falloff in the Details panel (Falloff: None, Illus. 43).

The rendering now shows the ceiling's undersurface being slightly brighter (Illus. 44).

Render settings

Adjust some Render settings before starting your final image rendering to improve the images' graphical quality.

Open Render Settings (Render menu), and set Best Antialiasing in the General panel to achieve ideal edge smoothing (Illus. 45;

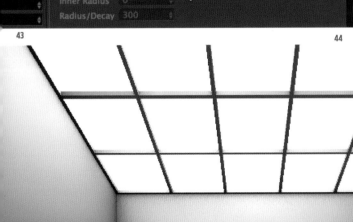

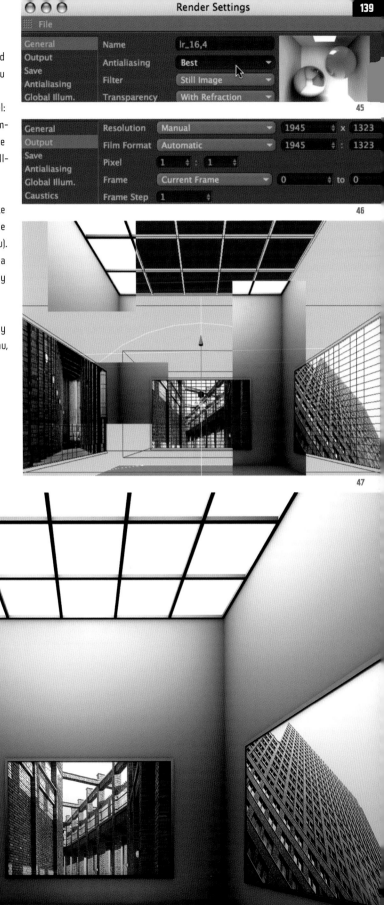

antialiasing was completely deactivated while setting up the scene to save you rendering time).

Set the image size in pixels (Output panel: Resolution), the values used create an image that covers the full width of a page in this book with a setting of 300 dpi. (Illus. 46).

Before rendering the scene in total, take time to render critical segments using the Render Region command (Render menu). This allows you to check if you forgot a setting or turned off a light source by mistake (Illus. 47).

When you're done with testing, you may Render to Picture Viewer (Render Menu, Illus. 48).

45

46

48

47

01

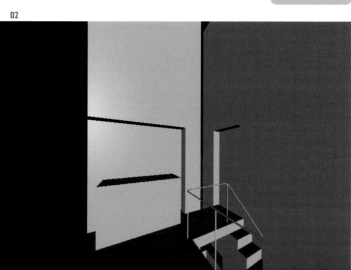

02

Sun and Diffuse Light II · Interior of the Tomba Mambretti by Guiseppe Terragni

The Tomba Mambretti is an unrealized project by the Italian architect Guiseppe Terragni (1904-1943). It is a subterranean grave in which the sarcophagi of the dead lie in shelf-like spaces.

The part of the tomb above ground is the entrance area. An altar niche was intended for meditation and prayer.

Light enters the structure through rectangular slits placed between the bordering wall and spaces between the walls and ceiling, as you can see in the rendering on the left (Illus. 01).

The gap of the entrance behind the viewer allows sunlight to penetrate the interior, it creates a striking ribbon of light that hits both floor and altar.

Hence the scene features both a set of layers of diffuse light and one direct light. Together they create a complex structure of brightness gradients with layers of soft shadows.

The goal in the following chapter is to re-create this scene with the appropriate light objects. Since you will only be working with area shadows, one of the main objectives will be to keep rendering time within reasonable limits as you develop and test your renderings.

Getting Started

Open the 12_start.c4d file (see p.236). It was created with Version 10.

You can see the room from an entrance perspective. You see the viewport image is clipped by gray rectangles - the image output to be rendered in the Picture Viewer will have an upright format.

Gouraud Shading was selected for the Editor image (Editor menu Display). For the view, there is a camera in use that is protected against position change. You may toggle the Editor camera if you want to navigate through the scene (Editor menu Cameras).

Render the scene. Although there are no light sources in the scene, you can see the room since the Cinema 4D Default Light is active to replace missing light sources (Illus. 02).

Diffuse General Light

We will use a hemispherical area light to visualize diffuse sky light.
Place a light and call it Diffuse. Select Area for the light's and the shadow's type, and increase its brightness sharply (General panel: Intensity = 1200, Illus. 03).

For Area Shape, choose Hemisphere with an Outer Radius of 400 (Details panel, Illus. 04). Use one of the side views (F3 or F4) to get a sense of the overall size and proportions (Illus. 06).

Go back to the Details panel and reduce the light Samples rate to 16 to keep rendering time as short as possible.
Reduce Accuracy to 50 in the Attributes manager's Shadow panel for the same reason, and adjust the Minimum and Maximum Samples values to 20 (Illus. 05).
Of course this will make the shadow very grainy, as you can see in the rendering, but it is accurate enough to assess the brightness gradient and ensures reasonable rendering time.

The settings I suggested are the result of a pretty long trial & error phase; feel free to change them if things look different on your screen.

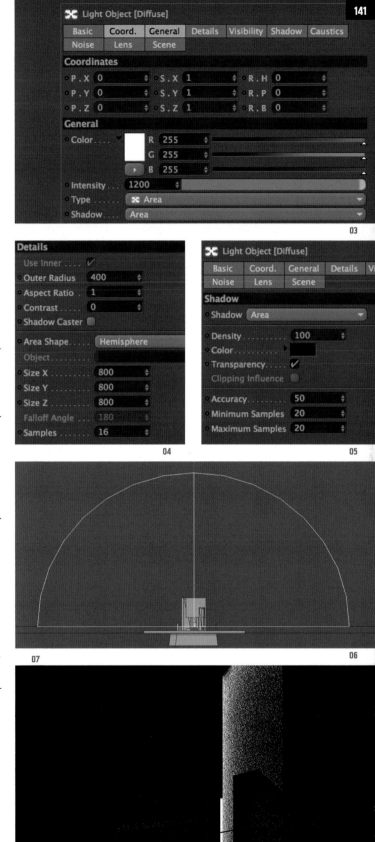

08

09

10

11

12

Sunlight

You will focus on sunlight now that you have worked on our diffuse daylight. Sunlight is set in a specific direction, as opposed to the Diffuse, and creates relatively hard shadows.

Direct sunlight, as in most cases, is the key light in your scene, i.e. it has the most peculiar look. But, as I mentioned before, it never comes alone, there's always a diffuse light supplying it.

To visualize sunlight in the given scene, place another light and name it Sun (Illus. 09). Choose Infinite for light and Area for shadow type (General panel, Illus. 08). Raise Intensity to 200.

Infinite light consists of light rays with parallel trajectories – this makes the light source's location secondary, the only thing left to be set is the angle (Coordinates panel: R.H = -80, R.P = -15, Illus. 10; also see Chapter 04, Light Sources in Cinema 4D).
The R.H value defines the rotation angle around the perpendicular Y axis the light comes from and the R.P value defines the inclination of the light rays.

Don't forget to reduce the shadow bitmap's resolution (Shadow panel: Accuracy = 50, Minimum and Maximum Samples = 20, Illus. 11).

Render the scene. The ribbon of light looks quite good; as you can see, your sunlight only appears in very limited size in this case (Illus. 12).
The diffuse light plays a much more dominant role in this scene, which is why you will have to spend some more work on this.

You have actually already installed a light source that is meant to transport the diffuse portion of skylight into your model's interior, but it still isn't enough – brightness near the openings should be stronger.

So we will place a few additional lights to support our light setup in these areas.

Diffuse Light from Above

For example, there is a gap between ceiling and wall through which light enters the room on both sides. The effect of this light will be a general brightening of the interior, especially along the right wall. This demands an additional light for the light entering the room from above. In this case, the best choice would be a cylindrical light above the gap that casts a soft, scattered shadow starting from the roof edge.

Place a light (Roof Right, Illus. 14), and increase its brightness sharply (General panel: Intensity = 500, Illus. 13). Choose Area for your light and shadow type in the same panel. Set Cylinder as Area Shape in the Details panel (Illus. 15). It should be 10 units thick (Outer Radius = 5), length (Size Z) should be set to 55. Make sure the light Samples rate is set to its lowest possible value 16. Rotate the cylinder around its Y axis (Coordinates panel: R.P = 90) and move it above the gap (P.Y = 65, P.Z = –21, Illus. 16).

The Editor camera view (Illus. 17) shows you whether position and size are correctly defined.

Switch off all lights except for this last light you installed, and set the shadow bitmap resolution to a low value (Shadow panel: Accuracy = 50, Minimum and Maximum Samples = 20, Illus. 20).

The image result meets our expectations, but the effect reaches too far downwards (Illus. 18).

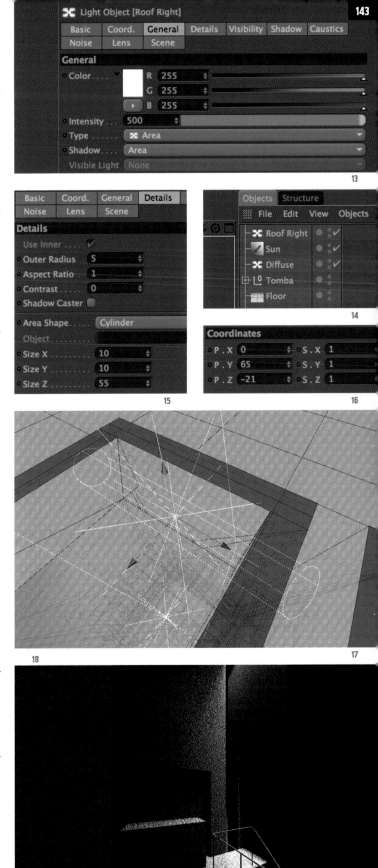

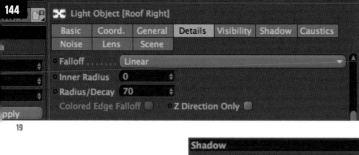

19

Again, falloff is the very feature in this case: activate Linear Falloff in the Details panel and define a relatively small range (Radius/Decay = 70, Illus. 19).

Render the scene again using your new light source – the image should be accurate now (Illus. 22).

Now turn on the other lights again and look at what you have achieved so far – the light situation looks more complex now (Illus. 21).

20

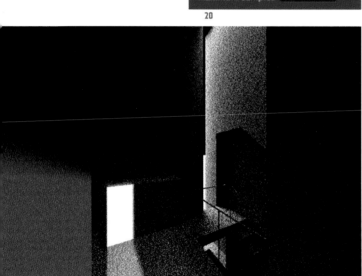

21

22

Light from the Basement

The basement is an important part of the tomb – light should shine from below to create connection to the hidden part of the building and at least give it a small roll in the scene.

Place a new light in the scene (named Basement, Illus. 23).

Keep the Omni type and set area shadow (in the Attributes Manager's General panel, Illus. 24).

Increase brightness significantly, which is almost always necessary when using area shadow (Intensity = 1000).

Drag the omni down to the gap between

23

24

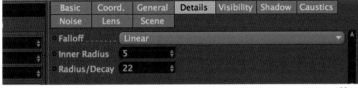

floor and stairs (Coordinates panel: P.Y = -15, P.Z = -15, Illus. 25).

25

Activate Linear Falloff to confine the light effect to the limited visible steps segment (Details: Inner Radius = 5, Radius/Decay = 22, Illus. 26).

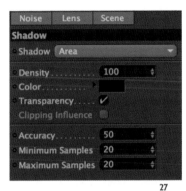

26

As far as the shadow graphics is concerned, in this stage you will have to stay with the pronounced graininess to save rendering time – make the necessary adjustments in the Shadow panel (Accuracy = 50, Minimum and Maximum Samples = 20, Illus. 27).

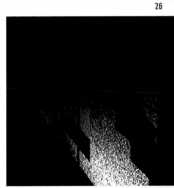

Render the scene with the newly placed light source to assess its effect (Illus. 28). The rendering with all lights switched on shows that the right side of the room looks pretty good, whereas the left side up to now is dominated by your "sunlight" (Illus. 29).

27   28

Keep in mind that we are planning to use an upright format for your final rendering, the gray bars on the left and right will disappear.

29

Diffuse Light from the Left

There is a door opening on the left that allows light to enter the room as well.
Our first diffuse light should be able to take care of this, but the effect isn't as explicit as we would like – just another situation to use additional fill lighting.

30

31

Place another light source and call it Door (Illus. 30).
Set a high value for brightness in the Attributes Manager's General panel (Intensity = 1000, Illus. 31), and select Area for both light and shadow type again.

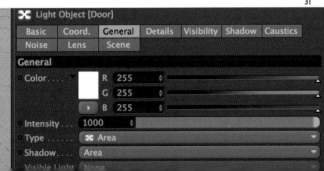

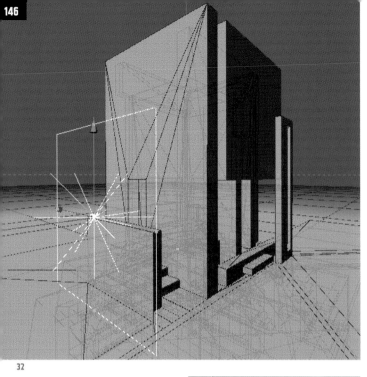

32

33

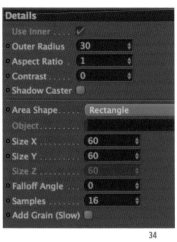

34

Drag the light object outwards (Coordinates panel: P.Y = 12, P.Z = 50, Illus. 33). Reduce the size of the rectangle in the Details panel (Outer Radius = 30, Illus. 34). Make sure the resolution of this light is as low as possible (Samples = 16).

Switch to the Editor Camera viewport to check the placement of the light source (Illus. 32).

The effect of this light is supposed to be limited to a specific range again, so activate Linear Falloff in the Details panel and set 45 for Inner Radius and 75 for Radius/Decay (Illus. 35).
Don't forget to reduce the shadow's resolution as well (Shadow panel: Accuracy = 50, Minimum and Maximum Samples = 20, Illus. 37).

35

36

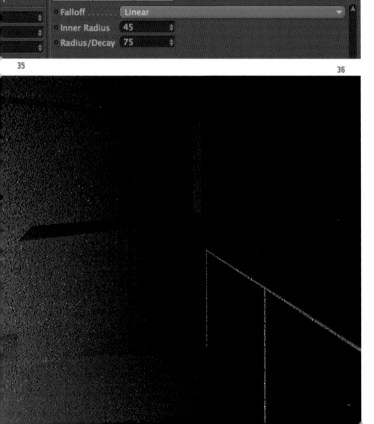

37

Switch off the other lights and render the scene – the amount of light seems adequate (Illus. 36).

The overall view – all your lights turned on again – looks well-balanced (Illus. 38). The lighting setup is complete now, so you can focus on preparing your final rendering.

Final Rendering Settings

Before we start, let me discuss one detail: although you could insert a background in post-production using Photoshop, you might want to create a white sky in Cinema 4D.

Select your Diffuse light and check the option Show in Render (Details panel, Illus. 39).

This makes the area light hemisphere appear in its assigned color which is white in this instance.

Since you won't have to worry about saving rendering time now that you're finished, please set a global shadow resolution increase.

Select all your lights (Illus. 40) – they share the same shadow type and resolution – and adjust the shadow sample settings they have in common.

Now set higher resolution values in the Shadow panel (Accuracy = 100, Minimum Samples = 100 and Maximum Samples = 400, Illus. 41).

38

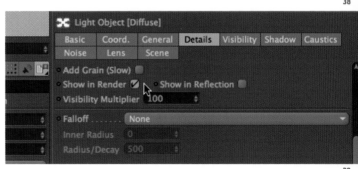

39

40

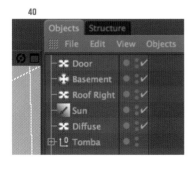

41

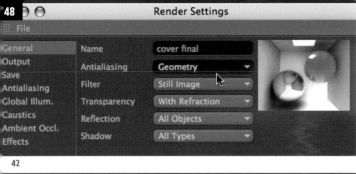

42

43

44

45

Time to focus on the appropriate rendering settings: it is best to define a new set (Render menu: New Render Settings), and call it Final, or something of that kind. Clearly defined, verifiable setting render sets help you save time and avoid mistakes arising from inconsistent adjustments.

Choose Antialiasing in the General panel – select the Geometry option so the contours in our image are adequately smoothened (Illus. 42), this will also result in finer shadow maps.

In the Output panel, set the image size in pixels – the given measurements lead to a picture with a resolution of 300 dpi over the entire surface of the cover of this book (Resolution, Illus. 43).

You may disregard the rest of the Render settings, e.g. you don't need Ambient Occlusion in this case since your scene is rather diffuse and shadowy, so additionally darkened room edges would barely be recognizable.

Cinema 4D needs a decent amount of time to render the final image, as you defined highly resolved area shadow for five light objects, so use the Render Region command (Render menu) to render critical image segments first (Illus. 44 and 45).

Go through the settings of all your area lights one more time and make sure the Samples rate is 16 for each light before finally rendering the image to the Picture Viewer.

This process takes a bit of time, but you can recognize how both the shadow's high bitmap resolution and antialiasing have an obvious impact on the image's quality (Illus. 45).

Chapter 12 · Sun and Diffuse Light II · Int. of the Tomba Mambretti

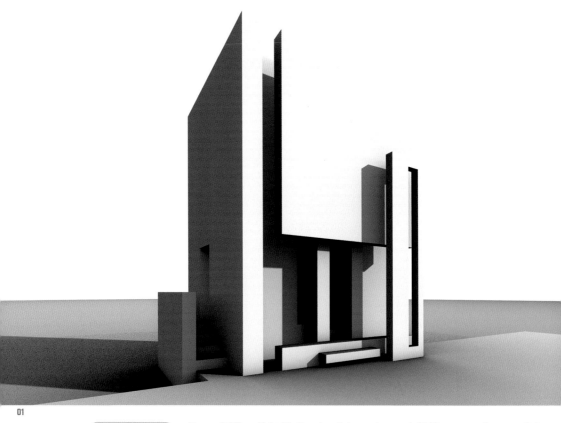

01

Sun and Diffuse Light III · Exterior of the Tomba Mambretti by Guiseppe Terragni

13

In this chapter, we are going to leave the inside of the tomb and concentrate on an outside scene for a change. The primary goal here is to create an atmospherically appropriate relationship between diffuse and directed daylight – Illustration 01 shows a possible result. Since the object is a more complex architecture model, part of your task will be to prepare the

02

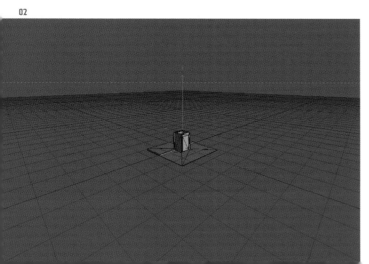

imported CAAD structure for your light setup, which makes this a review and practical application of the knowledge we gathered in Chapter 03, CAAD Import and Model Setup.

Open the 13_start.c4d file (see p. 236). You see a model that seems rather small and lonesome in the Editor (Illus. 02). As you know from Chapter 03, you can control the size of an imported model using import settings. But let's assume you skipped this subject and the result looks like our example. You would then have to check the size and quality of your model and change it as required. As it seems, the model is too small; place a camera, but stay with the Editor camera and steer around the model, so you can see both your 3d file and the new camera (Illus. 03) – the size relation between camera and model doesn't look correct, the model is to small and needs to be scaled.

Now select the entire Tomba object, a null object that contains all your construction components (Illus. 04), and in the Coordinates Manager, select the Scale option below the middle value column named Size. Scale will now be displayed as the column header, with all axis values set to 1. Raise these to 10 (Illus. 05), and confirm your selection by pressing Return. The Editor shows that your model has apparently grown by the factor of ten, just as defined by you. Zoom out of the scene a bit and assess the result – the camera-model size proportion looks completely different now (Illus. 06). When the Tomba object is still selected, you can toggle the Size+ option below the middle Coordinates Manager value column to read the size in units of your model in the middle column (Illus. 07; as I mentioned in chapter 3, here you'll find an answer to the size issue that is more exact than the comparison between camera and model:

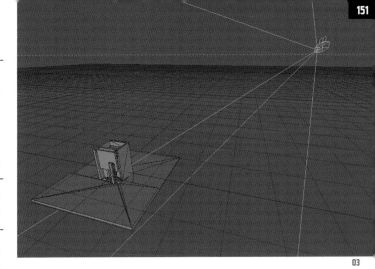

03

04

05

07

if the units shown in the Coordinates Manager match your model's original measurements in centimeters, the size is correct. And don't bother if any units like meter, millimeter etc are displayed, they don't mean a thing).

Now you will have to adjust your camera to create a good perspective. Turn it on, since you have only been using the Editor camera until now (Editor menu, Cameras: Scene Cameras – Camera). Make sure the camera object is selected and open the Coordinates and Object panel in the Attributes Manager (right-click on their tabs). Move the camera into the right position (P.X = -915, P.Y = 95, P.Z = 385, Illus. 08), and turn it (R.H = -120; the other two angles should be set to 0). Set your Focal

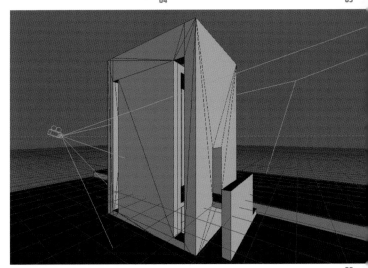

08

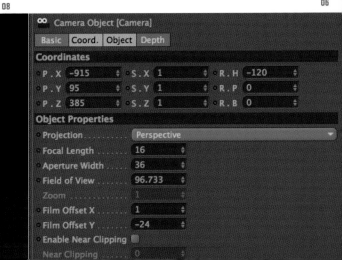

06

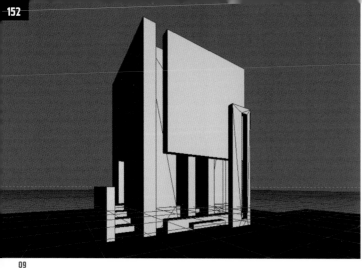

09

Length to 16. The perspective looks quite good - yet tune the Film Offset values (Offset X = 1, Offset Y = -24, Illus. 08) to see the building completely.

The perspective should look like the image on the left (Illus. 09). Fix the camera with a Protection Tag (Object Manager's Tags menu: Cinema 4D Tags, Protection, Illus. 10). This protects the camera against movement and rotation, focal length and film offset stay adjustable, though.

To continue, hide the coordinates grid. From the Editor's Edit menu, choose Configure All, and toggle the Filter panel in the Attributes Manager. Here, please remove the checkmarks for Grid and World Axis (Illus. 11). As you may already have noticed, you see the word Perspective displayed in the Viewport - this is because HUD is activated in the same Filter panel (Illus. 11) HUD (Head Up Display) is meant to inform you about certain aspects of your scene in the viewport windows, and in the HUD panel (the Attributes Manager should still show the Configure settings)

10

12

13

11

you may define which of these you see, At present, Projection is checked, so this is the reason why the word Perspective is shown (Illus. 12). Switch to the Editor camera view before continuing to avoid changing your camera's focal length or offset by mistake (Illus. 13). Now you will

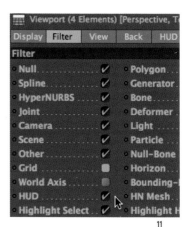

tackle a problem we already discussed in chapter 3 (CAAD Importing and Model Setup): the large number of triangular polygons on the object surfaces.

Toggle the four-window view (by clicking in the Editor viewport with your middle mouse button, or pressing F5) to gain a better overview. Define a different elevation view for each window (Editor menu Cameras – Left, Right, Front, Back, Illus. 14). Press Alt H so the model is shown completely in each window.

Pick the Configure All command (Editor's Edit menu, Illus. 15) to set the display mode for all windows – as you can see, its wireframe Lines mode for most of them up to now (Illus. 15). In the Display panel, set Constant Shading (Lines) for Active Object, and deactivate Separate Settings for Inactive Object (Illus. 16).

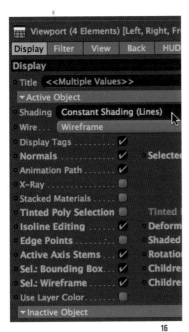

Since you want to remove needless triangular polygons, select the Polygon tool (left command bar, Illus. 17).

In the Object Manager, expand the Tomba null object and select all the objects in the folder (Illus. 18).

154

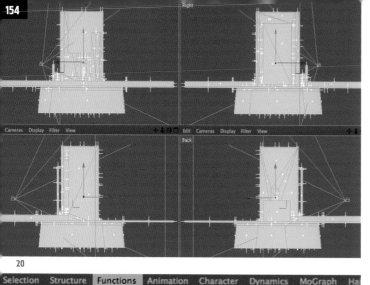

20

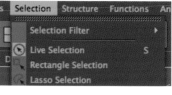

19

Now take the Select All command from the Selection menu (Illus. 19). All the model's surfaces should appear with orange edges, their normals displayed as small white lines (if you don't see them, Tinted Poly Normals is unchecked in the Display panel of the Configure settings; Illus. 20).

Select the Untriangulate command from the Functions menu to remove all unnecessary triangulations from the object surfaces (Illus. 21). Check Create N-Gons in the dialog that opens up (Illus. 22).

Explanation: Cinema 4D consolidates coplanar triangles into tetragons when it un-triangulates, but an object surface can of course have more than four corner points – thus it will still be divided in sub-polygons after combining triangles.
In this case, Cinema 4D can hide this internal subdivision for editing purposes (e.g. separation and extrusion) by displaying a so-called N-Gon.
Confirm the dialogue by pressing OK. As you can see in the Editor windows, the triangles have disappeared.
Now choose the Deselect All command (Selection menu). Surprisingly, the Editor still shows lines dividing surfaces (Illus. 23).
These subdivision lines can be hidden by unchecking N-Gon Lines in the Configure settings Filter panel (Illus. 24).

21

22

The objects in the Editor viewport now appear without subdivision (Illus. 25).

So, up to now, you have solved the scale problem and removed redundant triangles.

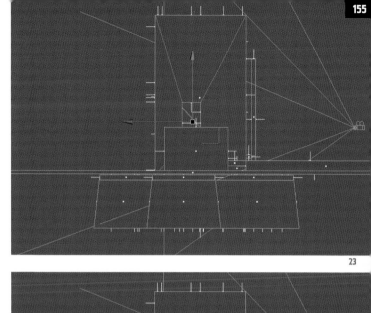

23

24

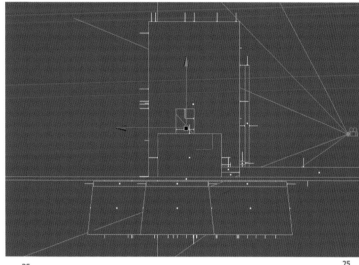

25

Now let's focus on the actual subject of this chapter, the lighting of the scene and embedding it in an adequate scenery.

You will refrain from using textures for the model, as we again want to stay with a rather abstract rendering, but it would be useful if our building were at least white to better assess the quality of the lighting setup.

The default material assigned to the surfaces of our building is gray. (As with default light and the Editor camera, there's no polygon without this material, though it's not indicated by a texture tag.)

To turn the surfaces white, select the New Material command in the File menu of the Material Manager (Illus. 26).

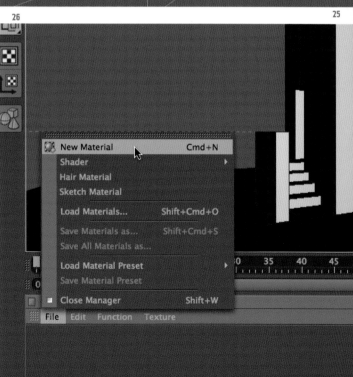

26

28

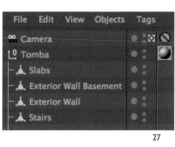

27

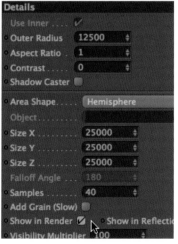

29

31

30

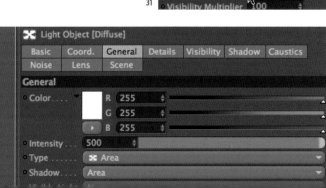

Assign this new material to your model by dragging its icon out of the Material Manager and on to the Tomba null object in the Object Manager. The corresponding texture tag should appear next to the null (Illus. 27).

Double-click on the tag to adjust the material settings in the Attributes Manager. The only thing you need to change is the brightness in the Color channel – set it to 100 (Illus. 28).

The model is definitely brighter now (Illus. 29).

By the way, you can deactivate the material's Specular channel (in the Basic panel) – it doesn't do any harm, but it is entirely unnecessary here.

Lightdome for Diffuse Light

Now let's focus on the light setup for our scene – first we want to concentrate on the diffuse portion of our sky light, i.e. the lighting that is always available at daylight, even under overcast weather conditions.

For this purpose, you will use a hemispherical light that vaults the scene like an artificial sky - rather the same way we used it in the preceding chapter (this kind of hemispherical light is also called a lightdome).

Place a light and name it Diffuse. In the General panel, select Area as light and shadow type (Illus. 30), and turn up brightness substantially (Intensity = 500). For Area Shape, choose Hemisphere with an Outer Radius of 12500 units (Details

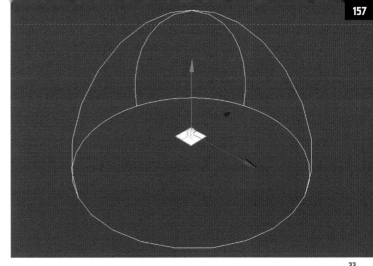

32

Coordinates

P.X	0	S.X	1
P.Y	−160	S.Y	1
P.Z	0	S.Z	1

panel, Illus. 31). In the same panel, you can make the light dome (the "sky") appear white by checking Show in Render.

Move down the lightdome (Coordinates panel: P.Y = -160, Illus. 32). You can assess the size proportion between lightdome and model in the Editor viewport after switching to Perspective again (Illus. 33).

33

Shadow

Shadow	Area	
Density	100	
Color		
Transparency	✓	
Clipping Influence		
Accuracy	75	
Minimum Samples	8	

34

Since you are using a light source that creates area shadow, you should minimize the shadow's bitmap resolution so your test renderings won't take too long. You can do this in the Shadow panel – set Maximum Samples to 10, and keep Accuracy set to 75 (Illus. 34).

Render the scene –the result is already pretty decent, although the shadow is too grainy (Illus. 35).

The diffuse lighting effect is obvious– the building's surfaces are evenly lit with soft shadows. If you want the shadow to be finer, increase the sample rate (for example set Minimum and Maximum Samples to 100, Illus. 36) and render the critical areas by using Render Region from the Render menu (Illus. 37).

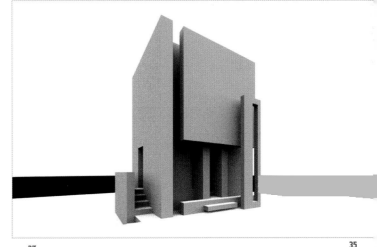

35

36

Basic	Coord.	General	Details
Noise	Lens	Scene	

Shadow

Shadow	Area	
Density	100	
Color		
Transparency	✓	
Clipping Influence		
Accuracy	100	
Minimum Samples	100	

37

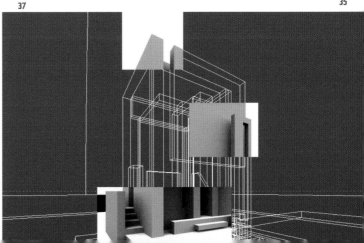

Light	Spot Light	Infinite Light
Area Light	Target Light	Camera
Target Camera	Floor	Sky
Sun Light	Environment	Foreground
Background	Selection	Stage

38

Direct Sunlight

Now you want to add direct sunlight to the scene you have just lit with a light-dome, and see the typical hard shadows this light creates – inventing sunlight will also result in a higher contrasted lighting of the building.

An infinite light source seems the most appropriate here. This time we will place it by choosing it directly from the Scene Objects menu (upper command bar, Illus. 38).

Now you will once again make use of the features Cinema 4D offers to create an easily controllable result.

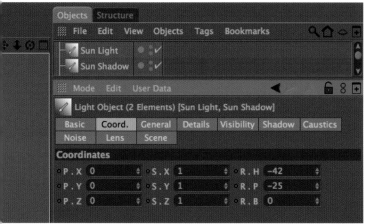

39

Your sunlight "competes" with the diffuse daylight (both as a light, and with the shadows it creates) – it shouldn't be too bright, because otherwise it will outshine the object surfaces, but it still should create strong hard shadows.

For this reason, it is easier to divide your sunlight into two objects: one which lights the object surfaces and one that only creates shadow (you remember Chapter 07, Sun and Diffuse Light I).

Duplicate the new light in the Object Manager – call one of them Sun Light, and the other one Sun Shadow (Illus. 39).

As you may recall (Chapter 04, Light Sources in Cinema 4D), the location of an infinite light source is irrelevant (hence it can remain at the zero point of the scene), its direction is the only important aspect here.

Select both suns, and set the light direction in the Coordinates panel (R.H = -42, R.P = -25, Illus. 40). This way you ensure both lights have the same direction.

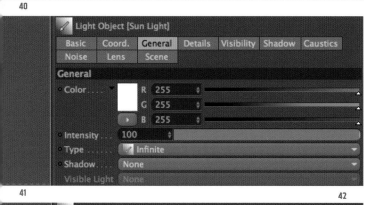

40

41   42

Keep the Sun Light's brightness (General: Intensity = 100, Illus. 41), and lower the Sun Shadow's a bit (Intensity = 75, Illus. 42).

For Sun Shadow, you have to check another option (Details panel: Shadow Caster, Illus. 43) to make sure this light only creates shadows, and keeps it from distributing light to the scene.

Select Area as the sun shadow's type (Illus. 42), so it isn't as sharp-edged and artificial – for a parallel light source, the transition between hard and soft shadow can be adjusted in the Details panel (in our example: Infinite Angle = 0.5, Illus. 43).

Make sure no shadow is defined for Sun Light (Illus. 41).

As always when you use area shadow, you have to lower its resolution to save time during your test renderings. For the sake of simplicity, you should do this for Sun Shadow and Diffuse at the same time.

Select both and set the Maximum Samples value to 10 in the Attributes Manager's Shadow panel, which now controls both lights (Illus. 44).

Switch off Diffuse and render the scene. You can see how both suns complement each other with different effects (Illus. 45) – without specifically defining the tasks of both infinite light sources, all surfaces in the hard shadow area would be completely black.

Lower the Diffuse's brightness so the scene doesn't become overexposed (Intensity = 225, Illus. 46). Turn Diffuse on again and render the scene one more time. The result looks pretty good. The diffuse and direct light complement each other successfully (Illus. 47).

43

44

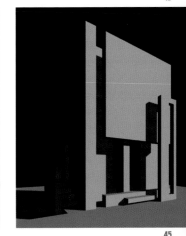

45

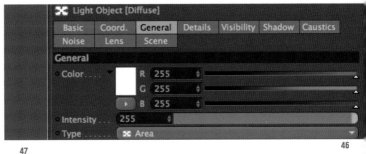

46

47

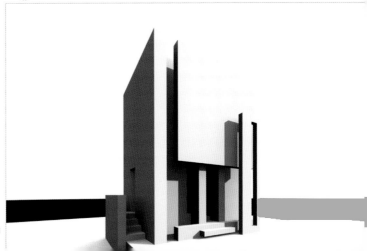

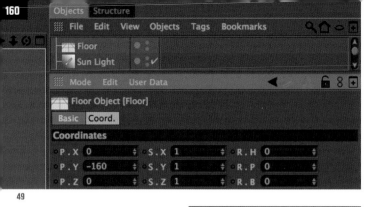

Scene Basis

Now you need a basis for your architecture scene, and both basis and hard shadows should be darkened a bit.

Place a Floor object in the scene (from the Scene Objects menu in the upper command bar, Illus. 49), and drag it downwards until it is at level with the model's Site object (Coordinates panel: P.Y = -160, Illus. 48).

Although the overall lighting seems to be balanced, the basis objects are overexposed.

To weaken this effect, we will use a light source with negative brightness, i.e. a light that withdraws lighting from the scene instead of contributing to it. As with lights in general, this negative light's effect can be limited to selected objects, too.

Again, an infinite light can be useful in this case – place this type of light in the scene and call it Fill Floor.

48

Rotate it so it shines downwards at a perpendicular angle (Coordinates panel: R.P = -90, Illus. 50). Since we need this light to darken the scene, you should set brightness to a negative value (General panel: Intensity = -75).

To limit this effect to the model Site and Floor, switch to the Scene panel. Set the Include mode and drag both objects from the Object Manager into the Objects entry field. (Illus. 51; you may have to expand the Tomba null object before you do this).

Settings for the Final Rendering

As usual, before launching your final rendering you have to make a few adjust-

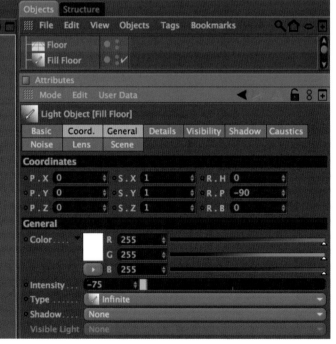

50

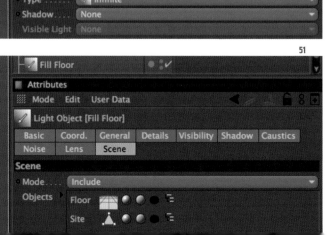

51

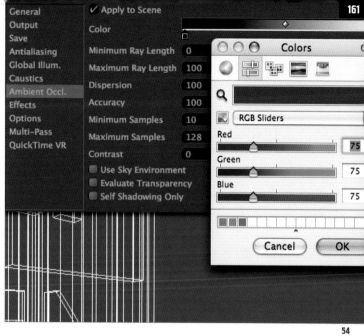

ments to improve the quality. Rendering time isn't as critical anymore.

For Diffuse and Sun Shadow, first increase the shadow's bitmap resolution (Shadow panel: Accuracy = 100, Minimum Samples = 25, Maximum Samples = 100, Illus. 52). Select Antialiasing in the General panel of the Render settings (Geometry, Illus. 53), and activate Ambient Occlusion (with a gray-to-white gradient, Illus. 54).

As you see in the viewport rendering, light distribution seems balanced now; the sun-created shadow looks defined, without being too sharp-edged (Illus. 55).

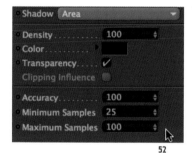

52

53

54

55

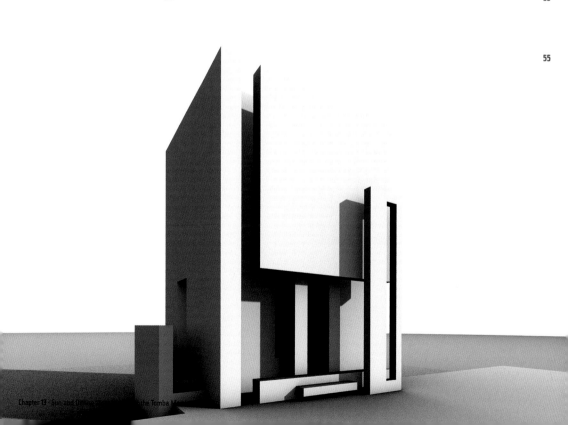

Image   Layer   Select   Filter   View   Window   Help

New ▶

Duplicate Layer...
Delete ▶

Layer Properties...
Layer Style ▶
Smart Filter ▶

New Fill Layer ▶
New Adjustment Layer ▶
Change Layer Content ▶
Layer Content Options...

Layer Mask ▶
Vector Mask ▶
Create Clipping Mask ⌥⌘G

Smart Objects ▶

Layer...   ⇧⌘N
Layer From Background...
Group...
Group from Layers...

Layer via Copy   ⌘J
Layer via Cut   ⇧⌘J

Feather: 0 px

Polygonal Lasso Tool (L)

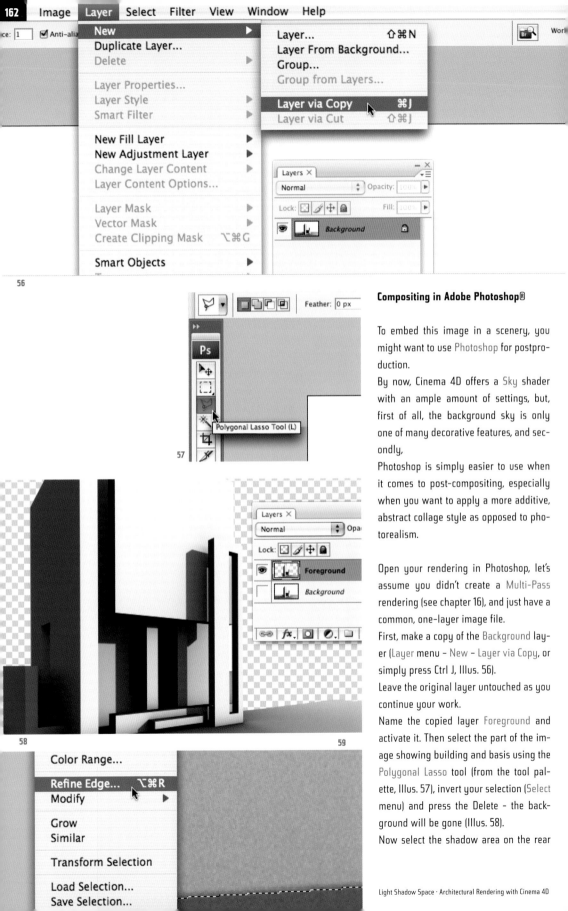

56

57

58

59

Color Range...

Refine Edge...   ⌥⌘R
Modify ▶

Grow
Similar

Transform Selection

Load Selection...
Save Selection...

Compositing in Adobe Photoshop®

To embed this image in a scenery, you might want to use Photoshop for postproduction.

By now, Cinema 4D offers a Sky shader with an ample amount of settings, but, first of all, the background sky is only one of many decorative features, and secondly,

Photoshop is simply easier to use when it comes to post-compositing, especially when you want to apply a more additive, abstract collage style as opposed to photorealism.

Open your rendering in Photoshop, let's assume you didn't create a Multi-Pass rendering (see chapter 16), and just have a common, one-layer image file.

First, make a copy of the Background layer (Layer menu – New – Layer via Copy, or simply press Ctrl J, Illus. 56).

Leave the original layer untouched as you continue your work.

Name the copied layer Foreground and activate it. Then select the part of the image showing building and basis using the Polygonal Lasso tool (from the tool palette, Illus. 57), invert your selection (Select menu) and press the Delete - the background will be gone (Illus. 58).

Now select the shadow area on the rear

part of the floor using the same tool. This
has to be done on the background layer,
since in your new layer it's already gone.
Keep in mind that Background has to be
the active layer to do so. Use Refine Edge
to tune your selection (Select menu, Illus.
59 and 60).

Press Crtl J again to move the selected
shadow to a new, separate layer you will
call Shadow (Illus. 61).

You have now completed the necessary
preparations for the addition of a background image. This image will have to be
located on a layer below the foreground
and shadow.

Open file 13_background.jpg. Press F several times until your picture is displayed
in a "normal" window. Move it sideways
so you can also see part of your rendering – the newly opened image still being
in the foreground.

Choose the Move tool from your tool palette (Illus. 62), click on your background
jpg image, hold down your left mouse key
and move your mouse over to the visible
part of your rendering.
When you release the mouse key, Photoshop drops a copy of the image you

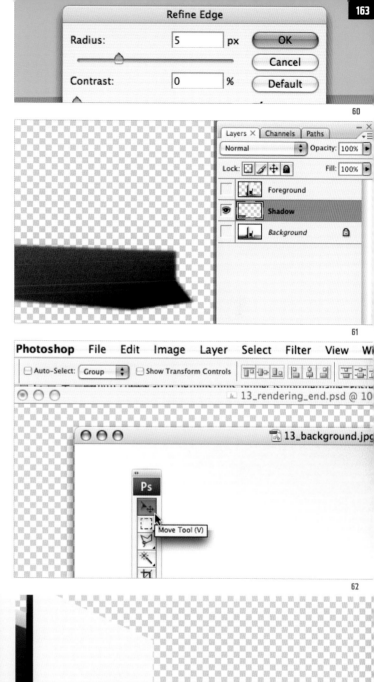

60

61

62

63

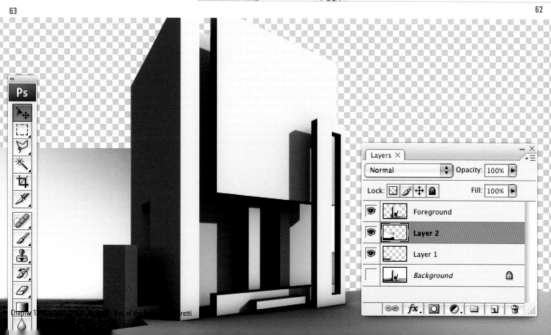

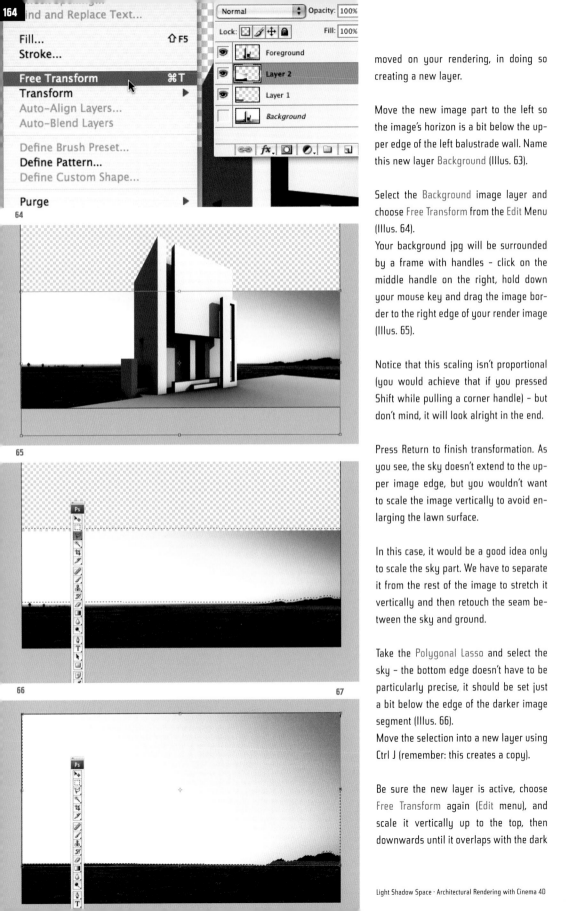

Find and Replace Text...

Fill...   ⇧F5
Stroke...

Free Transform   ⌘T
Transform   ▶
Auto–Align Layers...
Auto–Blend Layers

Define Brush Preset...
Define Pattern...
Define Custom Shape...

Purge   ▶

64

65

66

67

moved on your rendering, in doing so creating a new layer.

Move the new image part to the left so the image's horizon is a bit below the upper edge of the left balustrade wall. Name this new layer Background (Illus. 63).

Select the Background image layer and choose Free Transform from the Edit Menu (Illus. 64).
Your background jpg will be surrounded by a frame with handles – click on the middle handle on the right, hold down your mouse key and drag the image border to the right edge of your render image (Illus. 65).

Notice that this scaling isn't proportional (you would achieve that if you pressed Shift while pulling a corner handle) – but don't mind, it will look alright in the end.

Press Return to finish transformation. As you see, the sky doesn't extend to the upper image edge, but you wouldn't want to scale the image vertically to avoid enlarging the lawn surface.

In this case, it would be a good idea only to scale the sky part. We have to separate it from the rest of the image to stretch it vertically and then retouch the seam between the sky and ground.

Take the Polygonal Lasso and select the sky – the bottom edge doesn't have to be particularly precise, it should be set just a bit below the edge of the darker image segment (Illus. 66).
Move the selection into a new layer using Ctrl J (remember: this creates a copy).

Be sure the new layer is active, choose Free Transform again (Edit menu), and scale it vertically up to the top, then downwards until it overlaps with the dark

Light Shadow Space · Architectural Rendering with Cinema 4D

part of the background image (Illus. 67).
Now you are going to hide the lower part
of the new layer using a mask to reveal
the image underneath.

Activate the layer you just produced and

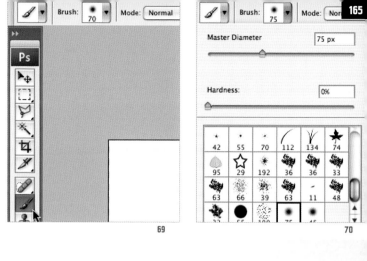

69

70

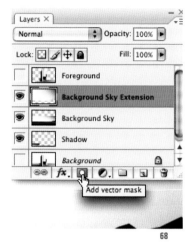

68

assign a layer mask (by clicking the corresponding button on the bottom of the
Layer panel, Illus. 68). The layer mask is
active now (the double edge on the miniature confirms this, Illus. 71), so you can
paint in it.

Select the Brush tool (Illus. 69) and give
it a larger tip (in the Options bar: 70px,
Illus. 70).
Make sure the foreground color is set
to black (see the left color square at the
bottom of the tools palette), and carefully paint over the border area between
"heaven" and "earth" (Illus. 71).

This will conceal image content of the upper layer (the one which is masked and
active) as you move your brush over it,
and reveal the image on the layer beneath.
The result should look like Illustration 72.

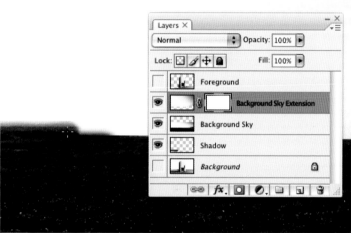

72

71

13_rendering_end.psd @ 25% (Background Sky Extension, Layer Mask/8)

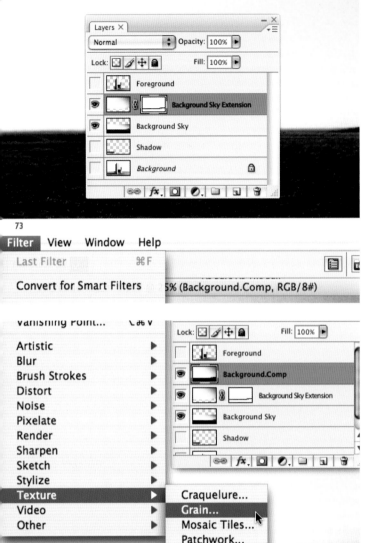

73

74

As you can see, it is possible to mount a background image with relative ease, and the mask feature is worth being used in a case like this.

You have even more mask-painting features at your disposal – it is possible to remove excess mask coloring (= Black): you may use either the Eraser tool, which is basically a painting tool that applies background color when used in a mask (White in this case) or, a more elegant solution, change the fore and background color by pressing X, which enables you to erase with the Brush tool.

According our desire to create a rather abstract instead of a photorealistic image, we will apply a filter to the background image.

Since this image is spread over two layers at present, you will combine both for this purpose as a copy.

Make sure only these two layers are visible, and activate the upper layer (Illus. 73).

Press Shift-Alt-Ctrl-E. Photoshop then adds a new layer that merges both image layers as a copy (this is an extension of the Merge Layers command).

Now you can apply filters on the new, merged layer to your heart's content,

75

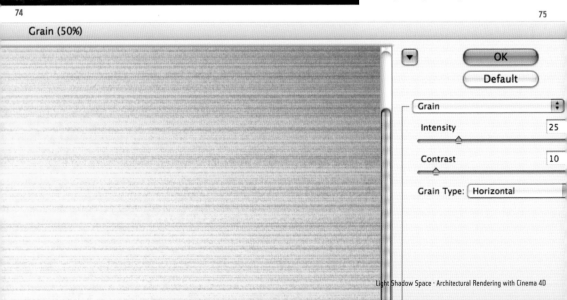

Grain (50%)

OK

Default

Grain

Intensity   25

Contrast   10

Grain Type: Horizontal

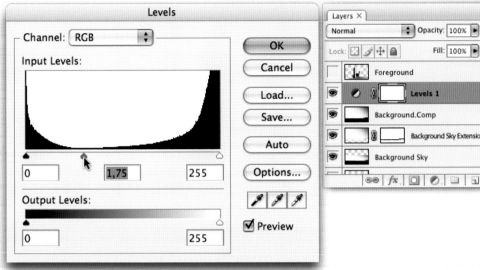

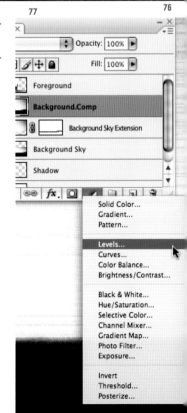

since you still have the originals in case something goes wrong.

Make sure the new layer is active and select the Grain filter (Filter menu: Texture - Grain, Illus. 74).
This is one of the filters that opens in the Filter Gallery, Illus. 75). Set Horizontal for Grain Type, Intensity to 25, and Contrast to 10 – the preview on the left shows you what the result will look like. Press OK to confirm and filter your layer.

The lower part of the image is still too dark.
Make sure the merged image layer is still active and place a Levels Adjustment layer (with the help of the black-and white button at the bottom of the Layer panel, Illus. 77).

If your image layer was correctly activated, the new Adjustment layer will land directly on top of it (Illus. 76) and the familiar histogram of Photoshop's Levels adjustment (Illus. 77) will open up.

To brighten the image move the middle slide below the diagram to the left until 1,75 appears in the value field (you may also enter the value directly).

You see how your image gets brighter as a result. But please focus on the dark parts of your image to check the result.

Press OK to confirm.

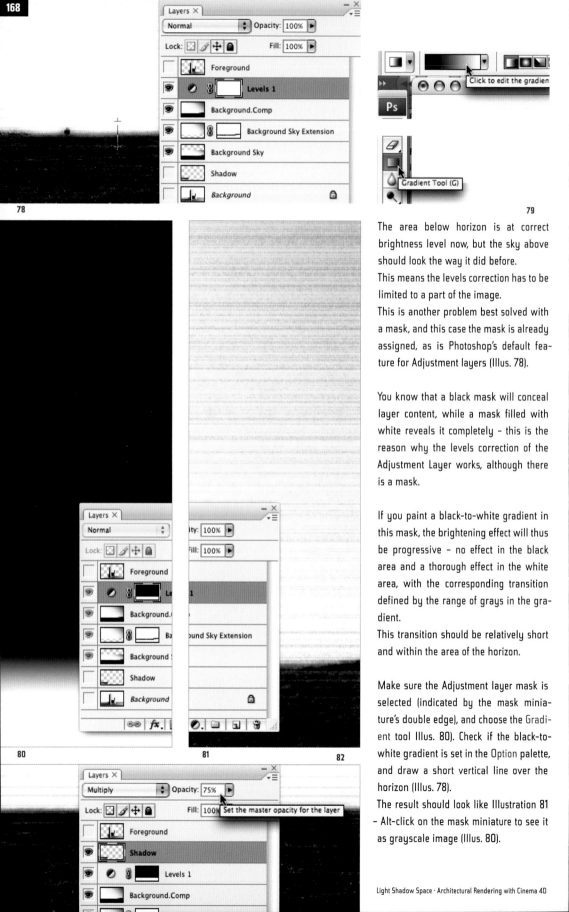

78

79

80   81   82

The area below horizon is at correct brightness level now, but the sky above should look the way it did before.

This means the levels correction has to be limited to a part of the image.

This is another problem best solved with a mask, and this case the mask is already assigned, as is Photoshop's default feature for Adjustment layers (Illus. 78).

You know that a black mask will conceal layer content, while a mask filled with white reveals it completely – this is the reason why the levels correction of the Adjustment Layer works, although there is a mask.

If you paint a black-to-white gradient in this mask, the brightening effect will thus be progressive – no effect in the black area and a thorough effect in the white area, with the corresponding transition defined by the range of grays in the gradient.

This transition should be relatively short and within the area of the horizon.

Make sure the Adjustment layer mask is selected (indicated by the mask miniature's double edge), and choose the Gradient tool Illus. 80). Check if the black-to-white gradient is set in the Option palette, and draw a short vertical line over the horizon (Illus. 78).

The result should look like Illustration 81 – Alt-click on the mask miniature to see it as grayscale image (Illus. 80).

The background is done now. Now turn the shadow layer visible again.

As you can see, the shadow surface fully covers the background image. Naturally this has to be changed; change the layer blending mode from Normal to Multiply, and reduce Opacity to 75 (Illus. 82).

Now show the level with the house again - you can increase contrast by copying the layer (Ctrl J) and changing the new layer's blending mode to Soft Light.

Now merge both foreground layers in a copy (Shift-Alt-Ctrl-E, see above) to give the foreground a bit of structure by applying a filter (Filter menu: Add Noise, Illus. 83).

Apply a gradient mask again to limit the grain effect to the basis in the foreground (Illus. 84).

You are finished with your postproduction phase. (Illus. 85).

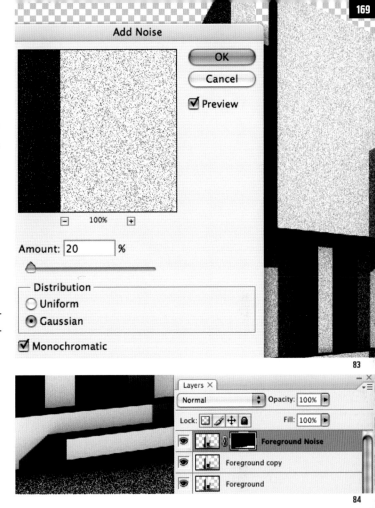

Add Noise

OK

Cancel

☑ Preview

100%

Amount: 20 %

Distribution
○ Uniform
⦿ Gaussian

☑ Monochromatic

83

Layers ×

Normal Opacity: 100%

Lock: ☐ ✎ ✦ ⬛ Fill: 100%

👁 **Foreground Noise**

👁 Foreground copy

👁 Foreground

84

85

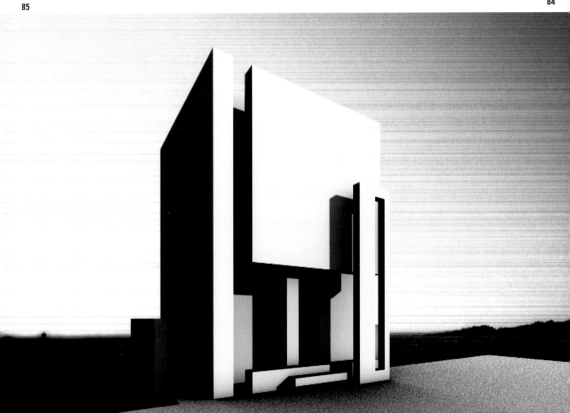

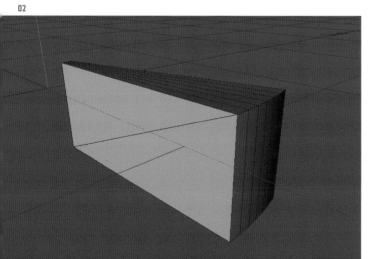

01

Rooms and Objects II · Spiral Staircase

Although this book is primarily about the lighting of architecture models I would like to show you at least a portion of the features Cinema 4D offers for creating your own models, since there is always a need for objects whose geometries are better designed in 3d software.

Let's take a spiral staircase, with a helicoid underside. Most CAAD programs may offer tools to create that type of object, but using them can be complicated, and the features they offer for designing details such as railings are limited.

Whatever the case, take the following as an example of how such or similar things can be realized using a 3D modeler.

We will also create a modest lighting set-up for this model at the end of this chapter (Illus. 01).

02

03

Basically, we will approach this task by modeling one step and copying it using an angle and position offset.

The step itself is the result of the subtraction of two basic objects followed by repairing and optimizing the ensuing polygon mesh. The geometry settings I suggest are based on predefined dimensions of our staircase.

First you need a step without a spiral undersurface. Place a Tube object in the scene (Illus. 03).

Reduce the object to a sector (Slice panel: Slice From 0 To 15, Illus. 04), make it smaller (Object panel: Inner Radius = 20, Outer Radius = 120, Height = 40), and drag it down a bit (Coordinates panel: P.Y = -5).

Reduce subdivision (Object panel: Rotation Segments = 6), to make optimizing easier later. The result is a first step, but without the curved underside (Illus. 02).

The construction of the subtraction object begins with the creation of a nurbs surface that should span over all the contour lines of the later spiral surface.

Place a so-called n-Side from the Spline Menu in the scene (upper command bar, Illus. 05).

Make it a straight line in the Attributes Manager (Object panel: Sides = 2, Illus. 06) with a length of 200 (Radius = 100).

Move the line so one end is on the scene zero point (Coordinates panel: P.X = 100), and down a bit (P.Y = -15).

The result is a horizontal straight line that lies on the front surface of our initial step (Illus. 07).

You'll need a few more straight edges to create your nurbs surface. The easiest way to get them is by duplicating the one you already have. However, you have to move its zero point beforehand.

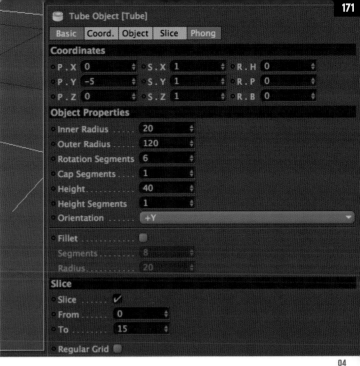

04

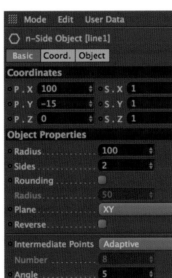

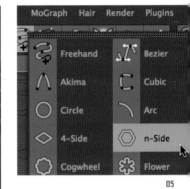

05

06

07

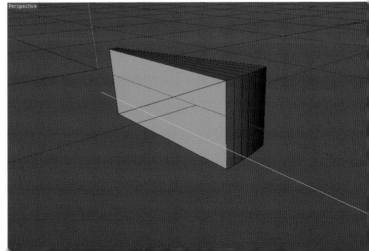

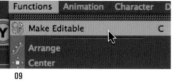

08

09

10

This doesn't work with a parametrical object like an n-side, it has to be converted first (Functions: Make Editable, Illus. 09).

Select the Object Axis tool (left command bar, Illus. 10), and set the X Position to 0 in the Coordinates Manager. Then press Return (Illus. 08).

The coordinates axis cross belonging to the line will jump to its beginning, and the line's position is 0 for X and Z.

Now duplicate this straight line three times – either by Ctrl-dragging it in the Object Manager or with the familiar copy & paste trick (Ctrl C - Ctrl V).

Rename the four straight edges, e.g. line1 – line4 (Illus. 11).

Move the first straight edge (line1) a bit further down (Coordinates panel: P.Y = -30) and rotate it clockwise (R.H = -15).
Leave the next straight edge (line2) where it is, drag the third (line3) up (P.Y = 0) and rotate it counterclockwise (R.H = 15).
Rotate the last straight line (line4) further up and counterclockwise using the same offset (P.Y = 15, R.H = 30).

The result should look like Illustration 12.

The placement of the lines had to be done this way to create a helical surface that is larger than the step; the increments chosen help avoid the creation of too many polygons when booled later on.

Check your straight line coordinates if your result doesn't look the same as shown on the left.

Now you will spread a curved surface over these straight lines. In principle, this will become the helical surface of your staircase's bottom.

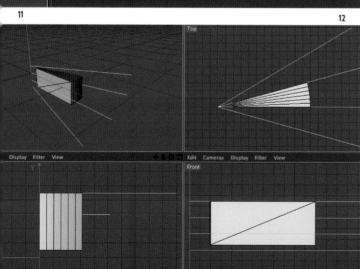

11

12

13

Place a so-called Loft NURBS in the scene (from the NURBS Object menu in the upper command bar, Illus. 13). Initially, this is an empty object that is listed on top of the Object Manager.

Select your four straight lines in the Object Manager and drag them onto the new nurbs object, Illus. 14), thus turning them into sub-objects to the nurbs.

Have a look at the Editor: you see a generously sized helicoid surface (Illus. 15).

Now reduce the subdivision of the nurbs surface. Make sure the object is selected, and set Mesh Subdivision U to 3 and Mesh Subdivision V to 6 in the Attributes Manager's Object panel (Illus. 14). Make sure that Subdivision per Segment is selected.

Your aim is still to subtract the nurbs surface from your initial step object to create the desired helicoid surface. However, this is not possible with the nurbs surface alone, what you need is a solid object.

The easiest way to get it is to convert the nurbs into a polygon surface first.
You will use this polygon surface and a vertically shifted copy to create your subtraction object.

Make sure your nurbs object is selected, and choose Current State to Object from the Object Manager's Object menu (Illus. 16). Cinema 4D then creates a polygon surface that looks exactly like the loft nurbs. Copy this polygon once and drag the copy down (Coordinates panel: P.Y = -30, Illus. 17).

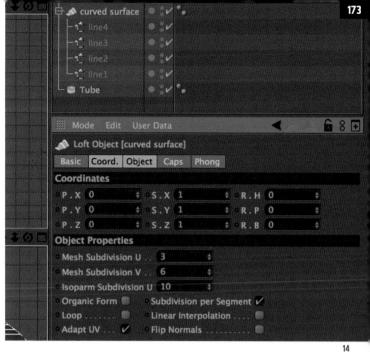

14

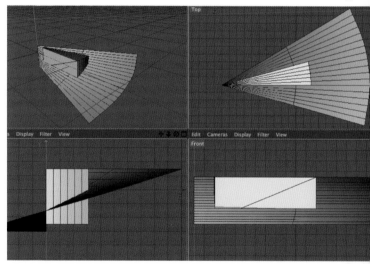

15

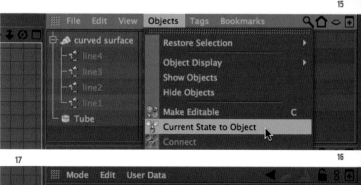

16

17

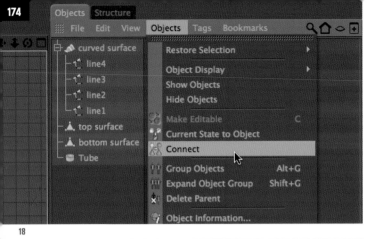

You now have two polygon surfaces; the upper surface is in exactly the same position the helical underside will be in later, while the other is way underneath the step.

You still have to unite these two polygon faces to use them for a boole action.

Select both and choose Connect from the Object Manager's Object menu (Illus. 18) Cinema 4D consolidates both of them in a new object that will be displayed at the top of the Object List – call it boole object (Illus. 19).

18

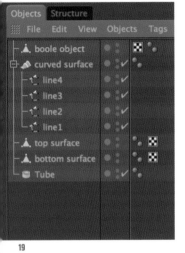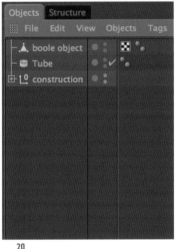

19

20

You are almost there now – you have the basic step and the body to be subtracted from it.
It doesn't matter that the sides of this boole object are open, booleing will work just the same. (The underside also doesn't have to be a helical surface, as is the case here. It was just practical to finish quickly by duplicating and dragging.)

Clean up the Object Manager before you continue.
Rename the Loft Nurbs curved surface. Combine the nurbs and the two individual polygons into a null object (Object menu: Group Objects), and rename it construction before excluding it from Editor and Render Display (Illus. 20).

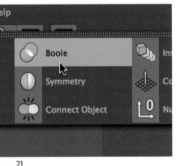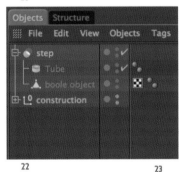

21

22

23

Pick a Boole Object from the Modeling Objects menu in the upper command bar (Illus. 21).
To subtract the helicoid body from the step, drag both the step (Tube) and the polygon object (boole object) onto the boole object, with the step on top (Illus. 22).

The result is your first step of your spiral stair (Illus. 23).

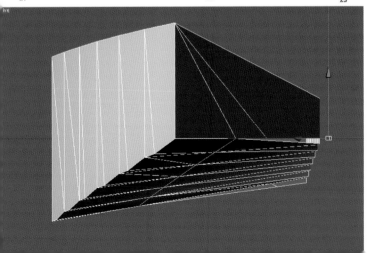

26

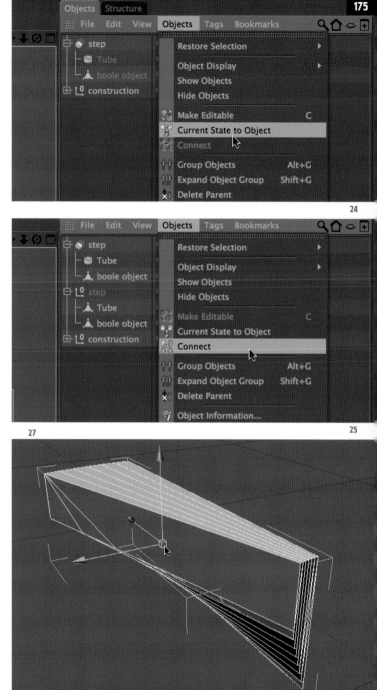

24

25

27

As you can see, the result isn't particularly neat yet. Since the entire later stair will be a number of copies of this step it would be wise to take some time and clean up the model now.

You should convert it into a polygon object for this reason (and because a boole construction takes more time to render than a polygon structure).

Use Current State to Object again (Object menu, Illus. 24).

Cinema creates a copy of the boole step as two polygon objects combined in a null.

Select both of them and unite them via Connect (Objects menu, Illus. 25).

Call this object poly step and delete the preliminary grouped objects; you should also hide boole object from display (Illus. 26).

Now you have to start simplifying the polygon object that represents your step.

Set the Radius of the Live Selection tool to 1 (in the Options panel your Attributes Manager shows after choosing the tool, Illus. 28), and make sure Only Select Visible Elements is checked.

Up to now, you know the points on the topside of the step are in the right position, and the points on the underside should have a height difference of 2.5 units (15 units / 6 subdivisions, Illus. 15).

Now you have to shift some points into the right position, consolidate coplanar polygons and delete unnecessary points. Zoom to see the step in full size (Illus. 27).

28

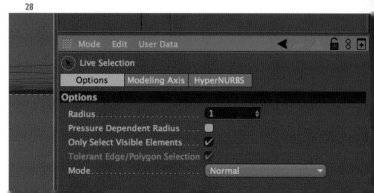

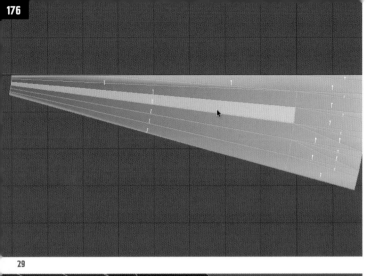

29

30

31

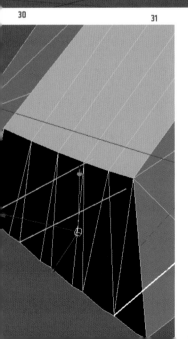

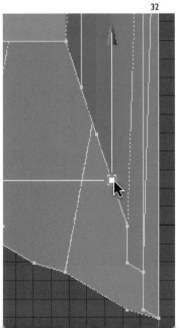

32

Now first take care of the underside of the step.

Switch to a bottom view (for example, switch to top view (F2) and select Bottom in the Editor Cameras menu). Press H to make the bottom view fill the viewport.

Select all the polygons you see with the Live Selection tool (you may "paint" over them with the tool and add selections while pressing the Shift key, Illus. 29). Delete all the surfaces once they are marked red.

Switch back to the Perspective viewport and look at the step from below. As you can see, some of the narrow, seemingly perpendicular triangles survived the deletion unscathed (Illus. 30). Select them carefully, and remove them (Illus. 30 and 31). The underside should be closed again using 6 quadrangular polygons, but you have to correct the inner side of the step first.

Zoom on to the narrow side of the stair so the bottom ends of the perpendicular lateral polygons are completely visible (Illus. 32). Choose Default Light from the Editor's Display menu and click on the sphere until the concerned surfaces can be easily distinguished.

Select the Move and Point tools (upper command bar and left command bar respectively). You have to straighten the zigzag bottom line until it looks like the left part of illustration 32.

Click on the points that are out of line; either delete them, or, if this makes polygons disappear, drag them on to neighboring points that have the correct position (Illus. 32; 3D Snapping should be activated, see the Snap Settings panel).

This trial and error strategy can't be avoided since it isn't always clear whether a point you deal with belongs to an existing or is just a leftover of an already deleted polygon.
If entire triangles are left over, delete them too. Of course you have to switch to the Polygon tool then (by the way, you can switch between the last two tools you used by pressing the space bar).

Now look at the opposite stair side; you will have to delete errant points here as well, or move them onto other points.
Always assume that the upper points are correct, and that the points underneath have to match up with them perpendicularly (Illus. 33).

If there are still triangular surfaces left over after cleaning up, delete them and draw new quadrangular polygons (Structure menu: Create Polygon, Illus. 34); this tool works just the way you would expect in a CAAD program, for a change.

Every click is a corner point, and the mouse conveniently snaps on neighboring polygon points (as long as 3D snapping is still checked, Illus. 35).

As an alternative you can delete one of the unnecessary triangles in each case and add a point on the hypotenuse of the remaining triangle (Structure menu: Add Point), and then drag it into the right position – the effect is the same.

It is decisive that there only remain 6 quadrangles – just as many as on the opposite inside surface – as a result of this operation (Illus. 36).

You certainly notice that sometimes there

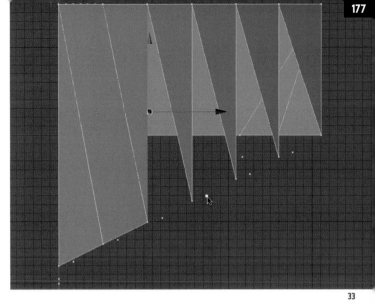

33

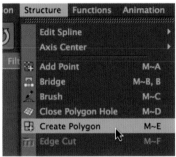

34

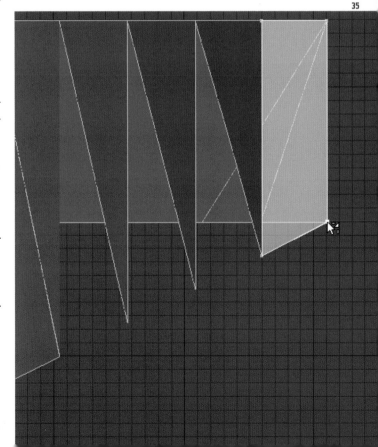

35

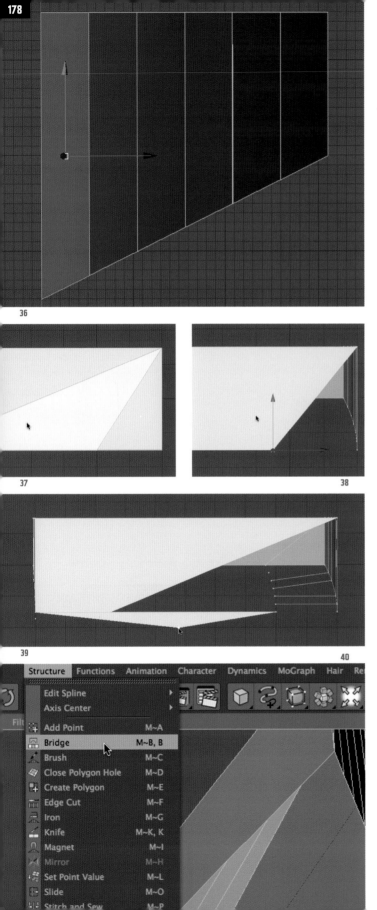

36

37

38

39

40

| Structure | Functions | Animation | Character | Dynamics | MoGraph | Hair | Re |

Edit Spline

Axis Center

Add Point   M~A

Bridge   M~B, B

Brush   M~C

Close Polygon Hole   M~D

Create Polygon   M~E

Edge Cut   M~F

Iron   M~G

Knife   M~K, K

Magnet   M~I

Mirror   M~H

Set Point Value   M~L

Slide   M~O

Stitch and Sew   M~P

are two points in the same position, and that there are even some points lying around without a corresponding polygon - later on you may remove them with an apt command.

Now let's focus on the remaining lateral surfaces. These surfaces are actually rectangles that are unnecessarily divided into a number of smaller polygons (Illus. 37). Delete the triangles on the front side, and drag the corner point of the remaining quadrangle to make it a real rectangle and thus close the side (make sure you are with the Points and Move tool, Illus. 38). You may by chance catch a point belonging to another, completely useless polygon that has up to now escaped your delete job - just remove it, and repeat your initial task.

The front side of the step should consist of one rectangle polygon when you're done, the back side may stay without any polygon, as this step will be duplicated later on.

(Using the Melt command in the Functions menu is an alternative to this process - Melt consolidates polygons lying in the same plane. The result is deceiving to an extent: just check N-gon Lines in the Filter panel of your Configure settings, and you can see that the surface is still triangulated. It is Cinema 4D's N-gon functionality that creates the impression of a real polygon reduction. You can get rid of this internal triangulation by removing the unnecessary points manually. However, this process doesn't seem easier than the first I described.)

Now continue and close the open sides. First navigate to the underside of the step, and select the Bridge tool from the Structure menu. You can bridge the spaces between points, edges and surfaces with new polygons using this tool (Illus. 40).

Make sure the Edge tool is selected in the left command bar.

You should connect the bottom edges of the perpendicular lateral surface polygons to create 6 new quadrangles on the underside.

You can click on the edge you want to draw the polygon from after selecting the tool.

The edge will then be displayed in white. Hold down the mouse button and move your mouse over to the opposite edge – Cinema 4D shows you a preview of the new polygon in light gray once you come

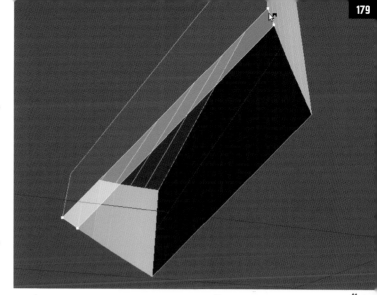

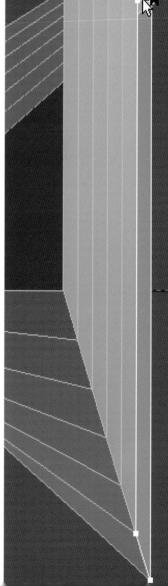

43   41

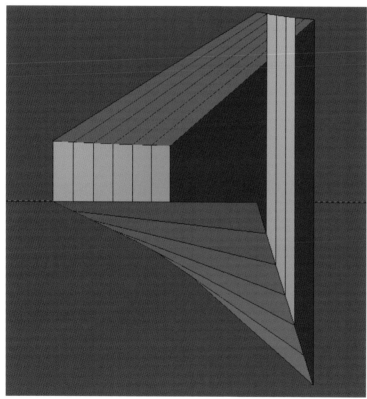

42

close to the edge (Illus. 40). Now release your mouse button, and the new surface is in the right place.

Repeat these steps 5 times until the bottom view of the step is closed (Illus. 41.)

Look at the narrow inner side of the step – there are still a few triangles there. De-

lete them and close the resulting holes with the Bridge tool (Illus. 42 and 43). You should also have 6 surfaces here in the end.

The step is almost finished now. Remember your step doesn't need a backside, since you will duplicate the step later on (Illus. 42).

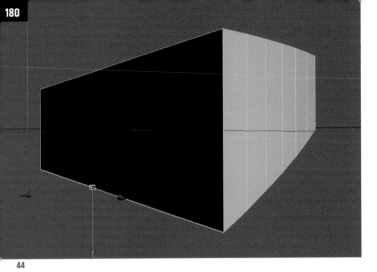

44

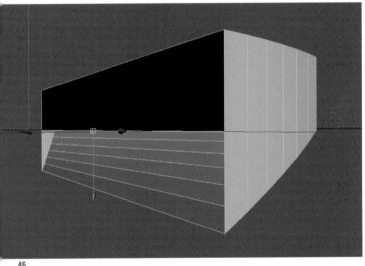

46

You may remove the part on the front that joins the next lowest step. You could use the Knife tool (Structure menu) to do this, but in our case it is enough to slide the lower edge up.

Make sure you are still with the Edge tool, and select the lower edge of the front surface with the Live Selection tool (Illus. 44). In the Coordinates Manager, you can see that the height (Position Y) of the selected edge is -15.

Set this value to 0 (Illus. 45), press Return, and the edge will jump into the right position (Illus. 46).

The step looks pretty neat now, but there are still some unnecessary leftover points resulting from the deletion of polygons. Obviously booleing caused the creation of some relatively complex structure, the traces thereof being still visible.

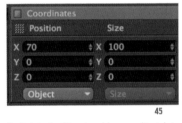

45

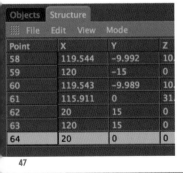

47

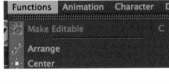

48

49

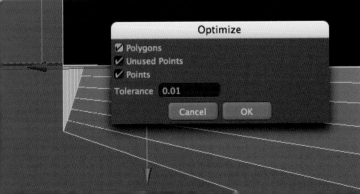

Switch to the Structure Manager (its tab is to be found right beside the Object Manager's).

By default, it shows you a list of all your active object's points and their position coordinates.

There are a lot of them at the moment; my example contains 64 (Illus. 47). Your scene may show a different number depending on the way you went about cleaning up.

We know that our object should have 25 polygons (4 x 6 polygons on the sides and 1 polygon on the front) and 30 points (7 x 2 on the top, 7 x 2 on the bottom, and two on the front), a considerably smaller amount.

The first thing you should do is remove all points that do not belong to any polygon. Choose Optimize (Functions menu), which enables you to do exactly that (Illus. 48).

In the settings field opening up you can define both elements that occur twice at the same place and elements that aren't being used. Just keep the settings as they are (Illus. 49), and confirm with OK.

You can see that the amount of points has dropped drastically in the Structure Manager. (Again, your result may differ from mine, Illus. 50).
But as you see, you aren't done with cleaning up yet, you still only want to have 30 points.

Look at the step again: the surface height is 15, the underside extends from 0 to -15. This means that the corner points of the 6 polygons that create the underside all have to be at a Y height of 0, -2.5, -5, -7.5, -10, -12.5 or -15.
You can correct the point coordinates in the Structure Manager by double-clicking on the respective value.
First make sure that all Y coordinates are changed to a flat value. E.g., in my example point 26 with Y = -12.498 should be set to Y = -12.5, Illus. 51).

To speed up the cleaning process take a look at your list of polygons. There should be exactly 25 of them, 6 for the sides and one for the front stair surface (Illus. 46).

In the Structure Manager, switch to Polygon mode (Illus. 52). The Structure manager may still display more than 25 polygons.

Choose the Polygon tool, and click yourself through the list – if you spot an errant polygon not belonging to the step, delete it (Illus. 53).

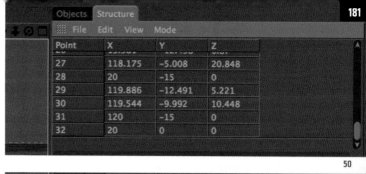

50

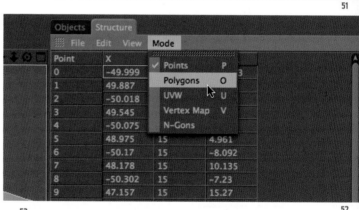

51

52

53

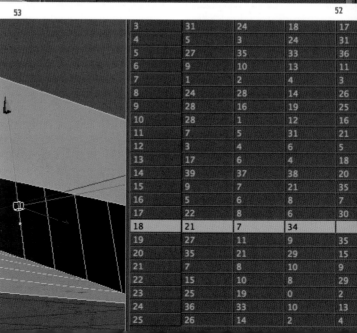

Structure
Edit · View · Mode

X	Y	Z
-50	15	-9.4
49.886	15	-4.165
-50.019	15	-8.527
49.543	15	1.059
-50.076	15	-7.656
48.973	15	6.264
-50.171	15	-6.789
48.177	15	11.438
-50.304	15	-5.927
47.156	15	16.573
-50.474	15	-5.071
45.911	15	21.659
50	15	-9.4
-50.681	15	-4.223
-50.019	-12.5	-8.527
-50.475	-2.5	-5.068
50	-15	-9.4
-50.076	-10	-7.656
-50	-15	-9.4
50	0	-9.4
49.886	-12.5	-4.178
-50.304	-5	-5.925
48.973	-7.5	6.264
45.911	0	21.659
49.532	-10	1.049
-50.171	-7.5	-6.789
48.175	-5	11.449
47.156	-2.5	16.573
-50.681	0	-4.223
-50	0	-9.4

54

Objects · Structure
File · Edit · View · Mode

Point	X	Y
0	-50	15
1	49.886	15
2	-50.019	15
3	49.543	15
4	-50.076	15
5	48.973	15
6	-50.171	15
7	48.177	15
8	-50.304	15
9	47.156	15
10	-50.474	15
11	45.911	15
12	50	15
13	-50.681	15
14	-50.019	-12.5
15	-50.474	-2.5
16	50	-15
17	-50.076	-10
18	-50	-15
19	50	0
20	49.886	-12.5
21	-50.304	-5
22	48.973	-7.5
23	45.911	0
24	49.543	-10
25	-50.171	-7.5
26	48.177	-5
27	47.156	-2.5
28	-50.681	0
29	-50	0

55

Now in the Structure Manager, change to Point mode again, and pick the Point tool again.

Go through the point list once more by clicking on the left number and check-ing the location of the selected point in the Editor. Erase the point if it is clearly superfluous.

Now continue optimizing your polygon body.

The points on the topside of the step have correct X and Z coordinates, since they stem from the original tube object – the coordinates on the underside don't match exactly, yet.

Select two points on one of the sides that should exactly be above each other (Illus. 54).

Check the Structure Manager to view the coordinates for both points. The one in which Y is 15 is the upper point, and the one in which Y Height is -5 is the lower point.

Now make sure the X and Z coordinate values for the lower point match the up-per point values. Double click on a value field to change a value and enter the cor-rect number (Illus. 54).

Repeat these steps for each pair of points that should have exactly the same X and Z values.

When you're done, use the Optimize com-mand again. The number of points should be 30 by now (Illus. 55).

When there are only 30 points and 25 polygons left, the result should look like the images in Illustration 56 and 57.

The lateral surfaces in the rendering ap-pear to be curved thanks to the Phong Tag (Illus. 58).

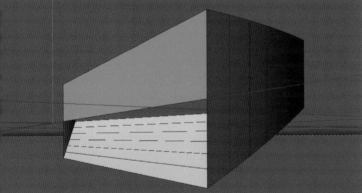

56

57

58

Objects · Structure
File · Edit · View · Objects · Tags
poly step
construction

Although it was hard work to create and clean up the step, it will be easy to make a staircase out of it.

The stair should consist of 18 steps with a rise of 15 units and a circle sector of 15° each.

At first, select your step object (Illus. 59). You need to use the Duplicate command in the Functions menu to create the staircase based on the step you have (Illus. 60; click on the three panels in the Attributes Manager with your right mouse button to see all the settings panels (Illus. 61).

The first setting refers to the amount of copies; you'll need 17 to make a stair with 18 steps.
If you put a checkmark next to the Create Instances option, you will create "intelligent" copies, which automatically adjust to size changes you may make on your original object later. (This actually isn't necessary in our case, since it is preferable to make decisive changes on the original tube object, or the nurbs surface. Since we would have to go through the entire polygon editing process again, the final duplication of the step is the least of out problems.)

Select Linear mode and Per Step for a duplication like the one in our example. This allows you to enter position, height and rotation values for the next step.
Make sure Position Enable is checked, and enter a Y value of 15 for the offset (in the middle field). Check Enable Rotation, and enter 15 in the first field (R.H).

If number of copies, duplication mode, height and angle offset are set correctly, click on Apply to launch the command.

A complete spiral staircase should appear in the Editor now (Illus. 62).

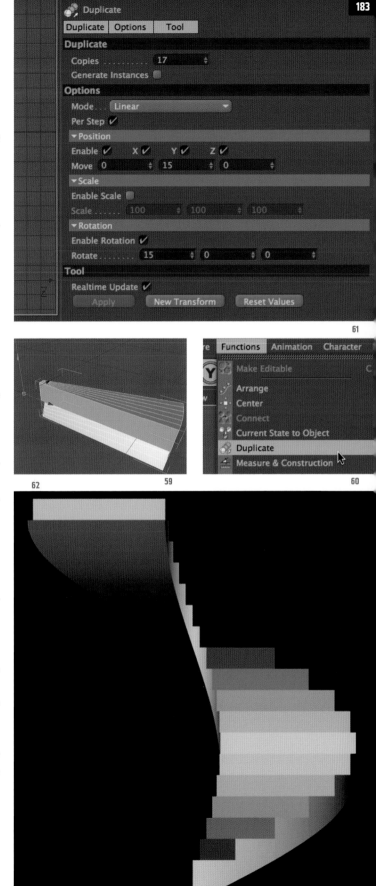

183

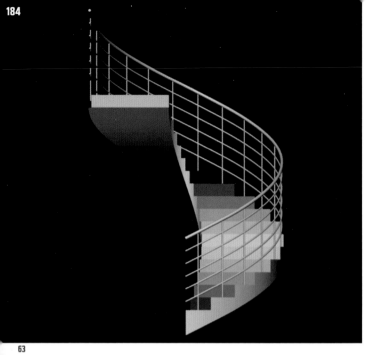

63

Now that the stair itself is done, you should add the railing. For the sake of simplicity, you will only build one for the outer side of the staircase.

The railing consists of a flight of bars and a number of spiral tubes (Illus. 63).

First you will build the handrail, using another mathematically generated shape (remember your helicoid), in this case a so-called Sweep NURBS.
A Sweep Nurbs allows you to extrude a two-dimensional figure along a curve.

In our case, the curve will be a helical line that follows the staircase rise. As such, it'll be the central axis of your handrail tube.

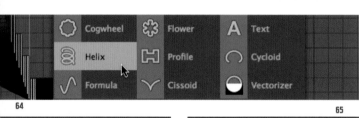

64

Select the Helix (Illus. 64) from the Spline menu (upper command bar), and toggle the Object panel in the Attributes Manager to make your settings (Illus. 65).

First rotate the helix into the right position (Plane: XZ) and limit it to a 3/4 rotation (Start Angle = 0, End Angle = 270).

65

The distance to the central stair axis should be 118 units (Start Radius = Final Radius), and the total height the spiral should reach should correspond with the height of the flight of steps (Height = 270).
Since the railing should be 1 meter above the steps, lift the helix to this height (Coordinates panel: P.Y = 100).

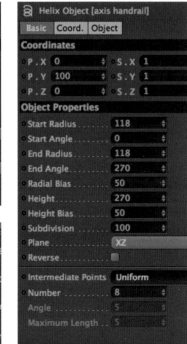

67

66

The handrail's profile should be circular, so select a Circle from the Spline menu as well (Illus. 66).
Enter Radius 2 in the Attributes Manager's Object panel so the rail has a diameter of 4 units (Illus. 67).

When used for an extrusion, the circle's position is irrelevant, so you don't need to

change a thing in the Coordinates panel.
Now to set up the rail, choose a Sweep
NURBS from the Nurbs menu (upper com-
mand bar, Illus. 68).

In the Object Manager, just drag both
splines you have just placed (helix and

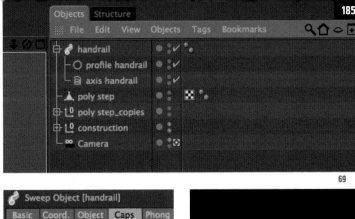

69

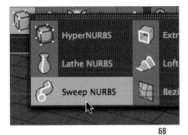

68

circle) onto the nurbs,

Keep an eye on the correct sequence so
Cinema 4D creates the right shape: the
circle should be above the helix (Illus. 69;

If you miss this, you'll see something un-
expected in the Editor). If you did it right,
you'll be able to admire an elegantly
curved handrail in your scene now (Illus.
70).

For sweep nurbs, there are some object-
specific parameters allowing you to finetune the rails shape.

What still needs to be shaped are the rail's
ends; you can edit them in the Attributes
Manager's Caps panel (Illus. 71).

Make sure you use the same settings for
the beginning and the end.
For Start and End, choose Fillet Cap from
the pull-down, so the tube isn't cut off too
sharply.

Surprisingly, the tube's profile will swell
considerably when you apply this option.

Just check Constrain to give it back its former diameter.

72

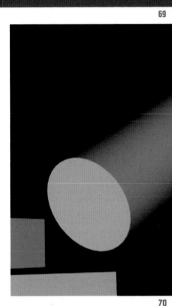

71

70

But the result still isn't satisfying, because
the fillet radius is larger than the tube radius.

For Start and End, set Radius to 0.5. For
Steps, set a value of 3, and the handrail
should be OK right now (Illus. 72).

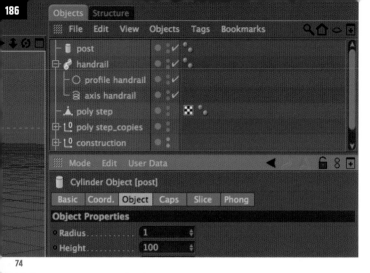

74

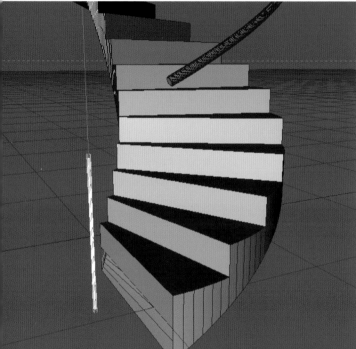

75

76

77

Before you copy the handrail to get the other railing elements you will take care of the perpendicular bars.

It seems reasonable to create one basic cylinder object, put it to the right position, and then duplicate it along the railing.

You'll see that Cinema 4D offers sophisticated features for this purpose that make your work easier, too.

First place a Cylinder in the scene (from the Primitive Objects menu in the upper command bar, Illus. 73).

Give it a radius of 1 and a height of 100 (Object panel) so it is thinner than the handrail and long enough to fit between it and the steps (Illus. 74).

As you can see in the Editor, Cinema 4D puts it in the middle of the scene as usual (Illus. 75).
Instead, it should actually be in the middle of the first step underneath the handrail.

Don't drag the cylinder into the right position by hand – you will make use of the fact that the handrail axis is a spline, which Cinema 4D allows you to align an object to at any position.

The point C4D uses for alignment is of course the object's zero; as you can see in Illus. 75, this is unfortunately in the cyl-

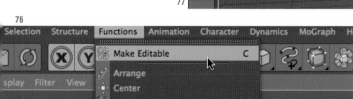

inder's middle, as is always the case with parametrical objects.

If you want to move point zero to the top (so the cylinder will be correctly fastened to the handrail axis), you have to first convert the cylinder into a polygon object.

Make sure your cylinder is selected and choose Make Editable from the Functions menu (Illus. 76; keep in mind that the resolution of the polygon object you create depends on the segment settings for the original parametrical cylinder.
More than one height subdivision is unnecessary, and 12 subdivisions are enough for the circumference, instead of the 36 in the default settings.)

As soon as your cylinder has been converted into a polygon object, you can move its zero.
Make sure the cylinder is selected, and activate the Object Axis tool (Illus. 77).

The Coordinates Manager shows you that Y Position is 0. Enter 50 (Illus. 78) and confirm by pressing the Return.

The Editor shows that the cylinder's zero has moved to the upper end now.

Now you have to assign a so-called Expression (coming as a tag) to connect the railing bar with the handrail.

Right-click the cylinder in the Object Manager, and select Align to Spline from the Cinema 4D-Tags flyout menu (you can also use the Object Manager's Tags menu, Illus. 79).

In the Object Manager, click on the Tag and look at the Attributes Manager. In the Tag panel, you see an entry field called Spline Path.

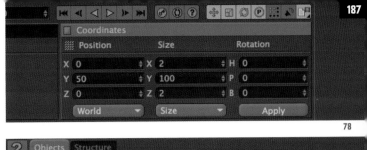

78

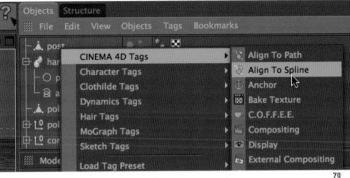

79

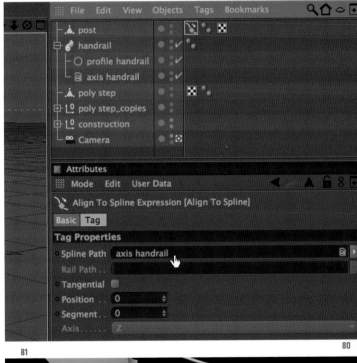

80

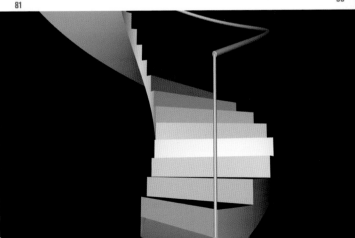

81

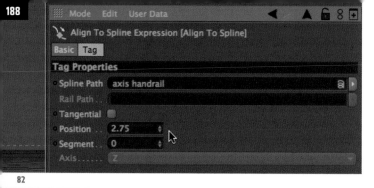

Mode   Edit   User Data

Align To Spline Expression [Align To Spline]

Basic   Tag

Tag Properties

○ Spline Path   axis handrail
Rail Path . .
○ Tangential   ☐
○ Position . .   2.75
○ Segment .   0
Axis . . . . . .   Z

82

83

Duplicate

Duplicate   Options   Tool

Duplicate

Copies   17
Generate Instances   ✔

Options

Mode . . .   Along Spline
Per Step   ✔
▼ Position
Enable   ✔   X ✔   Y ✔   Z ✔
Spline . . .   axis handrail
Start Pos.   2.75
End Pos.   97.25
▼ Scale
Enable Scale   ☐
Scale   100   100
▼ Rotation
Enable Rotation   ☐
Rail Spline . . . .
Align . . . .   +Y
Bank   0
Rotate   0   0

Tool

Realtime Update   ✔
Apply   New Transform

84

85

Now drag the helix (the handrail's axis) from the Object Manager into this field (Illus. 80).

The cylinder will immediately jump to the beginning of the handrail (Illus. 81).

Again, there's something left to do – the bar should be in the middle of the first step.

Whenever you set an object on a spline, you can define its position via percent – 0 meaning the object will be set at the beginning of the spline, 100 will put it at the very end.

Keep sure you still see the Attributes Manager's settings for the Align Tag, then enter 2.75 for Position in the Tag panel (Illus. 82), and see how the bar moves "inwards" to the desired position (Illus. 83).

Now that your first railing bar is in the right position you can duplicate it. Matching the number of steps, you need 17 copies, the last one should be set at Spline Position 97.25 (100 – 2,75).

This is just another chance to use the Duplicate command (Functions menu). Make sure the bar is selected, choose Duplicate, but now set Along Spline mode, not Linear (Duplicate panel, Illus. 84).

Keep 17 copies and be certain that Create Instances is checked, or all copies will be set in the same position.
(This is definitely one of the things you don't have to understand, in a case like this testing is probably the best way to find a solution. However, instances are good for you – the instances will e.g. adapt to the original's settings automatically.)

The most important settings are to be found in the Options panel: make sure that Enable X, Y and Z are checked, and drag the helix spline from the Object

Manager into the Spline entry field (after all, Cinema 4D has to know which spline the object should be duplicated on).

Limit the area the original and copies are to be distributed on setting Start (2,75) and End position (97,25). In this duplicating mode, it doesn't make a difference whether Per Step is checked or not.

Click Apply, and the 17 new railing bars should take their place along the handrail (Illus. 85).

Now take care of the remaining five railing tubes, which are supposed to spiral upwards parallel to the handrail.

The vertical spacing should be 15 units and their diameter should be the same as the perpendicular bars.

Actually, it makes sense to just copy the handrail once, give the circle extruded along the spiral spline a smaller radius, and then drag the copy downwards 15 units.

You can copy by either using the Copy & Paste command or by dragging the nurbs object inside the Object Manager while pressing the Ctrl key. Rename the copy, and open the group by clicking the plus sign.

Select the circle and change its radius to 1 in the Object panel (Illus. 86). Now drag the nurbs copy down (Coordinates panel: P.Y = -15, Illus. 87).

Repeat copying 4 more times since you need 5 of these tubes, and drag each of the copies 15 units downwards.

The last copy should be at Y height -75 (Illus. 88).

The staircase now has a complete railing (Illus. 89).

As you can see, it was possible to create this only with the help of splines and nurbs objects.

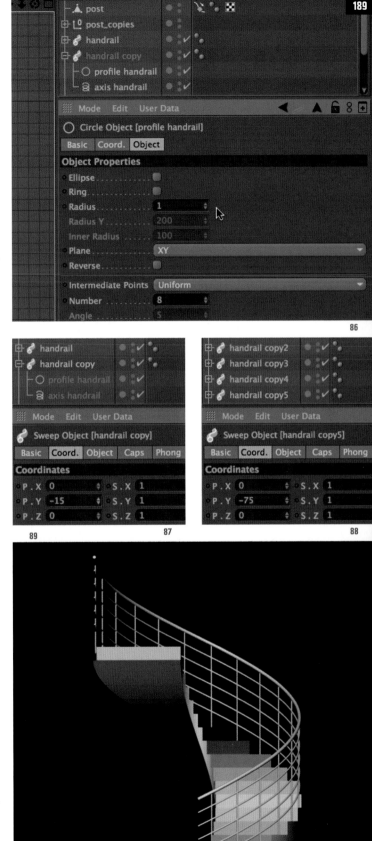

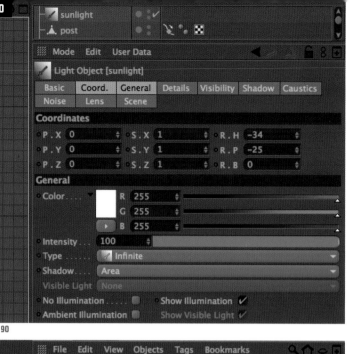

90

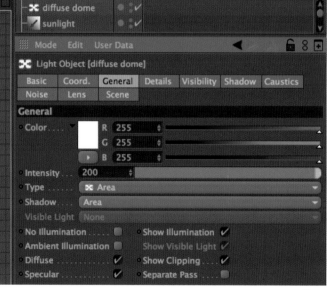

91

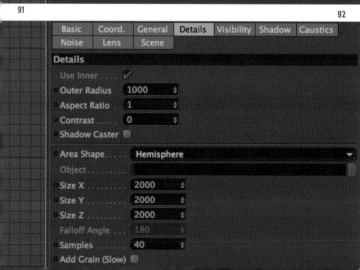

92

You only had to use polygon conversion once for the positioning of the first railing bar.

Notice that Cinema 4D has to convert the nurbs construction into polygons internally before it processes shading and other effects for rendering.

This can lead to a sharp increase in processing time when it comes to more complex scenes (or very fine nurbs object divisions and/or the splines they are based on).

So keep in mind that such nurbs objects are converted into polygon objects in a "real" scene (with the Current State to Object command) before you render the scene. You can simply keep the originals and exclude them from display and rendering.

We can afford some luxury in the last part of this chapter now that the staircase itself is finished – you might want to embed it in a modest scene that consists of two light sources, a ground surface and a camera.

You also want to assign steps and railing a material, so the model won't look quite as dull.

First place two lights in the scene (from the Scene Objects menu in the upper command bar).

We will call the first source sunlight and make it infinite with area shadow (Illus. 90).

The coordinates for the lighting direction are R.H = 34 and R.P = -25.

We will call the second light source diffuse dome. Assigned Area, it will contribute diffuse light to the scene, also coming along with area shadow (Illus. 91). It's best to use Hemisphere as Area Shape, with an Outer Radius of 1000 units (Illus. 92).

Still for the Diffuse, choose area shadow,

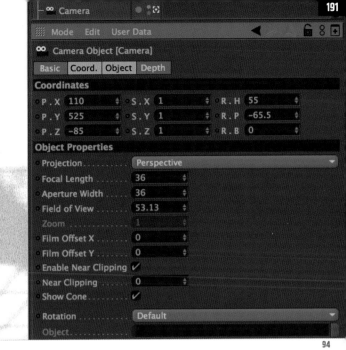

93

and increase its brightness considerably (General panel: Intensity = 200).

You will have to place a Floor object in the scene before having shadows on the ground.

Pick a Floor from the Scene Objects menu in the upper command bar and leave its position as it is.

You should use a camera to get a nice perspective.

Place one (from the Scene Objects menu as well) and enter the following values in the Coordinates panel (Illus. 94: P.X = 110, P.Y = 525, P.Z = -85, R.H = 55, R.P = -65,5. Keep the focal length at 36.

Now switch to your new camera (Editor's Camera menu: Scene Cameras) and – finally – render the scene.

The result is pretty nice; notice how the edge of the shadow created by your sun becomes softer as the distance increases – a pretty effect at the expense of longer rendering time (Illus. 95).

Now we'll focus on the materials. Create a new material (File menu in the Material Manager), and call it stair.

Assign it to the steps null object. Double-click on the texture tag in the Object Manager to tune the material.

In the Basic panel, deactivate the Specular and turn on the Bump channel.

Switch to the Color panel and set the color

94

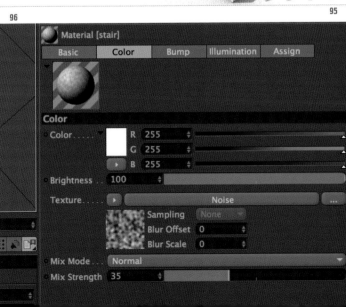

95

96

Noise Shader [Noise]

Basic | Shader

Shader Properties
- Color 1 . . . .
- Color 2 . . . .
- Noise . . . . Cell Voronoi
- Octaves 5
- Space . . . . Texture
- Global Scale 15
- Relative Scale 100 100 100
- Animation Speed . . 0
- Loop Period 0
- Detail Attenuation . . 100
- Delta 100
- Movement 0 0 0.001
- Speed 0
- Absolute . . . .
- Cycles 0
- Low Clip 0
- High Clip 100
- Brightness 0
- Contrast 0
- Use as Environment
- Project Environment

97

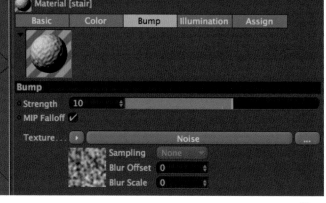

Material [stair]

Basic | Color | **Bump** | Illumination | Assign

Bump
- Strength 10
- MIP Falloff ✔
- Texture . . . Noise
  - Sampling None
  - Blur Offset 0
  - Blur Scale 0

98

99

Shader Properties
- Color 1 . . . .
- Color 2 . . . .
- Noise . . . . FBM
- Octaves 10
- Space . . . . Texture
- Global Scale 50
- Relative Scale 100 100 100
- Animation Speed . . 0
- Loop Period 0
- Detail Attenuation . . 100
- Delta 100
- Movement 0 0 0.001
- Speed 0
- Absolute . . . .
- Cycles 0

to 100 White (Illus. 96).

Select Noise in the Texture pull-down menu. This shader allows you to cover the steps with a structured surface.

Lower Mix Strength to 35 so the noise doesn't cover the white color completely. Click on the shader miniature to work on it. This takes you one level further down in your material settings.

You may select a specific noise type here; I suggest you take Cell Voronoi to achieve a Terrazo-type look (Noise, Illus. 97; a click on the small triangle all the way to the right gives you a visual overview of the shaders).

Aside from the color mix, which you should limit to black and white, you can also determine the noise grain size. Reduce Global Scale to 15 to make it smaller.

You can see a black-edged left arrow in the Attributes Manager's menu row. Click on the arrow to go back to the Color channel's top level, and then switch to the Bump Channel.

Select a noise in the bump Texture pull-down as well.
As the channel's name suggests, this noise will create a relief effect with a grayscale image (Illus. 98). In this channel you can define the strength of the relief effect, as well as the direction.
When Strength is positive, the light areas will appear to be raised; if the Strength slide is in the minus area, they will be recessed.

The direction is secondary in this case, but we don't want to overdo things with the relief strength, a value of 10 should be just fine.

Click on the shader miniature to access
the noise settings.

Choose an FBM this time with 10 Octaves
and a Global Scale of 50 (Illus. 99; According to the handbook, the octaves define
the level of detail).

You also want to define a characteristic
surface for the railing.

Create a new material and assign it to the
railing elements.

The easiest way to do this is to consolidate all of them in a null object (i.e., the
polygon object for the first railing bar, its
copies, the nurbs structure used to create
the handrail and its copies: Object Manager's Object menu: Group Objects).

Having created this new null object, you
may drag your second material onto it.

In the Basic panel of the new material's
settings, leave the Specular and activate
Reflection additionally.

In the Color channel, set Brightness to 100
(Illus. 100), in the Reflection channel, you
reduce the reflection strength (Brightness
= 20, Illus. 101).

For the metallic surface, a sharply contoured specular is characteristic.

Switch to the respective channel and set
the Metal mode. This turns the material
rather dark overall, while stressing the
specular (Illus. 10).

You can create a sharp-edged specular
by setting a relatively high value for Inner Width (40 in our case) and a negative
Falloff value (-25).

Render a segment of the scene - the material surfaces seem a bit abstract, but
distinct (Illus. 103).

100

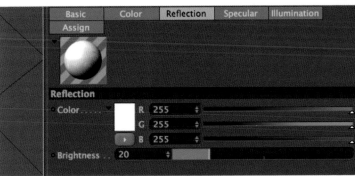

101

102

103

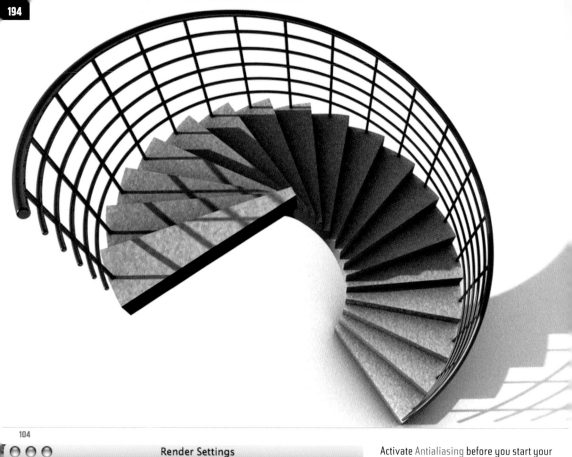

104

Render Settings

File

General	Name	New
Output	Antialiasing	Geometry
Save	Filter	Still Image
Antialiasing	Transparency	With Refraction
Global Illum.	Reflection	All Objects
Caustics	Shadow	All Types
Ambient Occl.		
Effects	Render As Editor	Off
Options		
Multi-Pass		
QuickTime VR		

Activate Antialiasing before you start your final rendering (Render settings' General panel: Geometry, Illus. 105). During your construction and test-render phase you could do without, which saved you a lot of render time, but for your final you want to get smooth edges.

Antialiasing also grants a higher shadow bitmap resolution.

Ambient Occlusion (Illus. 106) makes the image seem a bit more "real" later. It gives your model diffuse dark corners, unfortunately at the expense of considerably longer rendering time.

To reduce this disadvantage, reduce accuracy and resolution values (Accuracy = 50, Minimum Samples = 10, Maximum Samples = 40).

105
106

Render Settings

File

General	☑ Apply to Scene	
Output	Color	
Save		
Antialiasing	Minimum Ray Length	0
Global Illum.	Maximum Ray Length	100
Caustics	Dispersion	100
Ambient Occl.	Accuracy	50
Effects	Minimum Samples	10
Options	Maximum Samples	40
Multi-Pass	Contrast	0
QuickTime VR		
	☐ Use Sky Environment	
	☐ Evaluate Transparency	
	☐ Self Shadowing Only	

Increase the shadow resolution for both light sources (Shadow panel: Accuracy = 75, Minimum Samples = 20, Maximum Samples = 100).

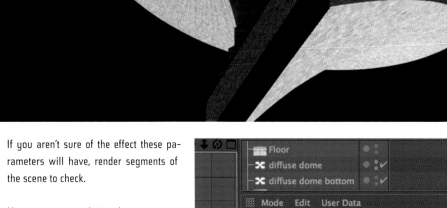

107

If you aren't sure of the effect these parameters will have, render segments of the scene to check.

Now start your rendering. As you can see, it takes a bit longer this time (Illus. 104).

I took the liberty of rendering a second perspective (Illus. 107). For this view, the sun and diffuse light were deactivated and an additional area light invented – in hemisphere shape as well, but inverted this time (Illus. 109). Since the view is from below as well, the ground had to be excluded from rendering.

The construction of the spiral case is complete. As you can see, you have to be very precise when modeling. An economical polygon structure that can be easily managed in the Editor without causing any mysterious shading problems, and which can be easily exported into a CAAD program, is definitely worth the effort.

109

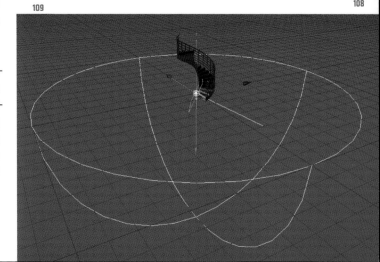

108

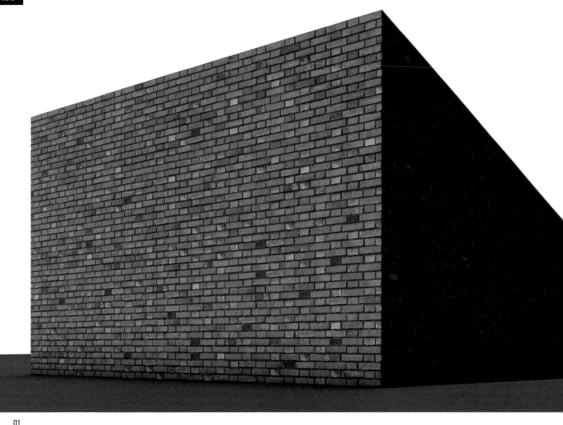

01

02

15

Texture and Object · Brick Wall

The subject of this book is light and shadow, other aspects of architectural rendering are only mentioned marginally. However, we nonetheless took some time to discuss modeling in the last chapter to become familiar with some of the functions Cinema 4D offers in this respect.

I would like to make another, equally brief exception now and discuss texturing - as an excuse for the creation of another object that will need a lighting setup.
This gives us the opportunity to at least briefly address texturing basics.

A brick wall is the object of this exercise, a square model with a brick wall surface.

Basically, this is an exercise that requires texture mapping with bitmap graphics projected onto the model.

Since normally bitmap graphics aren't large enough to cover the entire model surface they need to be tiled.
Image repetition is the result, an effect that makes computer-generated renderings often look a bit artificial, even when using high-quality textures.

To get rid of this problem for once, I prepared a relatively large texture image in Photoshop in which individual brick photographs were mounted - presuming

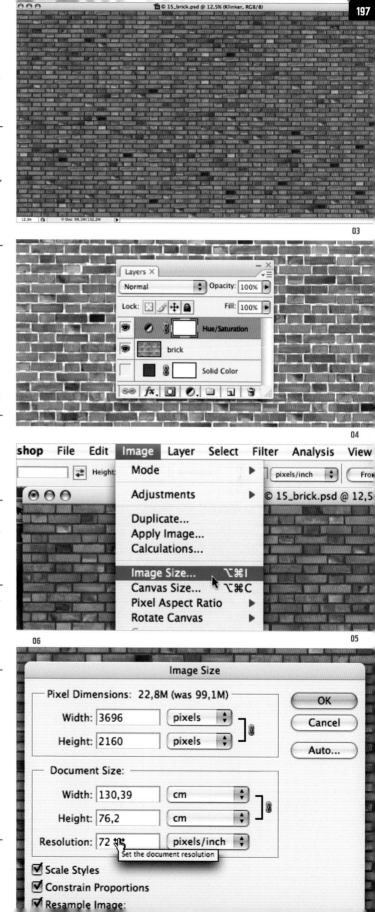

a standard German brick size my image would cover a wall surface of 5,50m x 3,20m in reality.

This kind of montage takes quite some time, but at least there will be no tile repetition in a wall this size.

Please note that my image, though huge, is not prepared for seamless tiling. Thus the transition at the wall corners where two graphics meet won't look perfect (a flaw you would definitely sort out in Photoshop).

Look at Illustrations 01 and 02, which show the finished rendering.

Keep in mind that the brick image is a Photoshop file, but the interstices were created using a Cinema 4D shader (a noise).

The interstice relief is not modeled, but the result of texture modulation (so-called bump mapping).

Open the 15_brick.psd file that shows the brick surface in Photoshop (Illus. 03).

All the stones are on one layer, the interstice space is transparent. The interstice's gray is created by the solid color layer underneath (Illus. 04).

Although the quality of the Photoshop image is impressive, it is hardly useful for texturing due to its size.

Take time to assess how large the visible wall segment will be in the rendering.

Divide the approximate size in centimeters by 2.54 and multiply the result by 150.

This is the maximum pixel size you will need (150 dpi should be enough for this kind of texture). Our Photoshop file would cover a 130cm-wide image based on this calculation!

Select the Image Size command from the Image menu (Illus. 05) – change the reso-

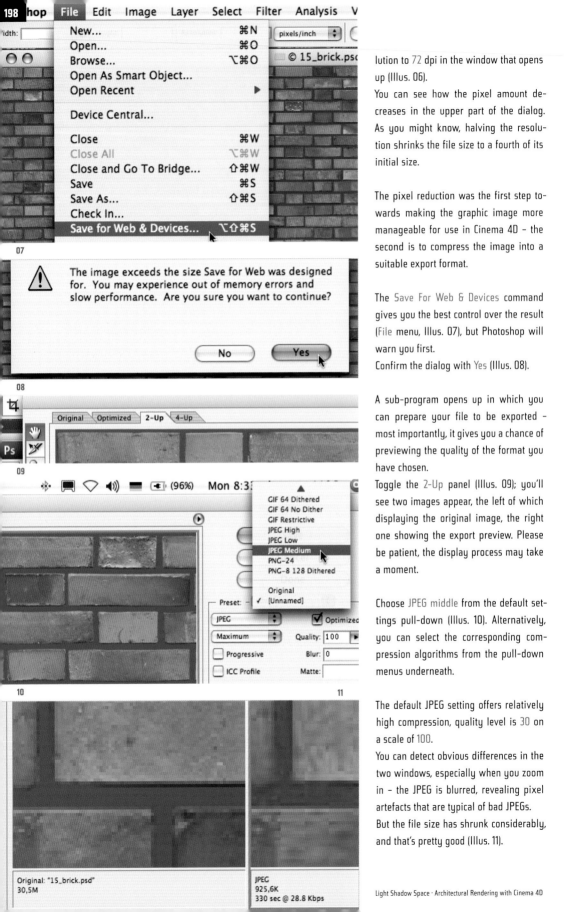

07

08

09

10

11

lution to 72 dpi in the window that opens up (Illus. 06).

You can see how the pixel amount decreases in the upper part of the dialog. As you might know, halving the resolution shrinks the file size to a fourth of its initial size.

The pixel reduction was the first step towards making the graphic image more manageable for use in Cinema 4D – the second is to compress the image into a suitable export format.

The Save For Web & Devices command gives you the best control over the result (File menu, Illus. 07), but Photoshop will warn you first.
Confirm the dialog with Yes (Illus. 08).

A sub-program opens up in which you can prepare your file to be exported – most importantly, it gives you a chance of previewing the quality of the format you have chosen.
Toggle the 2-Up panel (Illus. 09); you'll see two images appear, the left of which displaying the original image, the right one showing the export preview. Please be patient, the display process may take a moment.

Choose JPEG middle from the default settings pull-down (Illus. 10). Alternatively, you can select the corresponding compression algorithms from the pull-down menus underneath.

The default JPEG setting offers relatively high compression, quality level is 30 on a scale of 100.
You can detect obvious differences in the two windows, especially when you zoom in – the JPEG is blurred, revealing pixel artefacts that are typical of bad JPEGs.
But the file size has shrunk considerably, and that's pretty good (Illus. 11).

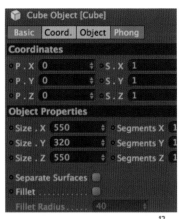

12

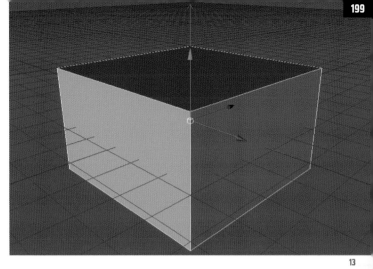

13

Since the file still has more pixels than we actually need, we will keep the selected format. Click Save and choose a path of your choice for your compressed file. Close your original PSD file without saving, to keep its initial quality.

Now we want to project this texture on a suitable model using Cinema 4D.

Open the program and place a cube from the Primitive Objects menu in the empty scene.

Make the cube large enough for the brick texture to fit on it in the correct proportion (Object panel: Size X and Z = 550, Size Y = 320, Illus. 12). The Editor shows you that half of the cube is under 0 level, but that doesn't matter (Illus. 13).

Pick a camera from the Scene Objects menu; set its position (Coordinates panel: P.X = 520, P.Y = -125, P.Z = 525, Illus. 14) and rotate it a bit (R.H = 15; the other angles should be set to 0).

Set the focal length to 21 (Object panel, Illus. 14), and shift the picture to get the right clipping (Film Offset X = -55, Y = -35).

Nothing has changed in the Editor – you have to switch to your freshly placed camera using the Scene Cameras flyout in the Editor's Cameras menu, Illus. 15) to change perspective (Illus. 16).

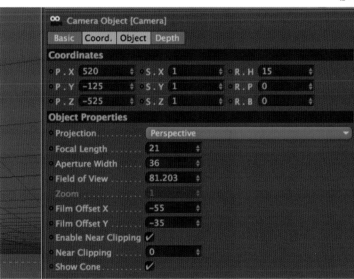

14

16

15

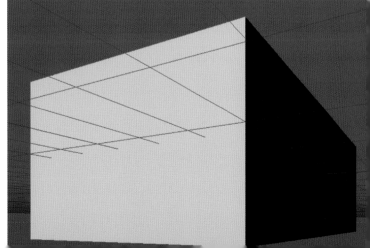

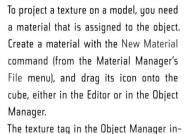

To project a texture on a model, you need a material that is assigned to the object. Create a material with the New Material command (from the Material Manager's File menu), and drag its icon onto the cube, either in the Editor or in the Object Manager.
The texture tag in the Object Manager indicates that the material has been properly assigned (Illus. 17).

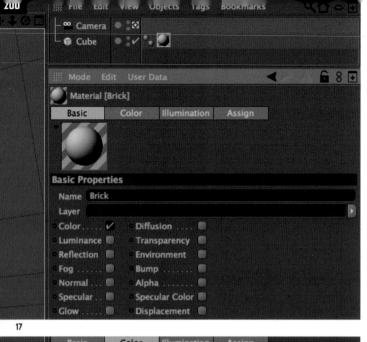

17

Double-click the tag to see the material settings in the Attributes Manager.
Switch to the Basics panel to give your material a name (e.g. brick) and deactivate the Specular channel (Illus. 17).

Toggle the Color panel. In most cases, this is the channel into which you load a bitmap texture that will be visible on the object.
Don't worry about the color and brightness settings, and click on the small black arrow next to the word Texture.
Choose Load Image from the pull-down menu that opens (Illus. 18). From the familiar file dialog opening up you should open either the JPEG file you just created or my brick.jpg picture (15:15_end:tex:brick.jpg).

18

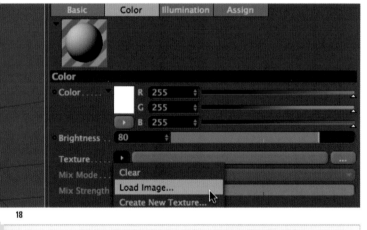

This image is not in the document search path. Do you want to create a copy at the document location?

No   Yes

19

20

Cinema 4D now asks a question about the texture path – click on Yes so your program "remembers" the file path (Illus. 19).

As a result, your cube will appear with the brick texture (Illus. 20).
It seems that the image has been projected on the front side of the cube in 1:1 scale. We will later see if this really the case, and why.
The other sides of the cube are also textured, but unfortunately they appear completely dark – you'll deal with that later.

The next step is getting rid of the blur on the brick image.

The default settings treat each projected bitmap with so-called MIP interpolation – a blur filter that is supposed to reduce texture flickering in animations.

Choose None from the Sampling menu (Color panel, right below the Texture pull-down) to make your texture appear sharp (Illus. 21).

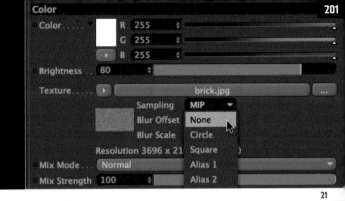

21

We have to differentiate between two things when working with materials and textures: the material itself the way it appears in the Material Manager, and the way it is projected on an object.

One and the same material can be assigned to a number of objects, and a different type of projection can be selected for each object. The material settings are accessed via double-quick, the projection settings with a single click on the texture tag in the Object Manager.

Single-click on the texture tag next to the cube object. The Projection type of your material is displayed in the Tag panel – at present, it's UVW Mapping (Illus. 22). This is a special way of projecting which fixes the complete texture on each polygon in the object.

The result looks right though, because the cube's proportions match the ones of the bitmap. We will leave things this way.

A "normal" projection type would be Cubic Mapping, which would allow us to rotate or move the texture (Illus. 23). If you choose this projection, end get lost after scaling, rotating etc., you can make the texture shrink back to the cube with Fit to Object, from the Object Manager's Tags menu Illus. 24).

Without "real" light sources we are dependent on Cinema 4D's Default Light. Select the corresponding command from the Display menu and click on the sphere until you are satisfied with the lighting (Illus. 25).

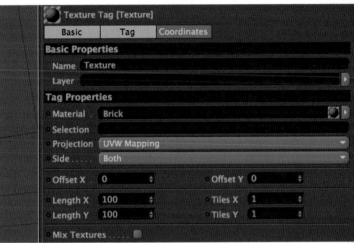

22

23

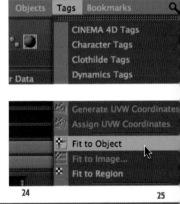

24

25

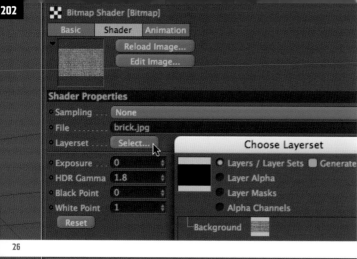

26

27

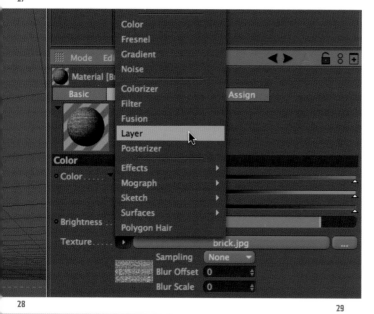

28

29

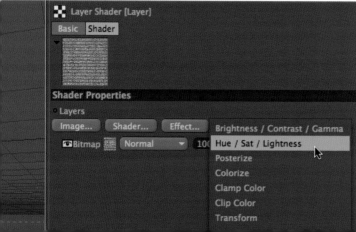

I want to give you a glimpse of what you can do with your texture in the Color channel before we tackle the interstice image and relief.

Click on the miniature of the brick image, the Attributes Manager will show you a few settings (Illus. 26).

You can select the type of sampling as well as modify the brightness (Exposure, Gamma) and brightness spectrum (Black or White Point), or even open the image in Photoshop to make changes (Edit Image; the application which will open when you hit this command of course depends on your OS settings).

The feature that allows you to select the layers of a Photoshop file is particularly interesting. After clicking on Select Layerset, a window opens that shows the graphics' layers. Since you loaded a JPEG image, the only layer shown is the Background. We could have made good use of this function since we are going to use a grayscale copy of our image in the course of the chapter.

Click on the left arrow on the upper right edge of the Attributes Manager to move up to a higher level, back to the material's Color channel (Illus. 27).

Open the Texture pull-down again – the one you used to load the image – and select the Layer option this time (Illus. 28). As you can see, the appearance of your cube hasn't changed.

Click on the miniature image again. A different set of settings appears this time (Illus. 29).

The layer function serves to stack images, shaders and effects on one another the same way Photoshop does. It allows you to use the same fill methods and create the same layer blending modes Photoshop offers (Normal, Multiply, etc.). Your texture is the only item so far, if you click

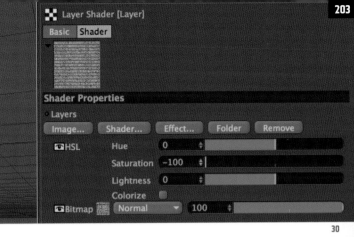

on its miniature, you will again see the settings you've seen earlier.

But now select Hue/Sat/Lightness from the Effects Menu (Illus. 29). You probably know this adjustment tool from Photoshop; it works the same way here.
Lower Saturation all the way (-100, Illus. 30). As you can see, your texture loses its color with this setting, it is reduced to a grayscale image (Illus. 31).

Remember: Saturation stands for the purity of a color - if it is minimal, there is no color in the image's pixels, maximum Saturation leads to the complete disappearance of gray.

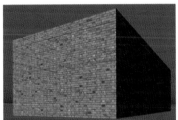

31

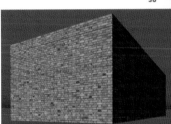

32

Set your Saturation back to a mid-range value (0, Illus. 33) and Hue to 30. This will change the pixels' color - the seemingly linear movement of the hue slide in fact corresponds to the circular movement in the color circle, which is why the outmost left and right hue values are the same. Anyway, the cube's brick cladding looks different now (Illus. 32).
The Colorize option is another feature that reminds you of the corresponding Photoshop tool inside the Hue/Saturation adjustment (Illus. 34). This makes the image's color more homogeneous, i.e., the color selected with the color toggle mixes with a grayscale version of your image. The result is, in principle, a Duplex image (Illus. 35). The higher the Saturation value, the stronger the coloring appears to be (in our example: Hue = 200, Saturation = 25, don't forget to check Colorize).

There are more tools you can use to work on your texture in the Effect menu. Some of these are familiar adjustment tools, like Brightness/Contrast/Gamma, whereas others remind us of Photoshop's filters, like Distort.
Take your time testing these options.

30

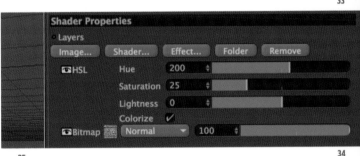

33

35

34

The Shader menu offers a different set of features that can also be stacked on one another. First click on the eye symbol next to the Hue/Saturation/Lightness effect you have already implemented (HSL, Illus. 36), to hide it.

Select Noise from the Shader menu – a mathematically generated structure with infinite modulation potential (Illus. 37). The default settings present the noise with 100% opacity when it is layered on the texture.
Before changing this, you should click on the small miniature noise icon.

A well-equipped settings panel opens up you're already acquainted with (see chapter 14).
In the first place, you can choose a noise type here, the default Cinema 4D offers you is but one of many (Illus. 38). Click on the black arrow next to the noise pulldown to access the miniatures selection panel.
Choose Box noise (upper left, Illus. 38). You can tune this noise by setting Global Size to 10 and Relative X Scale to 200 (Illus. 39).

The result of your selection is displayed in the Editor – the mathematically generated noise pattern is layered over the texture and covers the cube completely (Illus. 41).
Since you actually want to see your texture, move up one settings level in the Attributes Manager to access the settings of

the layer function once more. Set Multiply as your Noise layer blending mode and set Opacity to 50 (Illus. 40).
The Editor shows how the noise modulates the brick texture – hide the noise to study the difference (Illus. 42 and 43).

So much for the use of shaders in the Color channel – a glance at the Shader menu gives you a sense of the vast potential at your avail (notice the sub-menus for Effects and Surfaces).

You projected the bricks onto the model with the help of a bitmap texture. Now you will create the interstice image using a shader in Cinema 4D.

The reason for continuing this way is the fact that although the bricks look good as single images, the interstice frame around them won't, since repetitive tiling couldn't be avoided.

In Photoshop, the interstice area was displayed by a gray solid color level, just to make it look fine.
But this gray background does by no means resemble a satisfying realistic mortar structure – a surface whose characteristics you will now visualize with a noise shader.

Your first task will be to mask the brick image textured on the model, since the noise should only be visible between the bricks.

You'll see how this works later on; in the first place, for masking you need to create a black and white copy of your brick image using Photoshop.

In Photoshop, open the 15_brick.psd file again (it's better to create your mask using the initial high-resolution image).
Hide the Color and Adjustment layer to

42

43

45

44

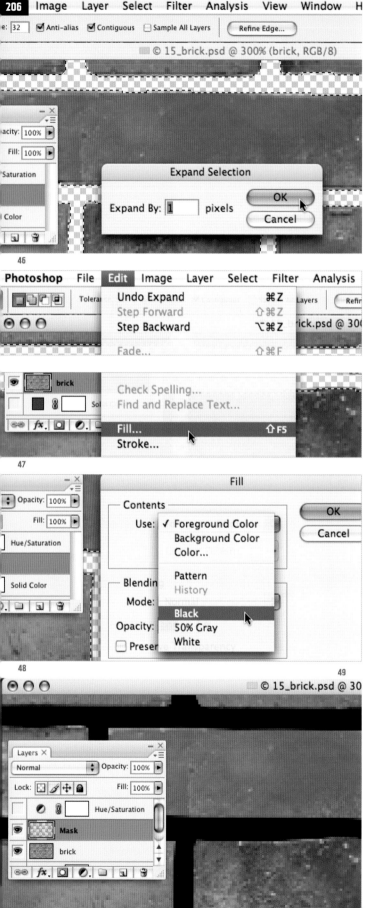

make the interstice space transparent (Il-lus. 44).

Choose the Magic Wand tool – select the lowest possible tolerance (1) – and un-check Contingent.
Make sure the brick layer is active and click on any spot within the interstice space – the magic wand will select every transparent pixel on the picture layer.

To be sure there will be no semi-trans-parent relics around your bricks, enlarge the selection by one pixel (Select menu: Modify – Expand – Expand By 1, Illus. 45 and 46; your selection should still be ac-tive of course).
Create a new layer before continuing which you name Mask.

The interstice space is still selected, and your new, empty level is active.
Select Fill from the Edit menu (Illus. 47), and select Black in the Use pull-down menu that appears in the command dia-log.
Confirm your selection by clicking on OK (Illus. 48; you probably figure you could have chosen the foreground color since it seems black too, but it might by some reason be only dark Gray instead of Black, and the mask wouldn't work precisely.)

Your selection on the interstice mask layer is filled with Black now, your layer shows the respective miniature (Illus. 49).

On the same layer, fill the remaining im-age area (covered by the bricks a layer further down) with White.

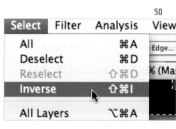

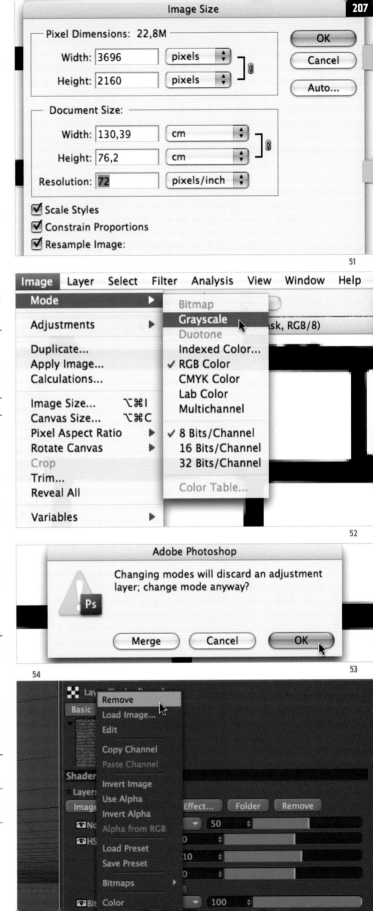

Inverse the selection (Select menu, Illus. 50; choose Reselect before if the selection is no longer active, from the same menu).

After inverting, fill the selection with White, again using the Edit menu's Fill command – just make sure it takes place in the mask layer.

The mask image is done for the moment, and you can export it as a JPEG file again (see the beginning of the chapter).
Once more, reduce resolution via Image Size (Image menu); as before, set the resolution to 72 dpi (Illus. 51; of course, you can do without downsampling if you dealt with your mask business in your already downsized brick.jpg).

Just keep in mind that brick and interstice mask image have exactly the same dimensions, otherwise you might get confusing results when using them in Cinema 4D.

Keep the brick layer switched off, and turn your image to Grayscale to save disk space and RAM while rendering later on (Image menu: Mode: Grayscale, Illus. 52).

Then, once more, Save for Web & Devices (File menu). Confirm Photoshop's timid question with Yes (Illus. 53).

You can close your original PSD file without saving as soon as you have saved a copy of your image as JPEG.

Back to Cinema 4D. With the Grayscale you just created (which is in fact black and white) you'll mask your brick texture and thus make way for the shaded interstice image.
Navigate downwards your material's Color channel to your Layer settings. Delete the Noise and HSL layers (right-click: Remove, Illus. 54).

55

Our sophisticated strategy to assign two different images in one material demands just another refined feature of Cinema 4D. Mixing two textures in one material channel, with a mask in between, asks for the Fusion shader.

Move to the top of your material's Color channel and replace the Layer with the Fusion shader (Illus. 55).

Quite scaringly, everything turns black – both the shader miniature in the Attributes Manager and the cube in the Editor.

Click on the Fusion's black miniature to access its settings.
The most important items you'll find here are three channels: the Base channel, meant to contain your brick image, the Mask channel, being the appropriate place for your grayscale picture, and the Blend channel, where you'll implement your interstice shader later on.

Up to now, the Base channel is occupied by your former Layer shader, which only consists of your brick image (here you are - it's not gone after all!).

56

57

Replace the Layer with the image itself, to keep a clean shader structure (although this practically doesn't make a difference). Just select brick.jpg from the Base channel's pull-down (Bitmaps flyout, Illus. 56).

Check Use Mask, and the mask channel is at your disposal (Illus. 57).

Load the mask image you just created in Photoshop (or use my 15_brick_mask.jpg

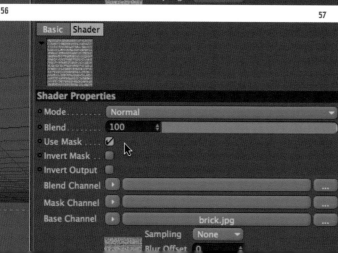

58

Light Shadow Space · Architectural Rendering with Cinema 4D

file instead, Illus. 58). Whatever image you choose, set Sampling to None.

Cinema 4D often does things we don't expect – unlike Photoshop, Cinema 4D by default applies a mask by concealing white image area; in your grayscale image, the brick's part of the image is white, instead of the interstices (Illus. 59).

But again, this is not really a problem – just check Invert Mask in the shader settings (Illus. 60), and the image will be displayed as expected.

The interstices aren't visible anymore, what you see instead is the black color of the empty Blend channel between the bricks (Illus. 61).

Now please load a Noise into the Blend channel (Illus. 62).

Switch to the noise settings and select Poxo from the shader overview (Illus. 64). Leave the settings as they are.

To finish implementing the interstice image, set the Blend slide to 35 (Illus. 63).

The Mask channel affects the Blend channel and only becomes effective if Blend is set to more than 0.

If the value is 0, the Blend channel remains invisible, the mask turns ineffective, and you see the gray area between the bricks in your Base channel image.

A Blend value of 100 would show your noise completely.

Instead, for the interstices we prefer to see an even mix of gray background and noise, so you are advised to use a midrange Blend value.)

Toggle a side view (e.g. F4), zoom in and render the image. The result looks pretty realistic, although there is still no relief (Illus. 64).

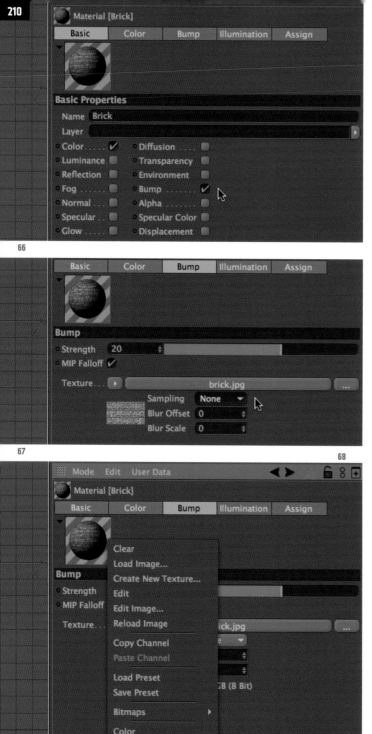

66

67

68

The texture looks right, what we miss is relief. The interstices in particular should be a bit further back.

As you might already know, such a relief doesn't have to be modeled, it's rather done with texture modulation.

You can set the appropriate settings in the Bump channel of your material. Switch to the Attributes Manager's Basic panel and check Bump (Illus. 66).

Switch to the Bump panel. Basically, what you need to achieve a relief effect is a grayscale image or shader.

The bump simulation is controlled by the shader's or graphic's grayscale values; white pixels in the Bump channel make the texture pixels look convex, black pixels concave, gray areas behaving respectively according to their brightness.

This process also works the other way round, depending on whether Strength is positive or negative (Illus. 67).

In your case it is best to use your brick image as reference – but only in a more contrasted grayscale version, so the relief effect will be easier to adjust.

You will create this copy in Cinema 4D with the help of a Layer shader, which you are already familiar with (see above).

Additionally, you will blacken the interstices via the Fusion shader so they step back more dramatically.

Load the brick.jpg file into the Bump channel. Set Sampling to None before you do anything else (Illus. 67).

In the Texture pull-down, replace the texture with the Layer shader (Illus. 68). Click on the shader miniature to access the Layer shader's settings.

From the Effect menu, select the Hue/Sat/Lightness adjustment tool, and set Saturation to –100 (Illus. 69; remember: sliding the Saturation toggle all the way to the left drains the color out of the image).

To achieve a convincing image, the interstices have to be recessed to quite a degree, so their area has to be blackened in our texture.

Switch back to the Bump channel's upper level and replace the Layer with the Fusion shader (Illus. 70). Click on the black miniature to access its settings – you see your Layer shader has „survived" the change by turning into the Base channel. Check Use Mask again, and load the black-and-white brick_mask.jpg image into the Mask channel.

Keep the Blend value set to 100 and check Invert Mask. Don't forget to switch off the blur for the mask image (Sampling: None, Illus. 71).

Now the interstices are black, the way they were earlier in the chapter (Illus. 61) – this is exactly what you want in the Bump channel now.

At last, you will adjust the relief effect – switch yourself back to the Bump channel's upper level and set Strength up to 100 (Illus. 72).

Render the side view again – the relief effect is quite intense, even on the brick surfaces (Illus. 73).

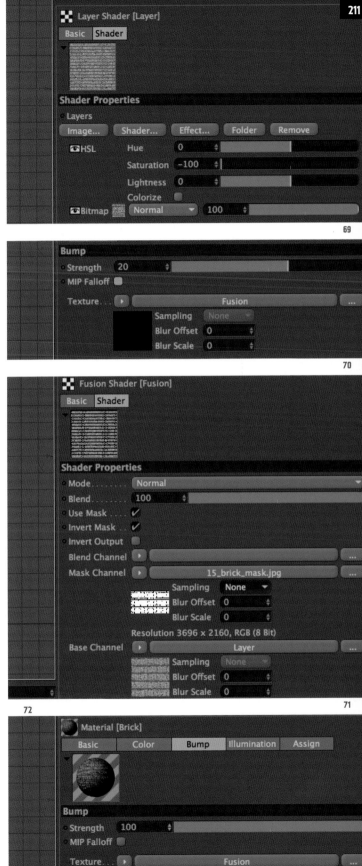

73

75

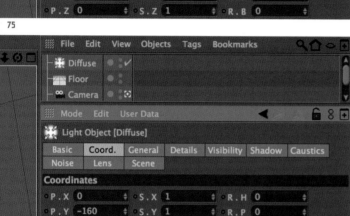

76

77

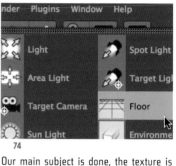

74

Our main subject is done, the texture is complete now, including the relief.

To finish up, we will focus on the scene a bit, especially on lighting. You won't learn something new, you just will apply things you already have exercised a number of times.

To get a shadow on the floor, you have to place one in the first place. Pick a Floor object from the Scene Objects menu (Illus. 74) and move it down until it is on the same level with the cube ground level (Coordinates panel: P.Y = -160, Illus. 75).

Now you may add your first light simulating diffuse daylight.
We will use a lightdome once more, a hemispherical area, which is meant to be an abstract reconstruction of the sky.

Place a light and name it Diffuse with Y = 160 (Coordinates panel, Illus. 76).

Raise its brightness a bit (General panel: Intensity = 125, Illus. 77), and for Type, select Area – shadow should remain deactivated.

Take care of the lightdome shape in the Details panel – select Hemisphere (Area Shape, Illus. 78) with a diameter of 5000 units (Outer Radius = 2500).
Reduce the sampling rate here as well (set Samples to its lowest possible value = 16), to ensure reasonable render times.

78

A look through the Editor camera informs you whether model and lightdome have the right size relation; obviously they do (Illus. 79).

Make absolutely sure Antialiasing is switched off (Render setting's General panel) before starting your test rendering.
Though this may influence the display of edges as well as the relief effect, saving render time pays you off, after all you just want to study your light setup's quality.

The brightness is adequate, since you will have another light anyway (for direct sunlight, Illus. 80).

To do so, place another light, and call it Sun.
Select an Infinite creating hard shadow (General panel: Raytraced (Hard), Illus. 81). Keep Intensity set to 100.

You know it's not the position of a parallel light that is important, but the direction - set proper values in the Coordinates panel (R.H = -45, R.P = -25, Illus. 82).

The view through the Editor camera reveals the result of these settings (Illus. 83).

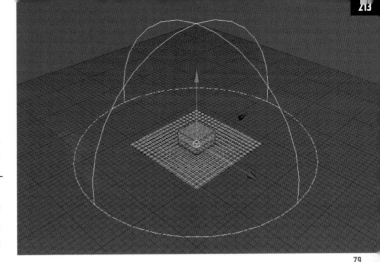

79

80

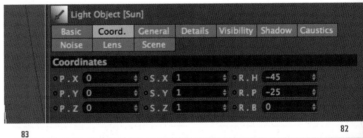

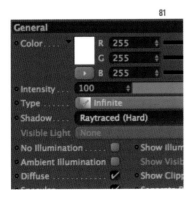

81

83

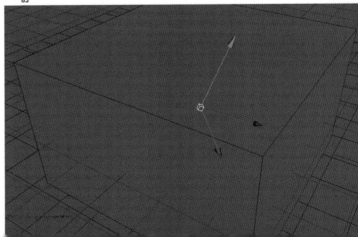

82

84

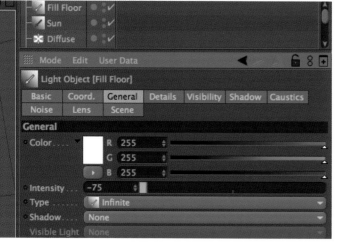

85

Render the scene, or more elegantly, just a segment of it (via Render Region in the Render menu).

The brightness distribution along the walls is quite pleasing, but the ground surface appears overexposed (Illus. 84).

You'll solve that problem with a third light, which will only darken the floor (sort of a negative fill).

In Cinema 4D, this is relatively easy to do, since you can define negative intensity for lights).

So place another light, and call it Fill Floor. Select an Infinite type in the General panel with negative brightness (Intensity = -75, Illus. 85).

It doesn't have to cast shadows, of course.

86

Again, the light's direction is crucial; set the R.P angle to -90 in the Coordinates panel, so the light rays hit the ground orthogonally (Illus. 86).

87

Make sure this "light" only darkens the ground, so switch to the Scene panel, set Include mode and drag the floor from the Object Manager into the Objects entry field (Illus. 87).

A test rendering (just a segment again!) shows you the result. Both ground and shadow are sufficiently darkened now (Illus. 88).

88

89

This marks the end of our scene setup. Our main focus this time was on handling the brick texture.

To close, we'll go through the Render settings once more to improve the final image's quality.

The first thing you should do for a final rendering is to choose Antialiasing (Best in this case, in the General panel of your New Render settings, Illus. 89).

This smoothens real object edges as well as the shadow's edges and the simulated brick relief.

In your scene, Ambient Occlusion is not a bad idea, either – check it in the respective panel (Illus. 90; keep the default settings).

But keep in mind that AO is nasty in terms of rendering times. Before you get mad at this, lower the AO Samples rates to abbreviate rendering time.

The rendering appears richly colored (Illus. 91). We have now solved a task that required a brick texture made of bitmap images of real bricks combined with a "blend" of mathematically generated interstice and relief surfaces.

A closer look shows you that the brick surfaces do not match up properly in the corners.

You can solve this problem by applying the brick material to these two wall faces separately. Then you can move the two textures until the corner looks right. (texturing separate surfaces of one single object is discussed on p.32).

Take time to try it out. Be aware that to move a texture you have to change its projection from UVW to Cubic mapping (see p.201).

Additionally, you'll have to pick the Texture tool (left command bar) before you can slide the brick image back and forth on the block.

90

91

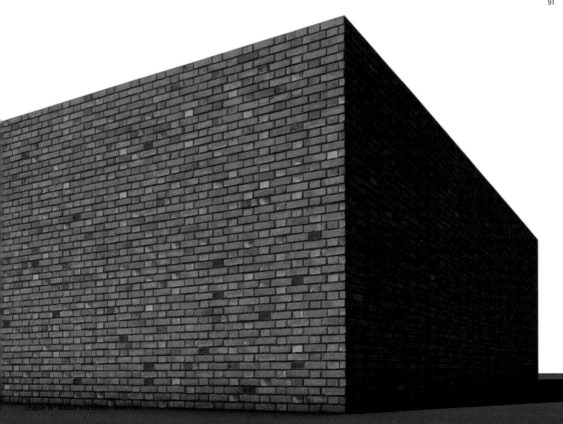

01

Multi-Pass Rendering in Cinema 4D · Compositing in Photoshop

The term rendering is often used throughout our workflow – while working on your scene setup, you use it to check your material and light effects (evaluating shadows, transparency and reflection makes only sense in a rendering, for example), and in the end you need it to calculate your final image or animation, which you can export and process further in post-

production. Right from the beginning, you should be aware of the fact that you can edit the result of your 3D work with a number of compositing programs.
In most cases, images and animations created in Cinema 4D are just not perfect enough to be used without postproduction.

Photoshop is without doubt the most important postproduction tool when it comes to optimizing a still image.

02

03

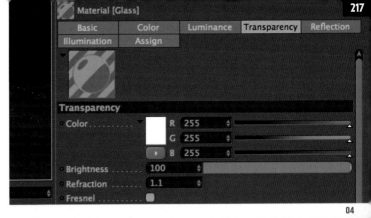

04

(Just imagine Cinema 4D produced a photo for you, not unlike a photo you shot with your digicam).

What is particularly convenient is that Cinema 4d is able to break down your rendering into layers containing separate aspects of the image (e.g. shadow), which can then be adjusted and retouched individually.

This feature is called multi-pass rendering. The only difference between this type of rendering and normal rendering is the final result, a multi-layer file.

As an example, let's use a color picture showing the New National Gallery in Berlin, by Ludwig Mies v.d.Rohe, that contains all the usual effects – shadows, transparency and reflection – it comes without a background too, which we want to add using Photoshop (Illus. 01).

If you open the 16_ng_start.c4d file and render it, you will see that the image looks a bit simpler, especially the shadows (Illus. 02).

I just created two alternative light setups. The respective version shown in Illus. 02 will save your resources during processing (fill floor test being active), while the version displayed in Illus. 01 uses the more refined, performance-intensive fill floor final light setup, which is hidden for the time being (Illus. 03).

The image's transparency, reflection and shadow effects result from corresponding settings for the textures and lights in use. For example, the glass material assigned to the window surfaces has a Transparency channel, transparency being set to its highest level (Brightness = 100, Illus. 04). Notice that Refraction is set to a value > 1. The terrace material (Granite) is reflective – a Noise shader in its Reflection channel adds a realistic amount of distortion (Illus. 05).

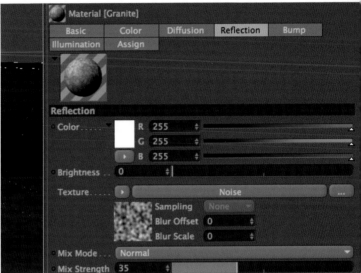

05

Fill floor test is the main light creating hard shadow (Illus. 06).

Take time to go through all the material channels and check all the settings, which textures and shaders are being used, etc. (double-click on the corresponding texture tag next to the objects in the Object Manager to see the respective material settings in the Attributes Manager).

You find more on texturing in Chapter 15, Object and Texture.

06

Render Settings

Use Render settings to adjust the size and set multi-pass mode for your rendering (Render menu).

For a start, first deactivate Antialiasing in the General panel. Edge smoothing and high shadow resolution are not crucial during your test phase at all (Illus. 07).

Define the dimensions of the image rendered in the Picture Viewer (Output panel). Keep the default 320x240 pixel size; it will keep rendering short, and you'll understand the essential multi-pass settings well enough (Illus. 08).

In contrary to what you may think, you don't need to enter settings in the Save panel (Illus. 09); you will define a file path further down.

In the same panel, we will later activate separate alpha channel processing for background compositing - but not at the moment.

However, the settings you enter in the Multi-Pass panel are decisive for your undertaking (Illus. 10).

In the first place, check Enable Multi-Pass Rendering so Cinema 4D "knows" that it has to render certain image aspects into separate layers.

You should also check two more options: Save Multi-Pass Image and Multi-Layer File.

The three options mentioned belong together in our workflow, they ensure your rendering will be saved without you doing anything.

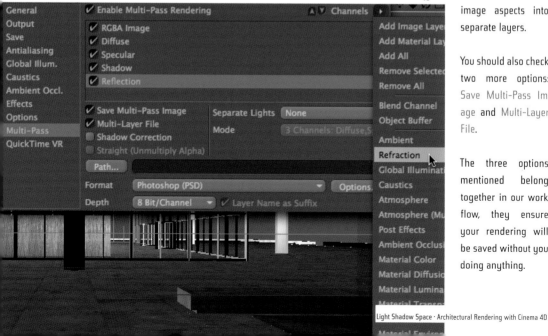

Light Shadow Space · Architectural Rendering with Cinema 4D

11

Now you can decide which aspects of your image should be calculated separately and turn into individual Photoshop layers later on.

Click on the little black arrow on the upper right (Channels) to open a pull-down menu for all the image items that can be rendered separately. (Notice that in Cinema 4D they are called channels, in Photoshop it's mostly layers, whereas Alpha and Object channels keep their label and are filed in Photoshop's Channel panel.)

Back to the pull-down: select RGBA Image, Diffuse, Specular, Shadow, Reflection and Refraction (Illus. 10). Refraction means Transparency, with one limitation (see below).

Enter a file path to have Cinema 4D save your image automatically. Don't forget to select Photoshop format (psd) and keep Color Depth set to 8 bits per channel (Illus. 11).

Now please launch your first multi-pass rendering (Render menu: Render to Picture Viewer, Illus. 12).

The Picture Viewer will open up in a new window - while rendering, its Channels menu allows you to see the single image channels you defined previously (Illus. 13).

As you can see, the Refraction channel displays everything that can be seen through the transparent glass panels. If it remains black, it is probably because Refraction is set to 1 in the glass material's Transparency channel. (For some reason, in multi-pass rendering Cinema 4D only displays objects in the Refraction channel that lie behind transparent textures with a Refraction value higher than 1).

When you're finished, you should open the image in Photoshop. All your selected channels are stacked in the Layer panel (Illus. 14).

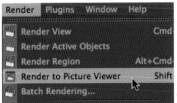

12

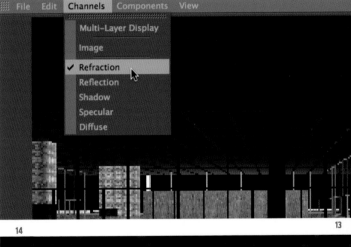

14

13

15

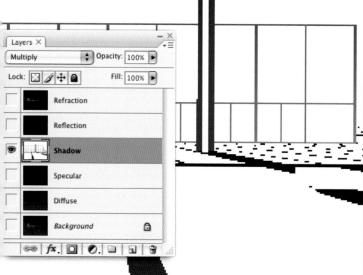

16

17

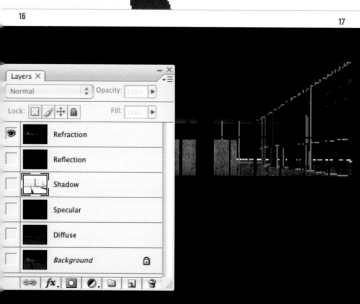

The RGBA channel, which contains all the image information in a single layer, has become Background layer. You should always keep this layer to compare the results of your image processing with the original later on. The RGBA = Background layer is good for checking if important image parts have not been rendered, too, since all the other layers put together should add up to the same image as displayed in the background image.

Sometimes though there are slight differences between the multi-layer composing and the background image. This happens when Cinema 4D is not able to put on display all its channels in Photoshop layers correctly. (But don't worry - the deviations are only marginal, and can easily be adjusted in Photoshop.)

Now hide the individual layers, then take a look at each of them consecutively.

The Diffuse layer for example displays the distribution of colored surfaces and their textures without additional effects, the image parts behind the window panes aren't visible (Illus. 15). The Diffuse layer is in Normal blending mode, so it covers the background layer underneath completely.

The Specular layer's image brightens the surface of all those objects having a Specular material channel.

Shadow is on its own layer too, with a white background. Multiply is assigned as the layer's blending mode, so the white part is invisible in the overall composing (Illus. 16).

The Reflection layer shows image parts that are only visible as reflections, not directly.

The image segment showing objects behind transparent surfaces is on the Refraction layer (Illus. 17). As blending mode, this layer features Linear Dodge, hiding the black area from composing, in contrary to the Multiply mode.

Once again: only transparency with a refraction value higher than 1 will reveal objects behind it in the Refraction channel (C4D) or layer (Photoshop) respectively.

This description covers the principles of how Cinema 4D converts image channels into Photoshop layers. Of course it may be necessary that even more channels have to be rendered (e.g. when using Ambient Occlusion). Just check Add Image Layers in Cinema 4D's multi-pass render Channel pull-down if you are not sure which channels are necessary. Cinema 4D may process useless channels when doing so, but it's easy to spot empty layers in Photoshop and delete them.

Now let's have a look at another cool feature which indeed is part of the multi-pass business, but not as obvious as image channels in the first place: by rendering a multi-layer image, Cinema 4D is able to produce an Alpha channel clipping image parts not occupied by objects.
This is very convenient when you need to mount a background image in Photoshop, since you can use it as a mask. To make Cinema 4D supply you with an image mask just check Alpha channel in your Render settings Save panel; but again, you don't have to check Save Image at this place (Illus. 19).

For a change, raise the image dimensions to 1024x768 pixels in the Output panel, just to make your image look a bit prettier in Photoshop (Illus. 18).
Now when you launch a Picture Viewer rendering again, you will be asked if you want to replace your first rendering file (remember you defined a file path in the Multi-Pass panel.) Confirm by pressing Yes (Illus. 20). While Cinema 4D is rendering, you can watch your mask evolving by choosing Alpha from the Picture Viewer's Channels menu (Illus. 21).

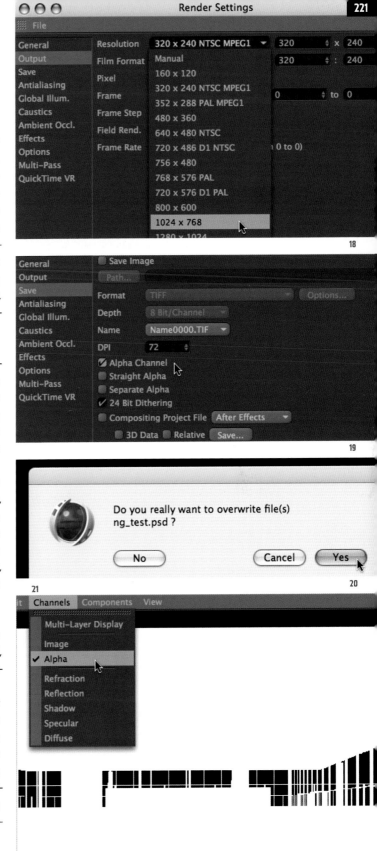

22

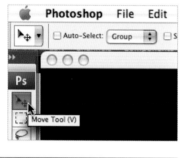

23

24

In Photoshop, you'll spot the mask Cinema 4D created in the Channels panel. It is listed below the RGB channels (Alpha, Illus. 22).

As you know, Photoshop saves its image color data in so-called channels that display the base colors' intensity (for an RGB image, it's Red, Green and Blue) as a grayscale image.

An additional channel shows the mix of all single Color channels, i.e. the overall image (RGB in our case).

The newly added Alpha channel has nothing to do with this – it is listed here for another reason: a selection you save in Photoshop is filed away in the channel panel – as a grayscale image. From here, it can be recovered (loaded) whenever you need it – to mask an adjustment, filter or image layer.

Every selection that has been saved in Photoshop is such an Alpha channel – or, in other words, your Cinema 4D-generated Alpha channel is just another mask that may be loaded for compositing purposes.

OK, now let's make use of this and add a background sky to our image.
Open the 16_sky.jpg file in Photoshop and move the window sideways, so you can see both images.

Make sure the sky image is in front and choose the Move tool (Illus. 23). Click on the sky image, keep your mouse button pressed and drag it onto the render image.
„Drop" it as soon as the mouse cursor is over the multi-passed picture – the sky will be copied into the rendering. Its placement will be centered if you press Shift when dropping (Illus. 24).

As you can see, Photoshop has set up a new layer to store the freshly imported image, above the last active layer (Illus. 25; you should drag the new layer to the top of the Layer panel list if it's not there already).

The sky covers the entire rest of the image. To limit it to the very scene background, you will assign a layer mask that you will create using your Alpha channel.

Choose Load Selection from the Select menu (Illus. 26).
You may now choose channels from any Photoshop file, which will then appear in the image as hovering selections (the familiar ants).

Of course you will use your own file, and select the new Alpha channel from the Channel pull-down (Illus. 27) – you see

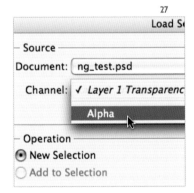

your background selection appear hovering above the image.
Now turn it into a mask by clicking on the corresponding button at the bottom of the Layer panel (Add Layer Mask, Illus. 28).

Photoshop will instantly turn the selection into a mask, although the wrong way (Illus. 29). Obviously, the Alpha channel's black part conceals the image.
Press Ctrl Z and repeat this step, changing a bit; just press the Alt key while clicking on the button for the new layer mask.

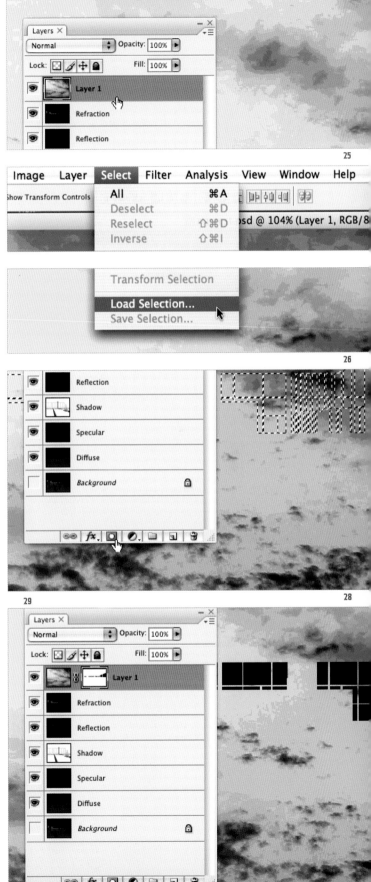

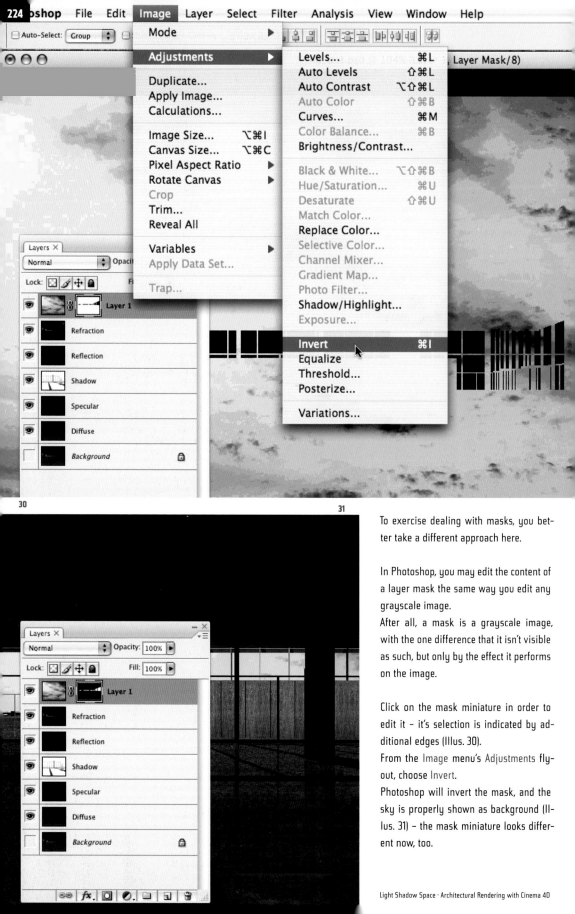

To exercise dealing with masks, you better take a different approach here.

In Photoshop, you may edit the content of a layer mask the same way you edit any grayscale image.

After all, a mask is a grayscale image, with the one difference that it isn't visible as such, but only by the effect it performs on the image.

Click on the mask miniature in order to edit it – it's selection is indicated by additional edges (Illus. 30).

From the Image menu's Adjustments flyout, choose Invert.

Photoshop will invert the mask, and the sky is properly shown as background (Illus. 31) – the mask miniature looks different now, too.

You have learned how you can make Cinema 4D process a background mask using the Alpha channel option in the Save panel.

You may refine the whole procedure and have Cinema 4D create a channel for each individual object, so you may edit it separately in Photoshop.
Let's assume you want to see a more dramatic brightness gradient on the Gallery's ceiling to add more depth to the image.

In Photoshop, you will use Levels to do this, but only for the image part showing the roof. As brightness will have to increase from back to front, choosing an Adjustment layer with a mask containing a black-to white gradient would be the appropriate strategy.

You will use Cinema 4D to create an Alpha channel for the roof, a decisive contribution to this task.

In Cinema 4D, select the roof object, right-click its name in the Object Manager and select Compositing from the Cinema 4D Tags flyout menu (Illus. 32).
This compositing tag will help you control the object's properties when you render the image, e.g. whether it will cast or receive shadow.
In your case, your sole concern is to assign this object its own Alpha channel for Multi-Pass rendering – make sure the Tag is selected, and check the first Enable in the Object Buffer panel. For Buffer, keep 1 (Illus. 33).

Now open your Render settings again and add an Object Buffer channel to the list of channels in the Multi-Pass panel.

A pop-up window appears in which you can enter an ID for the channel – enter 1 here as well (Illus. 34).

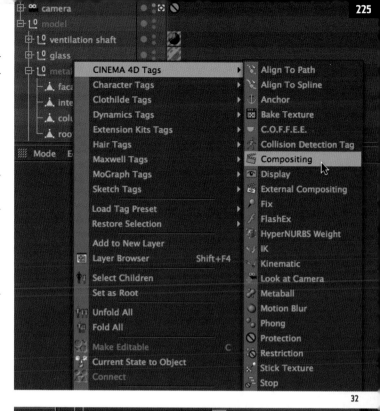

32

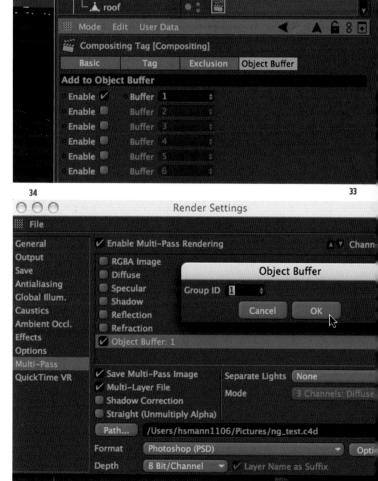

34

33

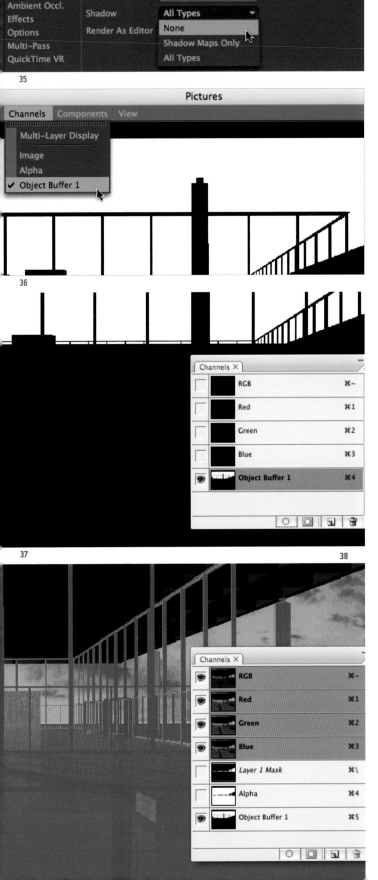

35

36

37

38

This ensures a mask will be created for the roof.

Since most of your rendering is already done, you may uncheck the other channels, because they don't need to be processed again.

Also, there's no need to display transparency, reflection and shadow again - uncheck these effects as well, in the General panel (Illus. 35).

Save your Photoshop image under a different name (Save As...) before rendering your C4D file with the object channel to make sure it isn't replaced with the new rendering.

Now render to the Picture Viewer, while waiting for the result you can watch the roof mask evolve choosing Object Buffer 1 from the Channel menu, Illus. 36).

Open the file in Photoshop - the roof mask is again displayed in the Channels panel with its original name (Illus. 37).

As you know, you can copy parts of images between open Photoshop files by dragging the corresponding Layer panel entries from one file to the other - the layer contents are then added to the target file as a new layer. This neat feature also works with channels.

In Photoshop, make sure the previously edited image file is open and partially visible behind the new mask image.

Then drag Object Buffer 1 from the mask image's Channel panel into the original image's window.

The copied channel will appear in the Channels panel of your original picture. Besides the RGB channels, display the new Buffer channel - it appears as a red mask set over the actual picture (Illus. 38).

Hide it from display again to continue editing the image, make sure your RGB channels are active, and switch back to the Layer panel.

Now let's get back to our actual goal of brightening the roof. As said before, you will do this with an Adjustment layer, which should be above all other layers.

Pick Load Selection again (Select menu, Illus. 39). The file you are currently working on will then appear as Document in the settings window. Keep this setting, and select your Object Buffer 1 from the Channel pull-down menu underneath (Illus. 40; as you have already noticed, Photoshop almost always displays a channel name in italics followed by transparency. This isn't a channel strictly speaking. It is the selection of all non-transparent areas in the active layer).

The grayscale channel will appear as a hovering selection.
Now click on the middle button at the bottom of the Layer panel (Create New Fill or Adjustment layer, Illus. 41). Select Levels from the pop-up menu, which opens the corresponding settings window.
The so-called histogram shows the pixel distribution over the entire image brightness spectrum from Black (left) to White (right), but only of the image area defined by the selection.
As you can see, the image is pretty dark here (Illus. 42).
To significantly brighten this area of the image, slide the right toggle to the left, to the beginning of the pixel range.
Alternatively, you can enter a value way lower than 255 in the right Input Levels entry field (it's 81 in our example, Illus. 42).

The image shows that the roof area is much brighter now.

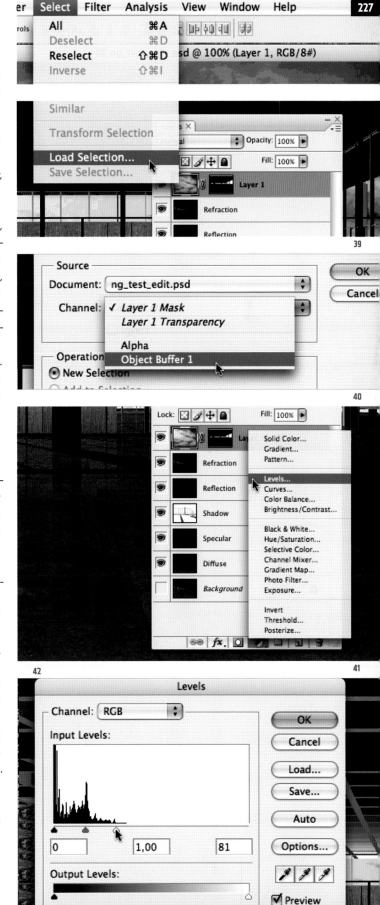

43

The Levels adjustment is listed as a separate layer in the Layer panel along with a mask whose miniature shows the Cinema 4D Object Buffer channel (Illus. 43).

But we want to go a step further and make the brightness decrease towards the rear part of the roof. To achieve this, you'll have to insert a black-to-white gradient in the white part of the mask.

Load the selection again to do so. It will be faster to choose Reselect instead of Load Selection (Select menu, Illus. 43). Make sure the Adjustment layer mask is selected for editing. (Again, the additional edge around the mask icon indicates whether this is the case.)

Now select the Gradient tool from the Tool panel. You will draw a gradient in the mask, and since there is a selection, it only works within the marked area.

In the Option panel above, you can see a black-to-white gradient icon - click it once to access the gradient settings (Illus. 45; as shown in my example, it's al-

44

45

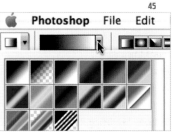

46

ready the right one, if by some reason it's not, just choose the black-to-white gradient from the settings and confirm with OK. And be sure you're in Linear Gradient mode, indicated by the row of smaller icons in the Options panel).

Now you are ready for drawing - click somewhere just beneath the selection, keep you mouse button down and drag the mouse cursor straight up (keep the Shift key pressed down so the gradient axis will be perpendicular, Illus. 46).

Stop drawing right beneath the selection's upper edge.

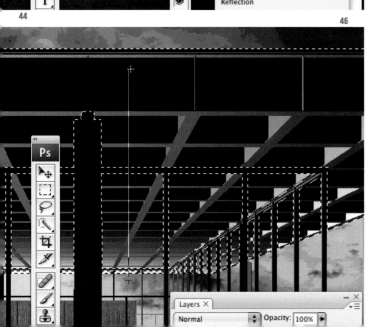

You may Alt-click the mask miniature to look at the mask itself - normally only its effect is visible in the image, not its gray-scale picture itself (Illus. 47).

You can see that the gradient only covers the area you selected. Another Alt-click on the mask miniature switches to the real image again, and an articulate brightness progression is now visible along the underside of the roof (Illus. 48).

As is the advantage of Adjustment layers, you may correct the brightness any time later on by double-clicking its layer miniature to access the histogram settings and sliding the toggles.
Redrawing the gradient - after reloading your selection - is possible at any time, too.

Now you will optimize details of the picture and see how the layer structure in multi-pass rendering helps you complete this task.

The shadow image is still very dark. Activate the layer it's on (Shadow, Illus. 49), and notice that the blending mode is set to Multiply.
Hence the white part of the shadow layer behaves like being invisible in the overall composing, and the black shadow surfaces do not cover the image underneath completely, but mix with it.
Set the layer Opacity to 50, to make the shadow brighter.

The next change concerns the background coloring - we want to trim it into more of a grayscale image.

Make sure the sky layer is activated in your Layer panel. Use the New Adjustment layer command (middle button on the lower edge of the panel) and select Hue/Saturation from the menu (Illus. 50).

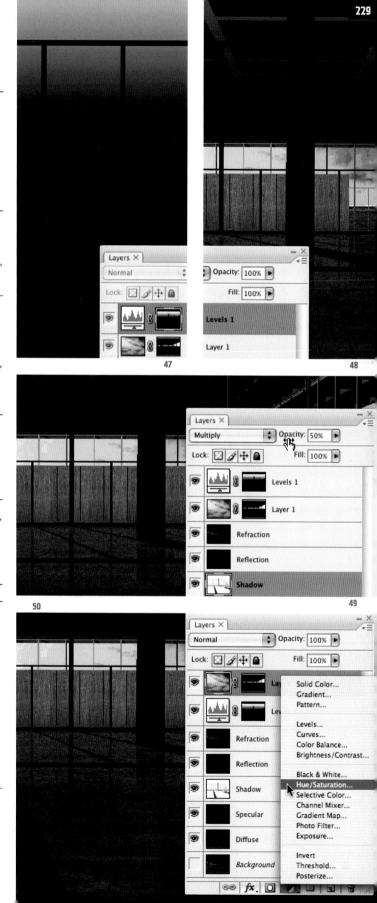

47

48

50

49

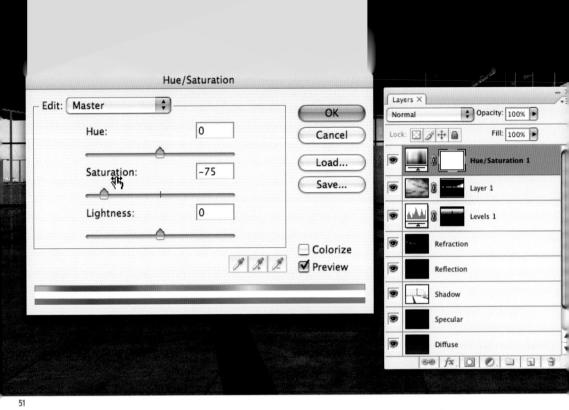

51

Photoshop will place the new Adjustment layer above the last active layer so you can control the coloring of all layers below.

The settings dialog (Illus. 51) basically offers you three parameters for tuning: Hue lets you change the color – take time to play around with it a bit, but our picture doesn't need any color changes.

As you may notice, the utmost left and right slider position result in the same

color, since in fact you are moving in a color circle.

The Saturation parameter is used to adjust the proportion between color and gray in each pixel – set the value to -75 to remove as much color as possible. Don't change Lightness.

Although you won't need it at the moment, notice that though you are in Edit Master mode, you may as well make changes for each Color channel individually (see top of the dialog). Hit OK.

As you can see, the sky now appears as the desired grayscale image with a slight colored tint – but unfortunately, so does the entire picture as well.

You can limit the effect to the image layer underneath with Create Clipping Mask (Layer menu, Layer panel, Illus. 52; as a more elegant alternative, in the Layer panel you can Alt-click the line between Adjustment and image layer).

52

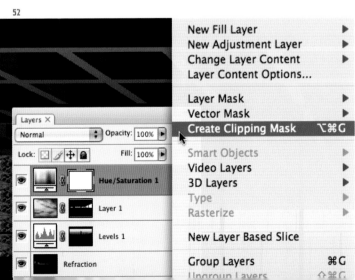

You see the effect in the Layer panel – the Adjustment layer is indented, it creates a so-called Clipping Mask for the image layer below, which means its effect is limited to it (Illus. 53).

As you can see in the image, the sky is the only part drained off color, the rest of the image still has its original coloring. (You can always dissolve this grouping by Alt-clicking the line between both layers again).

You have mounted the sky, lightened the roof's underside, and reduced the coloring of the sky.
The last step is to brighten the interior along the front glass façade with a filter.

To avoid changing the concerning image layer (Refraction) irreversibly, duplicate it using Ctrl J or by dragging it onto the New Layer button at the bottom of the Layer panel.

Since you are going to limit the filter effect to the colored areas of the layer image, you should set the copied layer's blending mode to Normal (Illus. 54).

Create a layer mask that hides the black background before filtering the layer.

Make sure the Refraction layer copy is active and select the Magic Wand tool from the Tool palette.
Set Tolerance to 1 in the Options panel and uncheck Contingent (Illus. 55).
Now click on any part of the black background to select it.

Remember: you use the Magic Wand to select surfaces that are the same (or similar) color – the lower the tolerance, the smaller the color spectrum selected around the marked pixel.

53

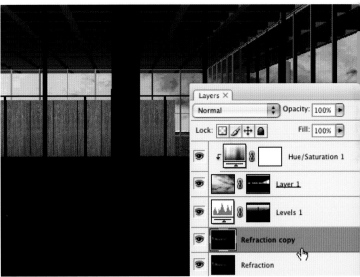

54

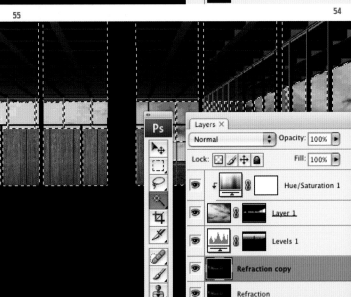

55

Lock: ☒ ✎ ✛ 🔒   Fill: 100% ▶

👁 ⤷ [Hue/Saturation gradient] ⑧ ☐ Hue/Saturation 1

👁 ⑧ Layer 1

👁 [Levels histogram] ⑧ ☐ Levels 1

👁 [thumbnail] Refraction copy

👁 ☐ Refraction

👁 ☐ Reflection

👁 [thumbnail] Shadow

👁 ☐ Specular

🔗 | *fx.* | ▣ | ⚫. | ☐ | ▣ | 🗑

56

Filter   Analysis   View   Window   Help

Unsharp Mask   ⌘F

Convert for Smart Filters   tion copy, RGB/8#)

Extract...   ⌥⌘X

Artistic   ▶
Blur   ▶
Brush Strokes ▶
Distort   ▶   Diffuse Glow...
Noise   ▶   Displace...
Pixelate   ▶   Glass...
Render   ▶   Lens Correction...
Sharpen   ▶   Ocean Ripple...
Sketch   ▶   Pinch...
Stylize   ▶   Polar Coordinates...
Texture   ▶   Ripple...
Video   ▶   Shear...
Other   ▶   Spherize...
                    Twirl...
Digimarc   ▶   Wave...
                    ZigZag...

Levels 1

Refraction copy

57

Diffuse Glow (113,5%)

58

▼   ⬭ OK ⬭
     ⬭ Cancel ⬭

┌ Diffuse Glow ─────────
│ Graininess   2
│   △
│ Glow Amount   ▶
│   △
│ Clear Amount   ▶
│   △

Now convert the selection into a layer mask. The fastest way to do this is by pressing the Add Mask button on bottom of the Layer panel (Illus. 56).

In the new mask, Photoshop will fill the selected area white and the rest black, which will leave the layer's background visible.
This is the same „mistake" you experienced when you first tried to mask the sky background. So undo your last action, and press the Alt key when you click on the mask button again.

Now that the selection is OK, choose the Diffuse Glow filter (Filter menu: Distort, Illus. 57).
This is one of the filters that opens in the Filter Gallery, a sub-program in which you can conveniently select and adjust some of the filter Photoshop offers.

To achieve the desired effect, i.e. softly brightening areas with shining white light, the background color has to be set to White (you can control this via the Tool panel).

For the filter, set a slight Graininess effect (= 2, Illus. 58), and a relatively high Glow Amount of 15. Adjust Clear Amount to 10.

On the left you can see a preview – you can zoom and move the image segment.

Light Shadow Space · Architectural Rendering with Cinema 4D

Select	Filter	Analysis	View
All		⌘A	
Deselect		⌘D	
Reselect		⇧⌘D	
Inverse		⇧⌘I	
All Layers		⌥⌘A	

59

However, it would be nice to stress the filter effect on the right side – without that, the image area on the left looks overly incandescent.

It seems a good idea again to use a gradient mask that will allow for a soft filter effect transition from left to right.

Make sure that your copied Refraction layer has a mask, and that it's activated.

Reselect the layer's colored parts (Select menu – Reselect, or use the Magic Wand again, Illus. 59). Inverse the selection (Select menu, Illus. 60) to get a correct mask this time.

Select the Gradient tool again, still a black-to-white. Now click-drag your mouse from left to right, from the wood surface's beginning to its end, while pressing the Shift key to keep the line horizontal (Illus. 61).

Now the filter effect concentrates on the right part of the picture, and you can see a respective transition on the wood surface (Illus. 62).
You can admire your gradient again by Alt-clicking on the mask miniature (Illus. 63).

63

Select	Filter	Analysis	View	Window	Help

All	⌘A
Deselect	⌘D
Reselect	⇧⌘D
Inverse	⇧⌘I
All Layers	⌥⌘A
Deselect Layers	
Similar Layers	
Color Range...	
Refine Edge...	⌥⌘R
Modify	▶
Grow	
Similar	
Transform Selection	
Load Selection...	
Save Selection...	

00% (Refraction copy, Layer Mask/8)

60

61

62

64

65

You've now seen some of Photoshop's post-processing tools for images rendered in Cinema 4D.
The Multi-Pass layers and Alpha channels were very helpful in this context.

The original lighting setup for the Cinema 4D scene was deactivated for the sake of shorter rendering times.

66

Turn back to your C4D file, and take a look at the Object Manager. You can see an object group called fill floor final (Illus. 65).

This contains basically an array of a number of Omni lights that create hard shadows, as well as an Area that contributes diffuse light to the scene, coming along with Area shadow.

The omni group was created by copying one original light as a number of instances, a strategy you've already applied several times before (e.g. Ch. 09, Rooms and Artificial Lighting).

Switch on this light group (for Editor and rendering), and hide fill floor test you have been using until now.

Now check all the settings that have a decisive effect on the rendering's quality (Antialiasing, Output Size, Transparency, Shadow, Reflection, etc.).

Seize the opportunity to render small image segments beforehand to get a quick impression of the result.

Rendering the whole image will take much longer now, which is definitely justified by the result however (Illus. 64).

Now, this is an image you definitely would like to try Photoshop on.

Compile imported, processed and newly created layers into one layer (Shift Alt Ctrl E) - this will serve as a basis for our experiments.

The first step might be to choose a Threshold Adjustment layer (Illus. 66) to create a posterized black and white version of the image - I chose a Threshold value of 70 (Illus. 69). The layer blending mode should be set to Linear Dodge so the black and white graphics can mix with the image underneath. You also might want to mask the layer in the lower part of the image via a short black-to-white gradient (Illus. 67 and 68) - to make sure the terrace floor isn't effected by the Threshold.

Since you've almost created a grayscale image now, it may be apt to use a Hue/ Saturations Adjustment layer, but make sure Colorize is selected (Illus. 70). This allows you to colorize your rather grayscale image with any color you want, and to tune the result via Saturation and Lightness controls.

Launch a Wireframe rendering (have your Editor display the scene in Lines mode, choose Render as Editor in your Render settings General panel), and integrate the result in your Photoshop composing, again with Linear Dodge as layer blending mode.

For inspiration, just take a look at my 16_ finalrender.psd file; use the Layer Comp panel to switch between different layer combinations.

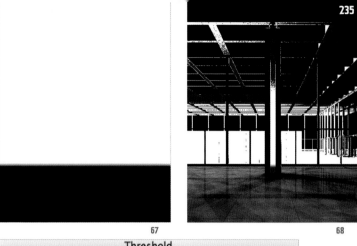

67

68

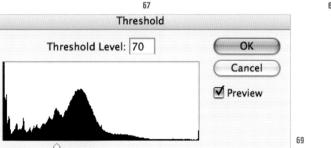

69

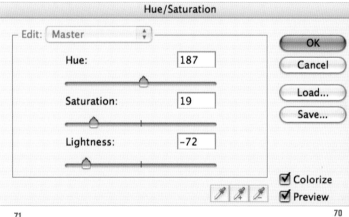

71

70

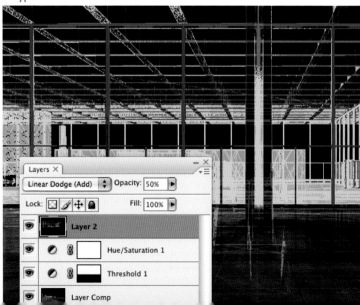

Software, Tutorial Files

Cinema 4D and Photoshop are protected trademarks of their manufacturers Maxon Computer AG and Adobe Systems Incorporated. You can download 30-day free trial versions of both programs at the manufacturer websites:

Cinema 4D R10: http://www.maxoncomputer.com/download_demo.asp
Photoshop CS3: http://www.adobe.com/downloads/

The files I provided you with in the book are available on my website. You have to log in as follows:

http://lsr.architekturdarstellung.info/en
ID: lumen
Password: umbra

Use http://www.architekturdarstellung.info/kontakt.php for any questions, remarks, correction suggestions or criticism you may want to share with me.

I wouldn't have begun this book hadn't I been incited and accompanied by a lot of people: my students who have endured various versions of my tutorials so far, the staff of Maxon Computer GmbH who supplied me with software and helpful hints, my poor colleague professors at the faculty of architecture at Stuttgart's UAS who more than once had to suffer from my absent mind, and David Marold in particular, editor at Springer, who has amicably accompanied me and my „first born".

However, I managed to finish this English edition only because Irmela and Leonhard treated me with great love and tolerance over the last weeks, although I must have been a pretty boring partner and father. I dedicate this book to the both of them.

Index

Rendering

Photoshop